ACTUALIZATION AND INTERPRETATION
IN THE OLD TESTAMENT

SOCIETY
OF BIBLICAL
LITERATURE

DISSERTATION SERIES

J. J. M. Roberts, Old Testament Editor
Charles Talbert, New Testament Editor

Number 86
ACTUALIZATION AND INTERPRETATION
IN THE OLD TESTAMENT
by
Joseph W. Groves

Joseph W. Groves

ACTUALIZATION AND INTERPRETATION IN THE OLD TESTAMENT

Scholars Press
Atlanta, Georgia

ACTUALIZATION AND INTERPRETATION IN THE OLD TESTAMENT

Joseph W. Groves

Ph.D.,
Yale University
New Haven, Connecticut

Advisor
Brevard S. Childs

Library of Congress Cataloging-in-Publication Data

Groves, Joseph W., 1944–
    Actualization and interpretation in the Old Testament.

    (Dissertation series / Society of Biblical
Literature ; no. 86)
    1. Bible. O.T.—Hermeneutics. 2. Bible
O.T.—Criticism, interpretation, etc.—History—
20th century. 3. Rad, Gerhard von, 1901-1971.
I. Title. II. Series: Dissertation series
(Society of Biblical Literature) ; no. 86.
BS476.G76   221.6'01   86-13926
ISBN 0-89130-966-7 (alk. paper)
ISBN 0-89130-967-5 (pbk. : alk. paper)

Printed in the United States of America
on acid-free paper

Acknowledgements

Although there are numerous people who contributed in many different ways to the production of this study, I wish to single out four men for a special debt of gratitude. The first three are my professors of Old Testament from Louisville Presbyterian Theological Seminary, who kindled my interest in Old Testament studies: Arnold B. Rhodes, Ulrich Mauser, and John Salmon. The greatest debt is to my advisor, Brevard S. Childs, who has been both an inspiration and a tremendous aid in the completion of the study.

Table of Contents

Introduction

Since the rise of the critical movement in Biblical scholarship during the eighteenth century, the major hermeneutical question has been how to bridge the gap between the historical-critical, "scientific" evaluation of the Biblical texts and their religious application.[1] Preceding the rise of this movement, questions of the objective historical validity of the Biblical stories are seldom asked of the texts. Instead, a unity of literal explication of the texts and religious application is presumed. However, in the eighteenth century new questions are addressed to the texts. They are concerned with the historical accuracy of the narratives, and especially of the miracles. They apply the general canons of linguistic meaning to the Biblical texts. They ask for externally verifiable data on the events being reported. In other words, what the texts say, their explicative meaning, is determined by the commonly held principles of historical and linguistic studies, with no reference to the religious sense of the texts.

However, few scholars in the eighteenth century are willing to declare the Bible religiously meaningless. Having done the work of historical criticism, the task of religious application remains. As the historical-critical method increasingly strips away the aura of divine authority from the text and dispenses with the idea of internal unity and cohesiveness, the problem of how to ascertain the religious significance of the texts becomes more and more acute.

Throughout the nineteenth and twentieth centuries, numerous options are explored in an attempt to bridge this gap. During most of the nineteenth century the concern with religious applicability is made wholly subsidiary to differing critical investigations of the texts. Mythic interpretation, epitomized by D.F. Strauss,[2] seeks to ascertain

---

[1]See Hans Frei, (*The Eclipse of Biblical Narrative* [New Haven: Yale University, 1974]) for a thorough investigation of this question.

[2]Strauss' seminal work was *Das Leben Jesu* (Tübingen: C.F. Osiander, 1835). For a study of his work, see Frei, *Eclipse*, 233-44.

the mythic consciousness of the authors who produced the texts and to understand the writings in terms of that consciousness. However, Strauss minimizes the actual religious meaning and application of these texts, being content to recreate the original milieu and as much of the inner consciousness of that milieu as possible. In the early phases of the history of religions approach (especially in the work of James Frazer)[3] the distinctive features of the Old Testament are completely lost in its comparison and collation with the folklore of other religions. While the religious nature of the tales is recognized, any applicability is subordinated to the fascination with the similarity of tales from different times, places, and faiths. The most important development of this century is that which culminated in Wellhausen's source criticism.[4] Here the interest lies in determining the parameters of the religious documents underlying the Old Testament and in studying the progressive development of Israel's religion. In each of these cases theological concerns are minimal, subordinated to other interests, be they mythical background, comparative studies, or historical development.

A new situation arises in the early twentieth century in Europe. Dogmatic theology is revitalized by the work of Barth, Brunner, and Bultmann. The high regard in which these theologians hold the scriptures and the extensive space which they allot to elucidating texts spurs a new interest in trying to relate textual explication and religious application. Since historical-critical studies are in firm command of textual explication, the problem is one of constructing a robust and convincing Old Testament theology on such an exegetical basis.

---

[3]James Frazer, *The Golden Bough* (New York: Macmillan Co., 1922); *Folk-lore in the Old Testament* (New York: Macmillan Co., 1923). John Vickery, in *The Literary Impact of the Golden Bough* (Princeton: Princeton University, 1973), demonstrates the governing influence of 19th century thought upon Frazer's work (pp. 3-67).

[4]Julius Wellhausen, *Prolegomena to the History of Israel* (Edinburgh: Adam & Charles Black, 1885). Also see Hans-Joachim Kraus, *Geschichte der historische-kritischen Erforschung des Alten Testaments von der Reformation bis zur Gegenwart* (Neukirchen Kreis Moers: Verlag der Buchhandlung des Erziehungsvereins, 1956) 235-49.

Numerous scholars attempt this exacting task.[5] Otto Eissfeldt[6] and Ernst Sellin[7] approach this problem by making a sharp separation between the historical and theological enterprises. Accordingly, the historical investigation of the Old Testament text lies in the realm of rational knowledge and cannot advance beyond relativity and immanence. While an historical investigation can provide insight into the text, set boundaries for feasible interpretations, and point out the incompatibility of many elements of the Old Testament with modern faith, it cannot connect directly to a faith-centered theological interpretation of the Old Testament. An historical investigation runs directly contrary to the needs of a theological interpretation to be focused firmly upon the present and to apprehend the absolute and eternal nature of God. A theological investigation is further conditioned by its confessional stance. Thus, its applicability is limited to one's own particular confession and to that specific time. Therefore, the historical and the theological have little connection between them. They are related only by juxtaposition and by the fact that the same person can perform both tasks, separate though they may be.

Wilhelm Vischer[8] and Hans Hellbart[9] do not merely separate the historical and the theological, but virtually eliminate the role of historical investigation by advocating Christological exegesis. In essence their approach is a return to a pre-critical Reformation theology which views the Old and New Testaments as a unified structure. The element which creates this unity is the pervading presence of the

---

[5]For a complete explication of these attempts, see Kraus, *Geschichte*, 382-94; *Die biblische Theologie* (Neukirchen-Vluyn: Neukirchener, 1970); Rudolf Abramowski, "Vom Streit um das Alte Testament," *TRu*, 9 (1937) 65-93; Walter Baumgartner, "Die Auslegung des Alte Testament im Streit die Gegenwart," *SThU* 11 (1941) 17-38; Emil Kraeling, *The Old Testament Since the Reformation* (New York: Harper & Bros., 1955) 178-284; Ronald Clements, *A Century of Old Testament Study* (London: Lutterworth, 1976); Robert Dentan, *Preface to Old Testament Theology* (rev. ed.; New York: Seabury, 1963).

[6]See in particular Otto Eissfeldt, "Geschichtliches und Übergeschichtliches," *TSK* 109 (1947) 37ff; "Israelitische-jüdische Religionsgeschichte und alttestamentliche Theologie," *ZAW* 44 (1926) 1-12; Kraus, *Biblische*, 311-13.

[7]Ernst Sellin, *Das Alte Testament und die evangelische Kirche der Gegenwart* (Leipzig: A. Deichert, 1921); Kraus, *Biblische*, 126-27, 311.

[8]Wilhelm Vischer, *The Witness of the Old Testament to Christ* (London: Lutterworth, 1949).

[9]Hans Hellbart, "Die Auslegung des Alten Testaments als theologische Disziplin," *TBl* 16 (1937) 140ff.

Messiah. The New Testament interprets the Old as Messianic prophecy and this interpretation is confirmed by a study of the Old Testament as a whole. Indeed, the true nature of the Old Testament is apparent only when one recognizes the pre-existence of Christ as the head of the Old Testament church. Consequently, both the unity of the Bible and the cause of that unity are beyond the scope of historical investigation, which can only end in confusion and uncertainty. One must approach the Old Testament through theological affirmation.

Otto Proksch[10] and Karl Girgensohn[11] take an approach which highlights many of the same elements as Vischer's Christological exegesis, but without the same radical devaluation of the historical. This method, called pneumatic exegesis, harkens back to the work of J. C. K. von Hofmann in the nineteenth century. While these scholars recognize both the validity and the value of the historical-critical method, they regard it as an inadequate basis for theological interpretation. They attempt to connect the two by proposing that the Old Testament has a real history, which may be discovered to a great extent by historical inquiry, but which is given theological import through selective and specialized interpretation. This specialized exegesis centers upon a view of Old Testament history as *Heilsgeschichte* in which the events have a typological significance that reveals Christ as the consummation of the entire Biblical message. This spiritual element is not present or is not easily elucidated for many portions of the Old Testament, so the interpreter must select those passages most easily conducive to pneumatic exegesis for special emphasis. Thus, Proksch's method leads to the devaluation of some parts of the Old Testament and the enhancement of others by his varied and peculiar combinations of the historical-critical method and spiritual emphasis.

Walther Eichrodt[12] integrates the historical and the theological more thoroughly than any of the attempts discussed so far. He consistently adheres to the historical-critical method and to a completely historical outline of the development of Israel's religion. He

---

[10]Otto Proksch, "Pneumatische Exegese," *Christentum und Wissenschaft* 1 (1925) 145ff; *Theologie des Alten Testaments* (Gütersloh: C. Bertelsmann, 1950); Kraus, *Biblische,* 128-30.

[11]Karl Girgensohn, *Grundriss der Dogmatik* (Leipzig: A. Deichert, 1924).

[12]Walther Eichrodt, *Theology of the Old Testament* (2 vols.; Philadelphia: Westminster, 1961); Kraus, *Biblische,* 126-35.

systematizes Israel's religious categories by taking cross-sections of its religion at various points in history. He demonstrates that the same theological concepts, especially the covenant, govern its faith at each cross-sectional point. This introduces the theological element, derived from Israel's own religious expression, into an essentially historical description of its religion. Eichrodt further enhances this faith perspective by contrasting it with the religions of Israel's neighbors. Therefore, Eichrodt connects the historical and the theological by conducting a thorough historical analysis and allowing the theological categories to emerge from the material of Israel's beliefs rather than from an outside system imposed by the interpreter.

Although each of these attempts to link the historical-critical method with theological interpretation has found its adherents, another model became increasingly prominent. It is best characterized by the term *Vergegenwärtigung,* which, although no English word fully conveys the sense of the German, may best be rendered as "actualization."[13] The word serves as a rubric for a methodological proposal by which the Biblical text is contemporized. The originator and chief proponent of the proposal is Gerhard von Rad. So many other Biblical scholars have appropriated or adapted it for their own hermeneutical method that it became the most prominent method for relating historical-critical and theological concerns during the decades of the forties, fifties, and sixties. Actualization holds sway particularly in Germany, as evidenced by the hermeneutics of Martin Noth, Claus Westermann, Hans Walter Wolff, and Odil Hannes Steck, as well as many other German scholars. However, its influence is also felt heavily both in England, through the work of Norman Porteous, Peter Ackroyd, Douglas Jones, and E.W. Nicholson, and in the United States through Bernhard Anderson, Walter Brueggemann, Brevard Childs, James Mays, and James Sanders.

---

[13]The concept of actualization has a varied vocabulary lying behind it, with *Vergegenwärtigung* and *Aktualisierung* being the two most common terms. In this study actualization will be used as a rubric for the entire concept and as a translation of both of these terms, which are used synonymously. The other technical terms associated with actualization will be introduced during the course of the study.

Yet, for all its prominence, the concept itself has received little scrutiny.[14] This study will seek to fill that void. Since the historical development of actualization has been completely neglected, the first chapter will concentrate upon this development in the work of von Rad. The second chapter will detail the contribution of other scholars to the concept, both in its development and in its adaptation, application, and expansion. The third chapter will critique actualization as a method of connecting historical and theological concerns, focusing upon the internal logic and consistency of the method. The final chapter is a series of three textual studies which concretize the criticisms of actualization and give some direction for a redefinition of the term which would make it more widely applicable to Old Testament interpretation.

---

[14]Some of the most significant critiques of von Rad are Hans Walter Wolff, Rolf Rendtorff, and Wolfhart Pannenberg, *Gerhard von Rad: Seine Bedeutung für die Theologie* (Munich: C. Kaiser, 1973); D.G. Spriggs, *Two Old Testament Theologies* (London: SCM, 1974); Walther Eichrodt, "The Problem of Old Testament Theology," in *Theology*, 1, 512-20; Hans Conzelmann, "Fragen an Gerhard von Rad,"*EvT* 24 (1964), 113-25; Martin Honecker, "Zum Verständnis der Geschichte in Gerhard von Rad's Theologie des Alten Testaments," *EvT* 23 (1963) 143-68; Douglas Knight, *Rediscovering the Traditions of Israel* (Missoula: SBL, 1973) 97-142; G. Henton Davies, "Gerhard von Rad," in Robert Laurin, ed., *Contemporary Old Testament Theologians* (Valley Forge: Judson, 1970) 63-90; James Barr, "Gerhard von Rad's *Theologie des Alten Testaments,*" *ExpTim* 73 (1962) 142-46; *Old and New in Interpretation* (New York: Harper & Row, 1966); Friedrich Baumgärtel, "Gerhard von Rad's *Theologie des Alten Testaments,*" *TLZ* 86 (1961) 801-16, 895-908.

Chapter One

The Development of Actualization in the Theology of Gerhard Von Rad

Since the origin and primary application of actualization as a method of relating historical-critical and theological concerns in the Old Testament lie in the work of Gerhard von Rad, we will first turn to his considerable corpus to study his particular expression of the concept. The organization of this chapter will deviate somewhat from a strict chronological progression. Since the term actualization has been so nebulous and ill-defined, we will seek to reach a preliminary understanding of the concept before tracing its development. We will do this by starting with a study of von Rad's initial formulation of actualization in *The Form-Critical Problem of the Hexateuch.* From there we will move back in time and seek the roots of the term in the work of three other men: Johann Gottfried von Herder, Hermann Gunkel, and Sigmund Mowinckel. The final sections of the chapter will deal chronologically with von Rad's development of actualization: the third section scanning his early work up to *The Form-Critical Problem of the Hexateuch* in 1938; the fourth covering from 1938 up to volume one of his *Old Testament Theology;* the fifth detailing the final formulation of the concept in *Old Testament Theology* and in the debates and elucidations which followed.

Von Rad's Initial Definition of Actualization

It cannot be maintained that this [Deuteronomy's recurring use of the word "today"] is merely an effective stylistic device which the deuteronomist has chosen to make more vivid *(Vergegenwärtigung)* what he has to say. On the contrary, it is a quite fundamental feature of Deuteronomy, reminding us that this is a vivid reconstruction *(Aktualisierung)* of the events of the redemption story such as only the cultus can furnish. No literary composition, however skillful, could ever bring events to life in this way.[1]

This passage from *The Form-Critical Problem of the Hexateuch* (1938) marks the first appearance of the term actualization in von Rad's work.[2] Not only is this the initial use of the term itself, but it is also his first attempt at tackling the problem of contemporization of the Biblical material.

In this particular passage he sets *Vergegenwärtigung* in opposition to *Aktualisierung*. However, the use of the two terms as opposites is only an apparent distinction; in the paragraphs which follow he employs *Vergegenwärtigung* in describing the phenomenon previously referred to as *Aktualisierung*. Then what is the opposition that von Rad has established, if it does not lie in the terms themselves? He is contrasting the use of actualization as a stylistic device, a simple literary technique, with a deeper, more profound use of the term in relation to the cult: the re-creation of the events of the cult and the re-experiencing of those events by the participants in the ceremony.

Here von Rad is making a distinction that is found in anthropological studies of cultic rites and which entered the realm of the Old Testament scholarship through the work of Sigmund Mowinckel.[3] Mowinckel (who clearly was von Rad's source for the distinction he is making and probably for the term actualization itself)[4] made the differentiation much clearer by using separate terms for the two phenomena and giving a more complete explanation. In the cult the primeval events are repeated and given a full reality *(verwirklichen Wirklichkeit)*, so that the participants are completely caught up in their identification with the events: the world is literally reconstituted and

---

[1]Gerhard von Rad, *The Form-Critical Problem of the Hexateuch,* in *The Form-Critical Problem of the Hexateuch and Other Essays* (New York: McGraw Hill, 1966) 28. The following abbreviations will be used hereafter: *Hexateuch* for the 1938 monograph; *Essays* for the 1966 collection of translated essays.

[2]To be more precise, this is the first technical reference in any of his major books and articles. It is possible that he used the term in the sense explained here in earlier sermons or obscure articles which are not readily available.

[3]Sigmund Mowinckel, *Psalmenstudien* (1921-24; reprinted, Amsterdam: P. Schippers, 1961) 2, 16-43. These pages not only show Mowinckel's use of the concept, but reveal his anthropological sources as well (p. 33).

[4]Von Rad refers frequently to Mowinckel both in this article (nine footnotes) and throughout his work, especially when dealing with actualization.

the cosmos held together until the next enactment of the cultic drama. This is called *Wiederholung*.

However, as one moves out of the pure, utterly primitive cult, this complete identity does not take place, since people have become more logical and have a different sense of time. Less vivid and less alive forms of contemporization take place in more sophisticated times:

> In dem protestantichen Gottesdienst ist nicht mehr viel vom Drama übrig. Von der dramatischen Wiederholung ist eigentlich nur die geistige Wiederbelebung und Vergegenwärtigung geblieben.... In spiritualisierter Gestalt lebt aber die Wiederholung fort als "Vergegenwärtigung."[5]

Vergegenwärtigung is a less real, spiritualizing means of contemporization than the pure *Wiederholung* of the primitive cult. Indeed, *Vergegenwärtigung* extends beyond the cultic realm entirely and can be used as a literary device for recalling a past time or event.[6]

Von Rad creates an ambiguous situation by applying *Vergegenwärtigung* to both the literary device of giving material contemporary relevance to its readers and to the re-experiencing of events through the cult. This should not be too unexpected, since von Rad does not regard the cult which lies behind the Old Testament materials as the pure, primitive phenomenon which Mowinckel is describing. The Israelite cult historicizes and spiritualizes its events. Thus, while von Rad wishes to retain the essential nature of *Wiederholung* for the Israelite cult, he also wants to indicate the distance between the Israelites and the other peoples of the ancient Near East. Therefore, von Rad used one term to encompass the characteristics of what Mowinckel considered two different phenomena. Despite the ambiguity of his terminology, it is quite clear that von Rad's interest lies in the application of *Vergegenwärtigung* to the cult and that this is the essence of actualization for him.

Von Rad's purpose in raising the issue of actualization at this point in his article is to show that Deuteronomy is closely related to the cult. Since actualization is a phenomenon that occurs during the cultic ceremony, its presence in the book of Deuteronomy signals its

---

[5]Mowinckel, *Psalmen,* 2.34.

[6]*Ibid.,* where Mowinckel applies the term to a modern poem.

connection to the cult. However, he makes a large leap in moving from actualization in a cultic ceremony to the same occurrence in a written document such as Deuteronomy. Therefore, he emphasizes that Deuteronomy's use of "today" is more than a mere literary device. For von Rad Deuteronomy must be more than a written document; it must be cultic material that even in its separation from the cult retains its vitality. Thus, although the book has passed through an extended history of growth, it has retained the pattern of the cultic ceremony and all its material refers to one cultic occasion, giving it both unity and vitality.[7] It is questionable whether von Rad gives adequate evidence that the gap is bridged. We will not pursue the point further at the present time since he returns to this problem later in his writings.

From this discussion of actualization two aspects of the concept have emerged. First, although we are dealing exclusively with written literature, actualization is far more than a mere rhetorical device. It involves a deep identification of the reader or listener with the material that is being actualized. The barrier of time dissolves and he becomes a participant in the very events being narrated. In this way the old material gains significance for the present age. The second point proceeds from the first: actualization is not an idle exercise, but an occurrence of great religious import, "determining the way of life of the very same people who receive it."[8] Thus, it is a theological move which takes old material and makes it religiously significant – indeed religiously determinative – for a later time. It is through actualization that the cult and history interact to keep Israel's faith alive and relevant.

In continuing our investigation of actualization in this article, we must ask what kind of material it is that Israel contemporizes. He gives two examples from Deuteronomy. In Deut 5:2-4 the sealing of the covenant at Horeb is made alive and present for those who listen to Deuteronomy. In this case an historical event is actualized. In Deut 29 it is more the validity of the covenant for the present-day audience than the giving of the covenant itself that is reaffirmed.

In von Rad's one reference outside of the Hexateuch, Ps 136, historical events are again the object of actualization. Here the entire

---

[7]Von Rad, *Hexateuch* 33.

[8]*Ibid.*, 29.

creed of Israel (plus the creation) is recited in a litany and thus made real for the audience.[9] A more significant use of actualization occurs in relation to the Yahwist. Von Rad does not refer to a specific example but to a more general problem faced by the Yahwist: do the traditions which he employs retain theological validity for Israel once they are divorced from the cult? Most of the material from which he shaped his work is of cultic origin. Now, however, it has been "historicized," removed from the cultic sphere. How has it retained religious meaning, since "the Yahwist speaks to his contemporaries out of concern for the real and living *(aktuellen)* faith"?[10] The means is none other than the actualization of the promise of the land, given to Moses but not fulfilled until the time of David.[11]

Several observations should be made on von Rad's use of the concept in this instance. First, it is manifestly a theological move. He explicitly states that it is used to give new religious significance to old traditions. Second, the process is central to the Yahwist's work. It is his method of handling a central problem: how to give his work the religious vitality with which he sought to speak to Israel. Actualization is not a methodological footnote, but the means used to bring to life his main point. Third, von Rad describes the material which is contemporized differently than in the previous examples. Now he speaks explicitly of actualizing traditions rather than historical events, litanies, or the general validity of the covenant. This will become a common designation in his later work. Fourth, actualization does not occur in the cult here. Instead, cultic material is given new validity apart from its old setting. This differs considerably from von Rad's discussion of actualization in relation to Deuteronomy, where it proceeded from the cult and indicated a continuing affinity that the material has for the cult. He makes no attempt to explain the relation of these two different kinds of actualization, nor does he indicate that he regards them as significantly different. Not until his *Old Testament Theology* does he acknowledge that he is discussing two different kinds of actualization and consider the relationship between the two. Here we

---

[9]*Ibid.*, 9-10. This is an offhand mention of *Vergegenwärtigung* (trans. as "presentation") with no elucidation.

[10]*Ibid.*, 69.

[11]*Ibid.*, 70. *Aktualisierung* here is translated as "reassertion."

can only note that a difficulty and a resultant imprecision in the use of the term exist from the beginning of von Rad's formulation.

The Form-Critical Problem of the Hexateuch has rightly been regarded as a seminal article in the development of von Rad's thought, especially in regard to his traditio-historical method and the centrality of the credenda to Israel's faith. That we have found it to contain his first use and elucidation of actualization is of no small importance. Its integral relation to the former concerns will become even clearer as we proceed with an analysis of von Rad's other work.

We have discussed this article first to give us a preliminary understanding of actualization for von Rad so that we can more easily discuss the roots of the concept both in his earlier writings and in the work of other men who influenced him. To summarize, three central elements emerge from this initial formulation of the concept. First, it is a process by which old sacred material is made vividly alive for a new generation – so much so that the barrier of time dissolves and they become participants in that which occurred long before. This most commonly occurs in relation to the cult, in the re-experiencing of the old saving events. However, it also occurs outside the cultic ceremony, although the mechanics of that process are unclear. Second, actualization is a process of great theological import; it is not a meaningless religious exercise, but one which shapes, renews, and validates Israel's faith. It lies at the center of the work of the Yahwist and is essential in understanding the form and function of Deuteronomy. This is von Rad's unique adaptation of the idea of actualization. As we noted, the concept already existed in relation to the cult drama in the work of Mowinckel. However, von Rad's application of it to the theological realm opened an entirely new field of exploration. Third, varied materials undergo this process. They may be historical events, litanies, old traditions, or other types of material. As we investigate the remainder of von Rad's corpus, we may keep these elements in mind as we search for clarifications, expansions, additions, and contradictions.

From the material presented, we can see that von Rad's concept of actualization in *The Form-Critical Problem of the Hexateuch* is far from clear. That should not surprise us, and indeed does not constitute a criticism of von Rad at this point, since the purpose of his article was not to explain actualization. Its primary focus is upon the credenda as the central element in Israel's faith. Actualization appears as part of the traditio-historical process by which this faith was kept alive. As such it plays an important role in the article, one which allows us to deduce much concerning the nature of the process. However, it is only as the concept grows in importance for von Rad that he feels compelled to explain it and expand upon this basic understanding. But before we proceed with that investigation, we must move back in time to discover its origins in the works of other scholars and its seeds in the earlier writings of von Rad.

Sources for von Rad's Concept of Actualization

As we noted in the previous section, the application of actualization to the Old Testament preceded von Rad. His genius lay in the new synthesis which he developed from earlier uses of the concept. In this section we will discuss briefly the three streams of thought which flowed together into von Rad's formulation. We will provide neither an exhaustive history of the idea of contemporization nor an historical analysis of central terms such as *Vergegenwärtigung* and *Aktualisierung,* since these endeavors would lead us far from our major point. Instead, we will choose one figure as an example of each stream of thought, describing his work in enough detail to demonstrate his contribution to von Rad's formulation.

1

Although the phenomenon of actualization as we have described it is a recent development, the general idea of contemporizing older materials stretches back to Johann Gottfried von Herder in the eighteenth century. His impact upon the world of theology and Biblical criticism can scarcely be overestimated:

> Without him the work of Schleiermacher and de Wette would have been impossible.... Without Herder there would have been no Erlangen group and no school of religious history. But for Herder there would have been no Troeltsch.[12]

In addition to Herder's widespread influence in breaking the grip of rationalism imposed by the enlightenment, he opened the door for the idea of contemporization in interpreting literature.

---

[12]Karl Barth, *Protestant Theology in the Nineteenth Century,* (Valley Forge: Judson, 1973) 316.

His first contribution stems from his philosophy of history. He refused to judge the events of history by modern criteria alone. Instead, he insisted upon the uniqueness of each age. A stage of history may be evaluated only after historians have immersed themselves empathetically in that milieu and formed a dialectical relationship between the earlier time and their own experience.[13] Consequently, there can be neither a single standard of judgment for history nor a single period of history (i.e., the Graeco-Roman era) which is deemed the highest. However, the uniqueness of an historical epoch does not mean that it is unrelated to the flow of history: "No one lives in his own period only; he builds on what has gone before and lays a foundation for what comes after."[14] Consequently, history has a sense of progress in which the transmission of tradition plays an important role.

Herder's philosophy of history also governs his attitude toward literature, including the Bible. The first step in interpreting the literature of any age is to recognize the uniqueness of thought and expression of that literature: "Moses could only speak in terms suited to his age, to his people, and to their apprehension, and it would be folly to demand of him more than this."[15] Consequently, the interpreter must not apply the criteria of other ages to the Biblical stories, but judge them "with reference to the peculiar nature of the feelings, sentiments and language, out of which they have grown."[16] To do this, the interpreter must enter into the spirit of that age as fully as possible.[17] While this process includes an intellectual grasp of the events and culture of an historical epoch, much more is involved, for the spirit of an age can only be tapped at an emotional, empathetic level:

> What is the critic to be to the author? His servant, his friend, his impartial judge. Seek to get to know him and to make a

---

[13]Johann Gottfried von Herder, *Yet Another Philosophy of History*, in Frederick Barnard, trans. and ed. *J.G. Herder on Social and Political Culture* (Cambridge: Cambridge University, 1969) 181-83. Also see Barnard's introduction, pp. 35-36.

[14]Herder, *Philosophy*, 188.

[15]Johann Gottfried von Herder, *The Spirit of Hebrew Poetry* (Burlington: Edward Smith, 1833) 2.92.

[16]*Ibid.*, 228.

[17]*Ibid.*, 182, 184.

thorough study of him as your master, but seek not to be your own master.... It is difficult, but just, that the critic should transfer himself into the thoughts of his author and read him in the spirit in which he wrote.[18]

In this way the spirit of the age enters *(Einfüllung)* the interpreter and the literature comes alive for him. Thus, the material becomes contemporized for the interpreter.[19]

However, this immersion of interpreters in the spirit of the literature does not complete the process. Now they must re-enter the spirit of their own age and seek to make the older material relevant and alive for it. Herder discovers this process of adaptation at work in the Bible itself: "[The Hebrews] do not repeat it [Moses' triumphal song] ... in endless litanies, as we often do, but adapt *(anwenden)* the ancient event to new occurrences."[20] Likewise, modern interpreters must use the old traditions in a manner meaningful to their own day. They accomplish this by isolating the "fruits of his spirit only, for the benefit of our own times:"[21]

> ... it does not matter alone what every splint and nail signified individually in its own place, but what it means to us now, beyond times and cultures, in the totality of the building in which providence has placed it. The purpose of the first is simply its own isolated knowledge, the second is necessary for its use for our time. The first makes the biblical antiquarian, the second the biblical theologian.[22]

Consequently, the contemporization of Biblical literature occurs not through dry, scholarly activity, but through the living application of the Bible's message in preaching and teaching. As the spirit of the times changes, so must the Biblical message be updated for each specific moment and never allowed to grow stale:

---

[18]Quoted in Alexander Gillies, *Herder* (Oxford: Basil Blackwell, 1945) 28.

[19]Frei, *Eclipse,* 184-89.

[20]Herder, *Spirit* 2.77. Also see pp. 113-159.

[21]*Ibid.,* 59.

[22]Quoted in Frei, *Eclipse,* 193-94.

... so ist's mit allen Situationen der Bibel. Sie verjüngen sich
für uns und wir verjüngen uns mit ihnen. Mich dünkt, man
dürfe, man könne keine zwo Predigten über ein Evangelium
halten, die in verschiednen Jahren sich völlig gleich seyn
dürften, gleich seyn könnten: denn wir schwimmen ja immer im
Strom der Zeit weiter, unsre Aussicht, unsre Beherzigung wird
also anders.[23]

The influence of Herder upon von Rad's work should be clear:
Herder sees each historical period, even those within the Bible, as
unique; he finds a process of adaptation of tradition in the Old
Testament; he views the interpreter as a contemporizing agent; he
evokes a deep concern for the role of preaching in contemporization.
However, to refer to Herder's sense of contemporization as actualization
would indicate too close a relationship between the two men. Herder
shows little interest in historical investigations which establish
different levels of tradition or different historical settings for the Biblical
materials. Nor is his sense of contemporization a specifically
theological one. While it may be used in preaching, it may also be
applied to any literature. The process is universal in nature.[24] No, for
Herder contemporization is an aesthetic process. It belongs to the realm
of nature and the spirit rather than to the specific field of historical
investigation. People are awakened to the literature by the act of the
preacher or teacher, not by the intervention of God. Through the
aesthetic sense the literature becomes alive and real – and contemporary.

Thus, we can see the birth of the idea of contemporization. While
von Rad's dependence upon Herder is far from direct, being filtered by
many years of theological and historical developments, that romantic
sense and aesthetic vision still shine through in von Rad's
formulations.

---

[23]Johann Gottfried von Herder, *Briefe, das Studium der Theologie betreffend*
(Weimar: in der Hoffmannischen Hofbuchhandlung, 1816) 2.18.   Herder's
vocabulary for contemporizing differs considerably from that of von Rad. He uses
such terms as *verjüngen, erneuen, beleben, immer lebendige,* and *anwenden.*

[24]*Ibid.,* 18-19.

The study of tradition criticism began with Hermann Gunkel and with it the concept of contemporization entered a new stage.[25] Essential to Gunkel's understanding of Biblical literature is that it is composed of several successive layers of traditionary material. Biblical scholars must take the final form of the text and peel back each layer until they reach the core of the material – the original story that was told. With each layer one should describe as closely as possible the situation in which it arose (either the historical circumstances or the particular institution which shaped it), the author, compiler, school, or group which composed it, the purpose of the layer, and the literary effect of the change in meaning that it wrought upon the earlier composition.

Gunkel made new and important strides because he was willing to push beyond the written text to the oral tradition underlying it, a move which Wellhausen and the other source critics had difficulty in making. Gunkel was able to take the stories of Genesis back to this oral stage and establish the circumstances in which the stories arose to a remarkable degree of fullness. Since source criticism had already done a great deal of work on the written documents which underlay the final text, Gunkel concentrated on the oral stage and made his most important contribution in relation to that stage of tradition. However, he has been unduly criticized for treating the original layer of the story as the most important, and as that which carries the meaning of the story. Several reasons existed for his emphasis upon the original layer: first, he was opposed by the Wellhausen school which saw no possibility for recovering the oral tradition and found it necessary to polemicize against this view, thus emphasizing the oral tradition. Second, this was an unexplored area, one open to a fertile and creative mind. Third, he had an undeniable interest in the early history of Israel's religion and its relation to and use of other religious traditions in the ancient Near East. These concerns led him to emphasize the original layer of material, especially in his early work on Genesis; but

---

[25]This study will not attempt a complete exploration of the work of Gunkel, but will merely highlight his contribution to the rise of actualization. For a more complete treatment of his work, see Werner Klatt, *Hermann Gunkel* (Göttingen: Vandenhoeck & Ruprecht, 1969); Knight, *Rediscovering,* 71-83; Kraus, *Geschichte,* 309-57.

his later work on the total composition of various stories reveals his wider concern for the total traditionary process.

While Gunkel emphasized the oral stages of development, he did not limit himself to them. Two excellent examples of his interest in the total history of Israel's traditions are his articles on the Joseph story and the Jacob cycle.[26] In both of these articles he traces the complete history of the development of the traditions. For the Joseph story he isolates four stages in the growth of the tradition: first, the single sagas, unrelated to the history of Israel; second, the historicization of the sagas based on Israel's history and the beginning of their coalescing into larger units around that history; third, the drawing together of the units into the J and E documents; fourth, the unification of J and E in the final composition of the Joseph "novella."

The picture which Gunkel gives of the Jacob cycle is similar, if more complex. He establishes that the kernel of the cycle is the first part of the Jacob-Esau stories (Gen 25:21-27:45), which were originally folk tales with the theme of shepherd against hunter. The first development was a coalescing of similar folk tales around this popular cycle: a second set of stories about a young shepherd (Jacob-Laban, Gen 29:15-32:1) were attached to the original nucleus; simultaneously a continuation of the Jacob-Esau stories arose (Gen 32:4-33:17). The second and most important development was the historicization of the stories: Jacob became the national ancestor of Israel, Esau was identified with Edom, and Laban with Aram. This actually caused a change in genre in the stories, from folk tale to saga. At the same time Jacob became associated with several stories of the holy places of Israel, and with the origin of the different tribes of Israel (who, of course, became his sons).[27] These three stages all existed at the oral level,[28] so that the entire cycle of stories came down to the compilers of the J and E documents. Therefore, later stages of development would be the writing down of the tradition in J and E and the combining of these traditions in the final literary form. Gunkel states that he assumes the validity of the prior source criticism of the

---

[26]Hermann Gunkel, "Die Komposition der Joseph-Geschichten," *ZDMG* 76 (1922) 55-71; "Jacob," in *What Remains of the Old Testament and Other Essays* (New York: Macmillan, 1928) 151-83.

[27]Gunkel, "Jacob," 185.

[28]*Ibid.*, 156.

Jacob cycle,[29] therefore he does not go into any discussion of these later stages of development. It should be clear from these articles that Gunkel does not absolutize the original stage of the oral tradition. This stage is the goal of his investigation, to be sure, because he begins with the final form and continually strips away layers until he reaches the original kernel. However, this is a methodological procedure and not a fixation upon that primary stage. After he recovers the kernel, he then reverses ground and gives a step-by-step development from beginning to end. With each layer of oral material he discusses the literary nature of the material, its probable setting and origin, and the most likely historical date. Thus, each layer is discussed at length.

The desire to reach back to the original kernel is motivated by what Gunkel considers the primary task of Biblical studies: the isolation, analysis, and exposition of literary types *(literarischen Gattungen)*.[30] However, there is no absolutizing of the original type: "the study of literary types, however, will only merit the name of Literary History *(Literaturgeschichte)* when it attempts to get at the history through which these types have passed."[31] This leads us to the most direct contribution of Gunkel to the concept of contemporization. He owes a great debt to Herder in his use of the aesthetic sense, for he believes one can only properly interpret these ancient writings if one is able to empathize with the authors and participate in their world to some extent.[32] However, he goes a step beyond Herder in his interest in the different layers of material that are present in the Old Testament. Now we must analyze each layer of Israel's literature. This is not a task of aesthetics, but of *Religionsgeschichte*,[33] and we can dissect the literature of Israel into layers of tradition on objective, scientific grounds.[34]

---

[29]*Ibid.,* 155.

[30]Hermann Gunkel, "Fundamental Problems of Hebrew Literary History," in *What Remains*, 59.

[31]*Ibid.,* 61.

[32]Gunkel, "Jacob," 157; *The Legends of Genesis* (1901; reprinted, New York: Schocken, 1964) 33.

[33]Klatt, *Gunkel,* 164.

[34]Hermann Gunkel, "The Close of Micah: A Prophetic Liturgy," in *What Remains,* 115.

However, within this tradition-building process in the history of Israel, one encounters contemporization:

> Occasionally it is even possible to see the same material passing through different literary types, being transformed *(umformen)* on each occasion in the spirit of a new age. For instance, the Saga can be seen passing into the Romance and into the Legend.[35]

While the aesthetic element is still present as the material is made contemporary for a new age in a new historical situation, the emphasis for contemporization lies in a new field: that of type study. The important element is that the material, as it is transformed, changes type. This is a process that can be studied objectively, analyzing the different layers and the changes that occur.

No longer is the link directly between the hearer and the written text. Now the fact that the process of contemporization has occurred within the Biblical material opens up an entire new world of analysis:

> And yet even these faithfully told legends are subject to the universal law of change. When a new generation has come, when the outward conditions have changed or the thoughts of men have altered, whether it be in religion or ethical ideals or aesthetic taste, the popular legend cannot permanently remain the same. Slowly and hesitantly, always at a certain distance behind, the legends follow the general changes in conditions, some more, others less. And here, consequently, the legends furnish us a very important basis for judging of changes in the people; a whole history of the religious, ethical, and aesthetic ideas of ancient Israel can be derived from Genesis.[36]

For Gunkel the primary interest in contemporization lies not in its aesthetic importance as a means of updating material in preaching or teaching for a present-day audience. Rather, it is a process that lies in the Biblical text itself and allows the scholar to uncover and reconstruct

---

[35]Gunkel, "Fundamental Problems," 66. Gunkel has his own vocabulary for the process of contemporization. Characteristic terms are *umbilden, umformen, aufnehmen, Veränderung, umdeuten,* etc. Most of these also appear in von Rad in relation to the tradition building process.

[36]Gunkel, *Legends,* 98-99. While the idea of adaptation of traditions within the OT also appears in Herder's work, it is not a primary concern for him.

the history of Israel and to reach beyond the written text to the long period of oral tradition preceding it. As he minimizes the aesthetic side of contemporization, he also minimizes the theological. There is little interest here in building a theology of the Old Testament or even expounding the theological ideas present in the text. His interest remains in the sphere of historical and literary analysis and reconstruction. When religious ideas and motifs surface they are related to the history of Israel and its religious institutions, not to a functioning theology. Gunkel's focus remained upon the process of tradition-building rather than upon the different traditions themselves. This prevents any sustained reflection upon the theological content of a particular tradition or even the general study of a tradition as a whole.

In conclusion, Gunkel's contribution to the concept of contemporization lies in locating it within the Biblical text itself as part of the tradition-building process. Thus, contemporization becomes part of the process of tradition criticism and is inseparable from it. When von Rad adopted the tradition-critical method, he necessarily inherited a general concept of the updating and enlivening of older materials.

3

We have already mentioned Sigmund Mowinckel and seen his influence upon von Rad at the seminal stage of his work upon actualization. However, this is only an isolated example of the relationship of the two men's work. A more complete explanation of Mowinckel's contribution is necessary, since von Rad drew upon other areas of his thought as well.

As we have seen, Mowinckel applies the terms *Vergegenwärtigung* and *Wiederholung* to the re-experiencing of the primeval events which occurs for the participants in the cult. This happens because any true cult is dramatic: "Nicht lediglich ein gespieltes Drama, ein Spiel, sondern ein wirkliches und Wirklichkeit hervorbringendes Drama, ein Drama, das mit realer Kraft das dramatisierte Ereignis verwirklicht."[37] It is this dramatic element that allows the full reality of the events to be made alive for the cultic participants. They find themselves transported back *(zurückprojizieren)* to the creation of the world.

---

[37]Mowinckel, *Psalmen* 2.21.

... durch die dramatische, "symbolische" /Darstellung und
Vergegenwärtigung und Wiederbelebung des betreffenden
Ereignisses wird dasselbe tatsächlich, real wiederholt; es
wiederholt sich, geschieht noch einmal und übt aufs Neue
dieselbe kräftige und heilbringende Wirkung, die es das erste
Mal am Morgen der Zeiten oder in der längst vergangenen
Vorzeit der Geschichte zu unserem Heile übte.[38]

As people emerge into the arena of history, they bring their cult
with them. The way for this move has been prepared by the
development of the cultic myth, which places the events of the cult in a
wider framework: it states that the events of the cult "happened
once."[39] Thus, as people become aware of history they can place the
cultic/mythic events in the sequence of historical occurrences. Myth,
which was once the totality of history, now becomes mixed with
history, with no clear distinction between the two. When this occurs,
there is a breakdown of the primitive *Wiederholung* and the total
reliving of the events which it spurred. In its place are the less
complete, more spiritualized experiences of *Wiederbelebung* and
Vergegenwärtigung.[40]

From this outline we may ask whether Mowinckel is really
discussing contemporization or archaizing, in which the people are
taken back in time rather than the material being brought forward to the
present day. In the case of the primitive *Wiederholung* the latter would
seem to be true, since the mode in which the events are presented
remains the same from generation to generation and part of their power
lies in this verbatim repetition. The events are, in fact, timeless and
eternal, and the participants are brought into their milieu – thus the use
of *zurückprojizieren* to describe the process. In contemporization the
opposite takes place. Past events are made consonant with the
contemporary historical situation either through a change in the words
used to express them or by the nature of the framework in which the
words appear. Mowinckel does not specifically state that this is what
occurs in *Vergegenwärtigung*, but one suspects that is is, since
Vergegenwärtigung can encompass even modern poetry. In both

---

[38]*Ibid.*, 21.

[39]*Ibid.*, 24.

[40]*Ibid.*, 34.

mechanisms one central element remains the same: the cultic material is made relevant in the lives of the participants.

Mowinckel's application of contemporization to the cult does not derive from either Herder's aesthetics or Gunkel's study of the traditionary process. It stems from work in cultural anthropology by such men as Söderblom, Grönbech, and Reinach.[41] From the work which these men did in primitive religious cults came both the concept of cultic drama and Mowinckel's specific terms for describing its phenomena. This adds an entirely new stream to the concept of actualization as it finally appears in von Rad.

Mowinckel was also aware of the occurrence of contemporization in the traditionary process. He views the Feast of Tabernacles not only as an example of cultic drama, but also as a reapplication *(Umdeutung)* of a fertility rite to the Israelite historical saving events.[42] He follows Gunkel in his description of the traditionary process in this instance.

He expands considerably on Gunkel when he studies tradition building in the prophets. Building upon the work of Harris Birkeland,[43] he sets forth a theory of the growth of the prophetic books based upon actualization. The original words of the prophets were preserved by a circle of disciples, who in turn adapted them to new historical situations:

> When the prophetic sayings have existed as a living spiritual force in the religious struggle and activity within a circle of transmitters who were themselves prophets and attributed to themselves prophetic inspiration, then it is evidently possible that the prophetic sayings ... during this use in the spiritual conflicts of the time have "marched with time" and have become to some extent transformed and stamped by new situations and requirements.[44]

---

[41]Mowinckel indicates his indebtedness to these men in *Psalmen* 2.26-35 (esp. p. 27, n. 1). Also see J.W. Rogerson, *Myth in Old Testament Interpretation* (Berlin: Walter de Gruyter, 1974) 78.

[42]Mowinckel, *Psalmen* 2.37-38.

[43]Harris Birkeland, *Zum hebräischen Traditionswesen, Avhändlinger utgitt av Det Norske Vikenskaps-Akademi* (1938) 5-96.

[44]Sigmund Mowinckel, *Prophecy and Tradition, Avhändlinger utgitt av Det Norske Vikenskaps-Akademi* (1946) 71.

These younger prophets found themselves inspired by the older "situation-determined" sayings and adapted them, either by rewriting them or by making additions, to their own situation, thus giving the old sayings "new life and actuality."[45] This became a common traditio-historical view of the transmission of the prophetic books, one which von Rad accepted, influenced by Mowinckel and Birkeland.[46]

The final area in which Mowinckel applies actualization is the theological sphere. It becomes a mechanism for bridging the gap between the world of the Old Testament and the present day: "God's word is always something *concrete* and *alive* ... God makes himself known to one definite man in his definite situation and gives him exactly what his situation demands."[47] The word is able to bridge the gap of thousands of years and become existential in people's lives.[48] Because of the nature of the Old Testament as the word of God, it is the interpreters' duty to themselves contemporary with the writers, to "draw up the clearest possible picture of the historical situation and the outward and inward, personal and general, circumstances that have influenced each of the Old Testament writings and sayings." Then they must "transpose" these experiences to our own day. This gives the word the opportunity to become concrete, relevant, and powerful in people's lives.[49] The influence of both a general neo-orthodox concept of the word of God and Herder's interpretive process emerge in Mowinckel's hermeneutics. Unlike von Rad he is content to give a general statement of interpretive procedure and never builds an Old Testament theology upon it.

In summary, Mowinckel made several important contributions to the concept of contemporization. First, he took the idea of cultic drama from the realm of cultural anthropology and applied it to Israel's cult and to its traditionary process. Second, he introduced *Vergegenwärtigung* into Old Testament studies as a means of describing the process of contemporization. Third, he, along with Birkeland,

---

[45]*Ibid.*, 71, 78.

[46]Gerhard von Rad, *Old Testament Theology* (New York: Harper and Row, 1962) 2.39-49.

[47]Sigmund Mowinckel, *The Old Testament as Word of God* (Nashville: Abingdon, 1959) 120. The original was published in 1938.

[48]*Ibid.*, 125.

[49]*Ibid.*, 131-32.

described the traditio-historical growth of the prophetic books in terms of actualization. Fourth, he applied contemporization to the theological significance of the Old Testament. In each of these areas, he exerted influence upon Gerhard von Rad to a greater or lesser degree.

4

This section has investigated three streams of thought which influenced von Rad's development of actualization. Herder's aesthetic theory, which originated the idea of contemporization, was the source of many studies of the hermeneutical process through which an interpreter seeks to grasp the meaning of the literature of prior ages. Herder's emphasis upon preaching and teaching is echoed by von Rad's theological concerns in relation to the Old Testament. Gunkel began the formulation of traditio-historical criticism and used the idea of contemporization in relation to it. This method with its focus upon the inner-Biblical nature of the traditionary process formed the basis for von Rad's entire enterprise. Mowinckel influenced von Rad in several areas, but his most significant contribution lay in the application of anthropological investigations into cultic drama to the religious traditions of Israel and its neighbors. Other scholars contributed to each stream which influenced von Rad. We have taken Herder, Gunkel, and Mowinckel as exemplars of the work of many people. Our investigation has shown that each of these elements – aesthetic theory, the traditio-historical process, and cultic re-enactment – has significantly influenced von Rad's unique formulation of actualization.

The Roots of Actualization in von Rad's Early Work

Not only did the other scholars influence von Rad's concept of actualization in *The Form-Critical Problem of the Hexateuch,* but his earlier work provided the basis for that formulation in 1938. These years between 1929 and 1938 were a creative and inventive period for von Rad, as he explored various approaches to Old Testament studies. Although he produced several significant works during this time, we will focus upon four of them which most clearly demonstrate the developmental roots of actualization: *Das Gottesvolk in Deuteronomium* (a revision of his doctoral thesis), *Das Geschichtsbild des chronistischen Werkes*, "The Levitical Sermon in I and II Chronicles," and "There Still Remains a Rest for the People of God."[50]

1

His earliest book, *Das Gottesvolk in Deuteronomium*, published in 1929, is interesting for its contrast to his later work in Deuteronomy. Although he expresses an interest in the forms in Deuteronomy, his major concern in this study is the history of a concept in the book and in other material influenced by Deuteronomy: the center of the content and the *Tendenz* of Deuteronomy is the relationship between Yahweh and the people. He investigates this relationship in the special vocabulary of Deuteronomy, in the cultic life of Israel, and in Yahweh's blessing for the people. In many places he touches on the same themes presented in his later studies in Deuteronomy, but in a wholly different manner.

For example, he deals with Deut 27:9, which he later uses as a prime example of actualization in its use of the word "today." In the present study he states that Israel is fully present *(völlig präsentisch)* as God's people at Sinai.[51] But this is used as a secondary point to show that Israel already existed at the giving of the law, rather than being constituted as a people by that gift. The phrase refers to the people, and says nothing about the literature or the process by which the people are made to experience presentness, as von Rad's later studies treat the phrase.

He also treats Deuteronomy in relation to the cult and discusses the change that occurs in Deuteronomy: here material originally associated with pagan cults has been removed from that sphere. In the present study he fails to evince the insight that Gunkel brought to such a

---

[50]Von Rad's other important works of this period are *Die Priesterschrift im Hexateuch* (Stuttgart: W. Kohlhammer, 1934); "Die falsche Propheten," *ZAW* 51 (1933) 109-20. Neither of these works displays any significant elements related to actualization. He also reviewed other scholars' attempts at Old Testament theology. However, these reviews also throw little light upon the development of actualization. See Gerhard von Rad, "Weiser: *Glaube und Geschichte im Alten Testament*," *Christentum und Wissenschaft* 8 (1932) 37; "Eichrodt, Walther: *Theologie des Alten Testaments*," *Christentum und Wissenschaft* 10 (1934) 427-28; "Das Christuszeugnis des Alten Testaments," *TB1* 14 (1935) 249-54; "Gesetz und Evangelium in Alten Testament," *TB1* 16 (1937) 41-47.

[51]Gerhard von Rad, *Das Gottesvolk im Deuteronomium* (Stuttgart: W. Kohlhammer, 1929) 25.

move: that it constituted a reinterpretation and usually an historicization of the meaning of the cult. Von Rad is content to state that the pagan significance is lost, the focus is now on the relation of Israel to Yahweh, and the purely cultic orientation has taken on an ethical dimension. Once again he demonstrates no interest in the traditionary process itself.

In the theological realm von Rad expresses ideas which later will be picked up in actualization. He sees a clearly existential element in Deuteronomy: "Straff ist die tatsächliche Gegenwart auf Gott bezogen. So finden wir zwei Gottessetzungen mit letztem religiösen Ernst erfasst: das *Hier* und das *Jetzt*. Darin ruht die Bedeutung des Dt.'s."[52] Here we see a phenomenon which recurs frequently in von Rad's work: through his analysis of the material, a modern philosophical or theological category emerges which contains the true meaning of the material – in this case, existentialism. His study of the language and concepts in Deuteronomy shows that it was a book that had contemporary relevance to the people of Israel; it is not a mere history book, but it put history in such a manner that it was existentially real. They experienced the "nunc aeternum," the "hic et nunc."[53] This is the same sense of contemporaneity that von Rad later treats as actualization. But none of the trappings of actualization are present at this time: there is no interest in the traditionary process; it is not related to the historical situation; there is no discussion of what it means to experience this contemporization; he never acknowledges that there might be a difference between this existentialism and a present day existentialism. The existential element which he introduces here is highly reminiscent of the early Karl Barth, with little effort to distinguish between ancient and modern categories.[54]

2

Von Rad's next book, *Das Geschichtsbild des chronistischen Werkes*, published in 1930, exhibits a considerable advance in thought

---

[52]*Ibid.*, 64.

[53]*Ibid.*, 61, 88.

[54]Kierkegaard's influence is also possible at this point. For his formulation of the ideas of contemporization and repetition, see Søren Kierkegaard, *Training in Christianity* (Princeton: Princeton University, 1944) 66-70; *Repetition* (Princeton: Princeton University, 1946) 81-159.

over the earlier one. Most importantly, he is aware of the traditionary process and sets Chronicles in clear relation to the previous traditions of Israel:

> Der grossen Aufriss von zweimal 480 Jahren der Königsbücher hat der Chronist nicht übernommen; er war von der Zeit überholt worden. Dieses Veralten eines theologischen Aufrisses war aber Ausdruck für eine grosse innere Wandlung. Der lange nach dem Exil schreibende Verfasser bedurfte, um zu seiner Zeit zu reden, einer grundsätzlichen Neuorientierung des alten Geschichtsmaterials. Indem er David und seine Thronfolger ins Zentrum rückte, glaubte er dieser Anforderung zu entsprechen! ... nein, der Chronist hat aus hochakuten Fragen und Tendenzen seiner Zeit heraus das Wort ergriffen und dadurch, dass er seine Gedanken, Wünsche und Abneigungen in ein konstruiertes Geschichtsbild projizierte, etwas wie eine Programmschrift für das nachexilische Israel geschaffen.[55]

Here he expresses a sensitivity to the time-conditioned changes that can cause a new history to be written, to the desire and need of an author to speak to the present day. He sees reflected in the Chronicler's work the questions relevant to that day. These questions have replaced the concerns of the older Deuteronomistic history. However, the Chronicler has continued to use the old traditions[56] and has imbued them with his own meaning. This reflects a clear understanding on von Rad's part of the traditionary process developed by Gunkel.

Von Rad follows both Gunkel and Herder in another aspect: the manner in which we understand the material today. We must search out the innermost thoughts and tendencies of a work, explore the origins of the old traditions which comprise it, try to understand the circles in which it circulated, and thus make it vivid *(lebendig)* for ourselves.[57] This is the arena of aesthetic contemporization to which both Herder and Gunkel belong. Von Rad's language still has not moved out of this general area of contemporization, although he connects it closely to the

---

[55]Gerhard von Rad, *Das Geschichtsbild des chronistischen Werkes* (Stuttgart: W. Kohlhammer, 1930) 120-21.

[56]Von Rad still rarely uses the word tradition; however, see *Geschichtsbild,* 24.

[57]*Ibid.,* 8, 132.

traditionary process, as does Gunkel.[58] One example of where von Rad stands in relation to his later work emerges in his discussion of Isa 55:3. Here he speaks of the passage being an unrealized promise which is retransmitted *(weitergeben)*.[59] While he recognizes the traditionary process which occurs, his understanding is far from that evinced by his concept of actualization. In a later study he states not just that there is a traditionary process operating in the verse, but that it is a radical one. The tradition is boldly reshaped *(umdeuten)*; it is "robbed of its specific content."[60] Thus, while *Das Geschichtsbild des chronistischen Werkes* shows a growing awareness of the growth of tradition, it still does not exhibit a mature understanding of the consequences of the process.

An article which should be discussed in relation to this book is "The Levitical Sermon in I and II Chronicles" (1934).[61] In *Das Geschichtsbild des chronistischen Werkes* von Rad discusses the coalescing of the offices of prophet and priest, the ecstatic and the cultic, into the office of the preacher, who speaks Yahweh's word which is received as authoritative.[62] His later article concerns the form of the sermons which this new office produced. From his discussion it is evident that the sermon form is one of the keys to von Rad's understanding of actualization. Here he first sees the linking of the actual contemporary situation with old tradition in a theologically meaningful sense. He says of Deuteronomy, "It is as if this writer feels himself driven by the problem of passing generations: how can later generations be kept loyal to Yahweh, and how can the link with his mighty acts in history be maintained? The deuteronomic sermon arose in response to this need."[63] He sees both the deuteronomic sermon and its direct descendant, the levitical sermon, as theological instruction which responds to a specific present situation by applying "a doctrine *(Glaubens)* long since established."[64] This is the same amalgam of concerns that we find in von Rad's formulation of actualization:

---

[58]He does this through such terms as *weitergegeben* (p. 122), *realisieren* (p. 122), *neue Formen* (p. 64), *Erneuerung* (p. 64).

[59]Von Rad, *Geschichtsbild,* 122.

[60]Von Rad, *Theology* 2.240.

[61]Gerhard von Rad, "The Levitical Sermon in I and II Chronicles," *Essays* 267-80.

[62]Von Rad attributes the initial insight to Mowinckel: *Geschichtsbild,* 114.

[63]Von Rad, "Levitical Sermon," 267.

[64]*Ibid.,* 269. Note the continued avoidance of the word tradition.

theological instruction, a specific historical situation, and a use of old traditions. However, the mix is still significantly different. There is still no thought of this leading to the hearer's re-experiencing the old traditions. Indeed, this would be impossible since von Rad is dealing with the re-use of doctrines rather than the historical events in the life of Israel. The centrality of these historical events has yet to be formulated and connected to the traditionary process. Also, von Rad is not dealing with the world of oral tradition. Instead, the sermons apply the written texts of older traditions to a contemporary situation, texts which have become authoritative for Israel.[65] The entire situation is not the one of vigor and vitality which von Rad attributes to actualization, but one of a decrease in originality and spontaneity, since it is written sources which are being utilized in a period of Israel's decline.[66]

These two works demonstrate von Rad's continued development in the direction of actualization. He not only sees the importance of the traditionary process, but links the re-use of doctrines (rather than traditions) to meet a contemporary need with a theological form, the sermon. In this synthesis he once again demonstrates his Barthian roots in the emphasis upon preaching as a theological vehicle. Most of the elements of actualization are present; however, the final integration is still lacking.

3

We will conclude our discussion of this formative period in von Rad's thought by examining "There Remains Still a Rest for the People of God" (1933).[67] This article develops different aspects of von Rad's thought related to actualization, developments that should be seen as concomitant with his two works on the Chronicler rather than as a linear progression.

In this article we find von Rad really grappling with the interrelations of the traditionary process, contemporaneity, and theology. He remains true to his theological roots as he continues to

---

[65]Ibid., 272.

[66]Ibid., 279.

[67]Gerhard von Rad, "There Remains Still a Rest for the People of God," Essays 94-102.

speak to Deuteronomy's message as *hic et nunc*.[68] However, he goes a step further in relating this existentialism more directly to the idea of contemporaneity: Israel is carried back (*zurückversetzen*) to the time of Moses, and God's redemption is made a present reality (*Gegenwärtigkeit*).[69] This backward movement is highly reminiscent of Mowinckel's explanation of actualization in the cult.

Von Rad also links the traditionary process to this development. The idea of rest undergoes several modifications in the history of Biblical thought. However, these changes are not developments, that is, they do not "supercede and exhaust (*entaktualisieren*) the force of its predecessor."[70] Instead of calling it development, he says: "Let us rather call this a chain of witnesses in which both the overall plan and the particular mode of expression are governed preeminently by the insight of each witness."[71] This is an awkward and groping expression of what will later be clearly developed as actualization by von Rad. The thrust of his comment is that later formulations of the idea of rest do not de-actualize the earlier expressions and that new formulations are guided by the freedom of the new interpreters and by their understanding of the old tradition.

A further lack of clarity is demonstrated by his continued avoidance of the word "tradition" for the material which is being updated. He uses vague terminology such as "theological conception" or "complex of ideas."[72] Even three years later he talks about "doctrines" and *Aktualität*, which he defines as a belief which has independent status.[73]

This article also exhibits the beginning of several theological interests for von Rad. The first hint of the idea of promise and fulfillment occurs. It is not discussed directly as such, but is mentioned in terms of the unfulfilled promises concerning rest which remain alive

---

[68]*Ibid.*, 94.

[69]*Ibid.*, 94, 96. *Gegenwärtigkeit* later becomes part of von Rad's standard vocabulary concerning actualization.

[70]*Ibid.*, 99.

[71]*Ibid.*, 100.

[72]*Ibid.*, 95, 99.

[73]Gerhard von Rad, "The Theological Problem of the Old Testament Doctrine of Creation," *Essays* 138-39.

even into the New Testament.[74] His explanation of the relationship between the Old and New Testaments is spelled out more clearly. The connection is seen as part of this chain of witnesses in the concept of rest; indeed, it is the final link in the chain. The New Testament offers a fresh understanding *(neu Verständnis)* of the idea of rest which omits theological elements present in the Old Testament and adds other elements which the Old Testament keeps entirely separate. It does not attempt to draw together all the Old Testament evidence, but exercises great freedom in choosing what to include and in using various references as proof texts.[75] This understanding of the testaments as one traditio-historical continuum and the charismatic use of the Old Testament by the New will appear as central features in von Rad's description of their relationship in his later work.

4

Although von Rad produced other notable works during this formative period of 1929-1938,[76] the ones discussed above are those most directly involved in the development of actualization. Most of the constituent elements of the concept are present in this period, at least in nascent form. From the beginning von Rad expressed a concern for the theological side of Old Testament studies. His theological outlook during this time shows the imprint of Barthian and Kierkegaardian existentialism, particularly in the immediate relevance of the Old Testament materials to their hearers. One element central to his later theological formulation, the creative word of God, does not appear in this period. Von Rad demonstrates a developing understanding of the traditionary process and the role which the contemporizing of old material plays in that process. Still lacking is the role of the credenda in the formation of the Old Testament traditions. Von Rad also begins to formulate his understanding of the relationship of the two testaments. In this period he expresses the relationship in terms of promise and fulfillment, with the role of typology yet to be discussed. Therefore, in this developmental period the roots of von Rad's concept of actualization are present. They merely await the mature mind to

---

[74]Von Rad, "Rest," 95-96, 100. For a fuller development of promise-fulfillment as an OT scheme, see Gerhard von Rad, "Christuszeugnis."

[75]Von Rad, "Rest," 99-102.

[76]For specific examples, see footnote 50 above.

synthesize them – a process which began forcefully, even brilliantly, with *The Form-Critical Problem of the Hexateuch* in 1938.

Von Rad's Development of Actualization

In the period between *The Form-Critical Problem of the Hexateuch* and his *Old Testament Theology* in 1957, von Rad did much to develop his concept of actualization. We will survey that development in this section. Since it would be impossible to touch upon each mention of the issue, we will concentrate upon the major advances, most evident in *Studies in Deuteronomy* (1947), "The City on the Hill" (1949), and his Genesis commentary (1950). During the same period von Rad also evolved his schemes of typology and promise and fulfillment. Since these are closely tied to actualization, especially in his *Old Testament Theology,* we will review them also by discussing "Typological Interpretation of the Old Testament" (1952).

1

Studies in Deutereonomy confirmed that von Rad had indeed embarked on a new approach to the literature of the Old Testament with *The Form-Critical Problem of the Hexateuch.* It clearly stands in the same line as that essay and is a stark contrast to his earliest work, *Das Gottesvolk in Deuteronomium.* This is not the place for a detailed analysis of the changes in von Rad's approach to Deuteronomy; suffice it to say that in contrast to the thematic study and direct theologizing of the earlier work, *Studies in Deuteronomy* displays a thoroughgoing interest in the form and origin of the book, and a sophisticated concern for the theological elements in the writings.

Von Rad had also refined the concept of actualization since *The Form-Critical Problem of the Hexateuch.* He no longer deemed it necessary to explain the nature of actualization or how and where it occurs in Deuteronomy. Its presence in the book is regarded as a fact; the concept is an integral part of von Rad's method because actualization is an inescapable element in the Biblical material which he is analyzing. With no explanation he assumes that the author of Deuteronomy is taking old material and making it relevant (*aktualisieren*) for his own historical situation. He does this for laws, the holy war traditions, the amphictyonic cultic traditions, the building of Solomon's temple, and the events at Horeb.[77] All of this disparate material, under the title of "tradition" is re-used by the Deuteronomist in the particular manner called actualization.

The nature of actualization differs somewhat from that described in *The Form-Critical Problem of the Hexateuch*. While von Rad still maintains Deuteronomy's relation to the cult, this connection does not assume the centrality for interpretation which it had in the earlier essay. The book consists of cultic material, but material that is presented to the lay community second hand, through priestly paraenesis.[78] This is a development of an idea presented in the earlier essay. In that instance von Rad described Deuteronomy as a collection of various materials, including homilies. While the homiletic material was an organizing mechanism for parts of the book, it was not the governing factor for the entire collection, nor was it specifically related to actualization. In *Studies in Deuteronomy* the homilies assumed a more important role. Now, Deuteronomy as a whole is "priestly paraenesis" and "preaching about commandments," with the homiletic material as the controlling principle of development and organization.[79] The paraenetic material actualizes the old traditions and commandments.

This constitutes a change from *The Form-Critical Problem of the Hexateuch;* there actualization was attached to the cult and directly related to cultic drama. Although the examples of actualization given by von Rad are generally considered paraenetic material, he did not draw the connection in the essay. He makes the connection abundantly clear in *Studies in Deuteronomy*. Consequently, actualization itself assumes greater importance for Deuteronomy. Von Rad sees it as central to the meaning of the book. The major question underlying Deuteronomy is this: Is Israel still the people of God, even though six centuries of apostasy separate them from Horeb?[80] Actualization wipes out the intervening period, places the current Israel at Horeb, and proclaims salvation for them. In connecting actualization with the central meaning of Deuteronomy, he also reveals the existential nature of the concept. Thus, we see a relation between *Studies in Deuteronomy* and

---

[77]Gerhard von Rad, *Studies in Deuteronomy* (London: SCM, 1953) 16, 52, 23, 50-51, 41, 43, 70.

[78]*Ibid.*, 13-15.

[79]*Ibid.*, 13, 15.

[80]*Ibid.*, 70.

Das Gottesvolk in Deuteronomium: Deuteronomy is still an existential tract. It makes salvation a present reality in a specific historical situation. In the later work, however, von Rad sees this existentialism as growing out of tradition criticism and actualization, as opposed to the connection with dogmatic theology that he demonstrated in the earlier work.

Von Rad introduces another theological concept which will assume an important role in his later work in the chapter "The Deuteronomistic Theology of History in the Book of Kings": the creative and vital word of God in history. The Deuteronomistic history is "really a history of the creative word of Jahweh."[81] This word begins as a word of prophecy, specifically a word of judgment in Kings, and, once uttered, moves inexorably to its fulfillment in history. This interrelationship with history means that the word cannot fail because of the "power inherent in it";[82] thus, it actually creates the history of Israel. At this point von Rad makes no explicit connection between the creative word of God and actualization, as he does later. The two concepts appear side by side and the possibility of a connection between them is apparent. They share the ability to renew old traditions and to make history alive for the people of Israel. Von Rad's ties to contemporary Protestant theology are evident in this concept which is closely related to the idea of the word of God which is inherently powerful, always renewed through preaching, always confronting the listener in the current situation.

2

During this developmental period von Rad first applied the concept of actualization to the prophetic literature. He briefly mentions the term in connection with prophecy in "Grundprobleme einer biblischen Theologie des Alten Testaments" (1943) and "Literarkritische und überlieferungsgeschichtliche Forschung im Alten Testament" (1947).[83] His first extended application of actualization to the prophetic literature is in "The City on the Hill" (1949).

---

[81]*Ibid.,* 91.

[82]*Ibid.,* 78.

[83]Gerhard von Rad, "Grundprobleme einer biblischen Theologie des Alten Testaments," *TLZ,* 68 (1943) 230; "Literarkritische und überlieferungsgeschichtliche Forschung im Alten Testament," *VF* 1947-48 part 3 (1950) 181.

Von Rad saw the need for a completely new evaluation of the role of prophecy's dependence on tradition. An important part of this evaluation is the role of actualization, since "the prophets laid claim to an unprecedented measure of liberty, both in their handling of ancient and accepted religious ideas and, even more particularly, in their application (*Aktualisierung*) of them to a particular situation and to a particular group of people."[84] This tension between freedom of expression and dependence upon tradition presages his later work in the prophets. His statement concerning the integral relationship between actualization and the present historical situation, which will be very prominent in his *Old Testament Theology,* is the most explicit expression so far. The interrelation of the historical situation and theological meaning has definite methodological consequences for von Rad. Historical reconstruction is necessary to understand a prophet's message:

> How could we possibly assess whether or not a prophet has properly discharged his task *vis-à-vis* his own generation, or whether he has used or abused his liberty of remoulding in his own way the traditional materials? To make any such judgment we should need at the very least a precise and detailed knowledge of the historical situation, and of its potentialities as well as its dangers.[85]

As in *Studies in Deuteronomy,* he sees no need to explain the nature of actualization and its use in the historical realm rather than the cultic; the concept is presumed. The entire article tantalizes the reader on the nature of actualization, since he refers to it obliquely in relation to the prophets' use of tradition, which is the main thrust of the article. Von Rad himself sees the article as a preview, a partial elucidation of one theme in the manner in which he wishes to restudy the prophets. We must wait until *Old Testament Theology II* to understand the full implications of his study.

3

In von Rad's commentary on Genesis (1950), as in his other works of this period, he does not so much discuss actualization as apply it.

---

[84]Gerhard von Rad, "The City on the Hill,"*Essays* 232.

[85]*Ibid.,* 241.

The selective manner in which he applies it is instructive. In his discussion of the growth of the Hexateuch around the basic credo of Israel's faith and in his outline of the narrative sources of Genesis he does not mention actualization. Nor does he deal with the concept in the exegesis of the text. In these sections he deals with the material in the normal terminology of tradition history and form criticism.[86] Only when he discusses the theological and hermeneutical problems of Genesis does he introduce actualization. This division of terminology helps clarify the role of actualization in relation to tradition criticism: it bears the weight of theological interpretation for what was originally a non-theological method.

The point at which actualization does arise is in von Rad's discussion of the relation of saga and history writing. The central difference between the two is that saga is characterized by an openness to actualization.

> It [saga] lives and grows at a time when the power of rational and logical, historical perception is not yet fully liberated, at a time, however, when the powers of instinctive, intuitively interpretive, one could almost say mantic, understanding dominate all the more freely. In its sagas a people is concerned with itself and the realities in which it finds itself. It is, however, a view and interpretation not only of that which once was but of a past event that is secretly present and decisive for the present *(gegenwärtsbestimmend).*[87]

The nature of saga affects our entire perspective on Genesis and its tradition history. We must not regard the book as history writing in the modern sense nor the transmission of the sagas as mere preservation of past events. The material has been altered and expanded continuously in its transmission, since it must at all times contain not only a core of

---

[86]Gerhard von Rad, *Genesis* (Philadelphia: Westminster, 1961) 17-20. When speaking of the origin of the material in the cult and its liberation from the cult, he uses traditio-historical terms which go back to Gunkel, such as "spiritualizing," "rationalization," "refashioning," "reform," "secularization."

[87]*Ibid.,* 32. The section on hermeneutics is considerably revised in the second edition (Philadelphia: Westminster, 1963) of the commentary. However, his revisions did not significantly alter the view of actualization presented in the first edition. One major alteration related to actualization was a virtual elimination of the role of typology in interpretation. While typology is a major element in this section of the first edition, the second edition stresses "continuity" between the testaments.

"historical *(historisches)* fact," but also "reflect a historical *(geschichtliches)* experience of the relevant community which extends into the present time of the narrator."[88] In this way the saga is a witness to the past, yet completely contemporary *(vollgegenwärtigung)* for the present community of Israel.[89] For von Rad the theological nature of the Genesis material can only be understood in relation to actualization. This is integrally related to the traditio-historical method, yet it requires a separate discussion and uses a distinct terminology, since we have now incorporated the realm of theology into the process.

This description of the nature of saga expands upon the understanding of actualization in relation to the Yahwist which von Rad first mentioned in *The Form-Critical Problem of the Hexateuch.* However, it neither alters the essential nature of the concept as a theological mechanism nor resolves the problems which the earlier article left unanswered. In particular von Rad does not broach the question of how one moves from actualization within the cult to actualization of material which has become separated from the cult. His discussion of saga may be seen as an attempt to explain the latter type, but it does not approach the problem directly. Von Rad's discussion of the process of the Genesis material separating from the cult is couched in the normal terminology of tradition criticism and fails to mention actualization.[90]

4

The final article to be discussed in this section is "Typological Interpretation of the Old Testament" (1952). This article does not mention actualization as such. However, it delineates von Rad's use of typology and promise and fulfillment, two concepts which he later relates to actualization. Since this is the seminal article for his understanding of both terms, this is an appropriate place to discuss them.

Neither concept appears *de novo* in this article. We have already mentioned that von Rad began to deal with promise and fulfillment as early as 1933 in "There Remains Still a Rest for the People of God."

---

[88]Von Rad, *Genesis*, (1st ed.) 33.

[89]*Ibid.*, 34.

[90]*Ibid.*, 17-20.

He continued to use and expand the concept in "The Promised Land and Yahweh's Land in the Hexateuch," and "Grundprobleme einer biblischer Theologie des Alten Testaments," both published in 1943.[91]

Typology began to assume importance for von Rad only after the appearance of Goppelt's book, *Typos*, in 1939. His use of the term is developed on the basis of Goppelt's work.[92] Von Rad's first use of the concept was in "Grundprobleme einer biblischer Theologie des Alten Testaments" in 1943. In his Genesis commentary he discusses it along with actualization: the continued actualization of the sagas has raised them to the level of a typical occurrence, which is especially clear when they are reused in the New Testament.[93] However, his elucidation of typology awaits the 1952 article.

In "Typological Interpretation of the Old Testament" the most significant move that von Rad makes is to limit the use of typology in relation to the Old Testament and to differentiate it from modern typology, ancient Near Eastern typology, and allegory. For him all typology is analogical thinking. Modern typology or analogical interpretation finds ultimate significance in the ordinary. It is both an aesthetic move, as in poetry, and a philosophical one, as in Plato's concept of the Ideal. Ancient Near Eastern typology found a direct correspondence between the heavenly and the earthly: an earthly structure is modeled upon a pre-existent heavenly prototype. Old Testament typology is neither of these; it rests upon a correspondence of *Urzeit* and *Endzeit*. In this case the eschatological events are modeled upon the events of the *Urzeit* and the future is understood in its correspondence to the past. However, the events of the *Urzeit* in the Old Testament are not so much the primeval events of creation, but the historical events of Israel's deliverance and formation as a people under Yahweh. Thus, Old Testament typology is historical typology.[94]

The historical element also allows von Rad to distinguish between typology and allegory. Allegory is also analogical thinking, but it is

---

[91]Gerhard von Rad, "The Promised Land and Yahweh's Land in the Hexateuch," *Essays* 93; "Grundprobleme," 228-29.

[92]Leonhard Goppelt, *Typos* (Gütersloh: C. Bertelsmann, 1939) 19ff.

[93]Von Rad, "Grundprobleme," 232; *Genesis*, 39-42.

[94]Gerhard von Rad, "Typological Interpretation of the Old Testament," in Claus Westermann, ed., *Essays on Old Testament Hermeneutics* (Richmond: John Knox, 1966) 19-20.

attached to the literal sense of the words and must find a full correspondence for each element of the text. Typology, on the other hand, has free rein with the literal sense of the text, but hangs closely upon its historical sense.[95] Rather than concentrating upon the religious ideas and teachings of the text, as does allegory, typology preserves the facts to which the Old Testament and New Testament texts witness.

The result of this limiting of typology in the Bible is that the object of interpretation is the kerygmatic intention of the text. Typology is not concerned with the historical, cultural, or archaeological similarities of the Old Testament and the New; nor is it concerned with models of piety or religious ideals. It focuses upon the historical kerygma of Israel's faith and its prefiguration of Christ.[96] Most important for our consideration is that typology is not stagnant theologizing. Each generation of Israel posed the problem of its relation to the kerygma anew. Ever fresh typologies arise as each new generation apprehends its relation to faith again.[97] In this element we see the beginning of a relation to actualization. Although it is not yet clearly articulated, both actualization and typology deal with the problem of Israel's existential comprehension of its faith. We must wait for von Rad's *Old Testament Theology* to see how these elements are linked.

Integrally related to typology in this article is a scheme of promise and fulfillment. Once again the Old Testament scheme is unique. It does not present a set of promises which are fulfilled and thus come to an end. Nor is there a set of promises which go on before Israel and will be fulfilled in the *Endzeit*. No, in the Old Testament we find a promise which is given manifold fulfillments. Each fulfillment is a witness to the trustworthiness of God. But the fulfillment also renews the promise, giving it new content, new life, leading it to a new and greater fulfillment: "Things are never used up, but their very fulfillment gives rise, all unexpected, to the promise of yet greater things ... Here nothing carries its ultimate meaning in itself, but is ever the earnest of yet greater wonders."[98] This is true because Israel's

---

[95]*Ibid.*, 21-22.

[96]*Ibid.*, 36-37.

[97]*Ibid.*, 34.

[98]*Ibid.*

history and this pattern of promise and fulfillment is a history of the creative word of God, which we discussed in relation to the Deuteronomistic history. Now, however, von Rad has expanded the role of the creative word of God to include not just the fulfillment of a promise, but also the renewing of that promise in its fulfillment. Thus, the promise is forever new, forever valid, depending only on the vitality of God's word and the reinterpretation of the present generation for its own time.

5

In this period of 1939-1952 von Rad expanded and developed his concept of actualization. Its application now permeates his work as he extends it to many different types of Old Testament material: the Deuteronomistic history, the prophetic literature, the entirety of the Hexateuch. While he does not give a detailed explanation of the concept, he moves in that direction by applying it outside the cult and discussing it in relation to the saga. But most importantly, during this period the separate strands of von Rad's thought – typology, promise and fulfillment, the creative word of God, and actualization – began coalescing into a coherent theological vision of the Old Testament. This period was a fruitful one of turmoil and growth as actualization assumed an increasingly central role and strove toward the full expression which von Rad achieved in his *Old Testament Theology*.

Von Rad's Full Exposition of Actualization

The full importance of actualization to von Rad's work did not emerge until his monumental *Old Testament Theology*. Even then he continued to develop the concept in the separate volumes and different editions of the book. We will take into account these developments as we outline his full delineation of actualization. Von Rad reflected upon actualization in other works during this period as well. Of particular value in understanding his clarifications of the concept in the face of criticism are "Offene Fragen im Umkreis einer Theologie des Alten Testaments" (1963), "Rückblick und Ausblick" (1965), his discussion of apocalyptic in the fourth German edition of *Theologie des Alten*

Testaments (1965), and *Wisdom in Israel* (1970).[99] We will refer to these works and others where appropriate in this section.

1

On reading the first volume of von Rad's *Old Testament Theology*, published in 1957, one is struck by the different role which actualization plays in comparison to his two earlier works which covered much of the same material, *The Form-Critical Problem of the Hexateuch* and *Genesis*. No longer is the concept limited mainly to explaining the relation of Deuteronomy to the cult, as in the former. (Indeed, the type of cultic actualization which that article set forth never appears in the first volume of the *Theology*.) Nor is it restricted to a theoretical discussion of the theological and hermeneutical problems of the Hexateuch, as in the latter. Now actualization appears as a central part of the hermeneutical method of the Old Testament texts, both in theory and in practice.

Von Rad applies the concept to a wide range of Old Testament texts and situations. He uses it in connection with the J and E documents (pp. 71, 117, 393ff), the law (pp. 199, 209), the narrator's conception of the Mosaic office (pp. 14, 290), the prophetic books (pp. 71, 117, 393ff), the cult (pp. 209, 253), Nathan's prophecy (p. 311), the psalms (pp. 321, 396), the Chronicler (p. 347), the promise of the

---

[99] Another work dating from this period is *Deuteronomy* (Philadelphia: Westminster, 1966), published in 1964. While it mentions actualization in the introduction, it does nothing to advance our understanding of the concept.

land (pp. 303-5), and Hebrew narrative in general (pp. 107-12, 365).[100] These widely divergent references demonstrate that actualization permeates his theological interpretation of the Old Testament. It is now central in practice as well as in theory.

However, the true importance of actualization becomes apparent only when we consider von Rad's discussion of his methodological presuppositions. He sets this discussion in the framework which we mentioned in the introduction to this study: the hermeneutical crisis occasioned by the growing divergence between historical criticism and theological application. Historical criticism has reconstructed one picture of Israel's history, while Israel's self-understanding has produced another, quite different, picture:

> Historical investigation searches for a critically assured minimum – the kerygmatic picture tends towards a theological maximum. The fact that these two views of Israel's history are so divergent is one of the most serious burdens imposed today upon Biblical scholarship.[101]

One does not solve this problem either by imposing a modern view of history upon Israel's faith or by saying that we must understand this faith apart from history. The key to solving this dilemma is to meet Israel upon its own ground and thus recognize that it had its own

---

[100]Gerhard von Rad, *Old Testament Theology* (New York: Harper & Row, 1962) 1. While Stalker states that his translation incorporates notes for the second German edition, most of the changes between the first edition of *Theologie des Alten Testaments* (Munich: C. Kaiser, 1957) 1, and *Theology* 1 are not made in the German until the fourth edition (Munich: C. Kaiser, 1962). One of the major differences between the first and fourth editions of *Theologie* 1 is that von Rad has added several very explicit references to actualization in the latter. None of the additions change the substance of von Rad's discussion, but they emphasize and clarify the role of actualization. For examples of the changes which von Rad made, compare the following pages:

Theologie 1 (1st-3rd eds.)	*Theologie* 1 (4th-6th eds.)	*Theology* 1
14	14	4
24	28	14
98-99	104	90
112-120	118-28	106-15
176	187-88	173

[101]Von Rad, *Theology* 1.21-22.

peculiar view of history – one shaped by faith and characterized by actualization:

> The kerygmatic picture too ... is founded in the actual history and has not been invented. The means by which this historical experience is made relevant for the time, the way in which it is mirrored forth in a variety of pictures, and in sagas in type form, are those adapted to the possibilities of expression of an ancient people.[102]

Israel's faith is not unhistoric; rather the historical kernel, which is essential and always present, is made subservient to the needs of faith.

The requirement of faith is that the material must speak relevantly to the time of the listeners and not be merely a dead, essentially meaningless relic of the past. This "problem of the generations" is the lynchpin of von Rad's method; it is constantly repeated as the means by which Israel theologized about its traditions:

> ... this did not exempt each generation from the task of comprehending itself in faith as the Israel of its own day, and from coming before Jahweh as this Israel. However, in this process of actualization *(Vergegenwärtigung)* the tradition here and there had to be reshaped.[103]

Thus, Israel bridges this gap by means of actualization.

Then, more explicitly than in any of his previous works, von Rad posits the question of how actualization is possible for narrative material. In *The Form-Critical Problem of the Hexateuch* he had explained only cultic actualization – and even then was more concerned with application than with explanation. In his Genesis commentary he approached the problem obliquely in his discussion of saga and history. Now he asks the question directly. The answer lies in the nature of the Biblical narratives: all of the Old Testament materials until the Deuteronomistic history are poetic.

---

[102]*Ibid.*, 108. Not in *Theologie* 1 (1st ed.). Compare *Theologie* 1.114 (1st ed.), with *Theologie* 1.120-21 (4th ed.).

[103]Von Rad, *Theology* 1.119. Also see pp. 4, 112, 125, 193, 199, 209, 226, 306, 311, 349.

Historical poetry was the form in which Israel, like other peoples, made sure of historical facts, that is, of their location and their significance. In those times poetry was, as a rule, the one possible form for expressing special basic insights.... poetry alone enabled a people to express experiences met with in the course of their history in such a way as to make the past become absolutely present.[104]

Faith and history are inextricably entwined in the poetic medium. The narratives demand not an understanding based on logic, but the assent of faith.

A further consequence of this medium of expression is that "the law of historical exclusiveness, according to which a certain event or a certain experience can be attached only to a single definite point in history,"[105] is not in effect. Historical events are intensified, combined, enlarged, individualized in such a way that they attain a typical significance and reach all the way to the narrator's own time with a stunning degree of contemporaneousness *(Gleichzeitigkeit)*.

Therefore, for von Rad actualization is at the center of a theology of the Old Testament. While a systematic study of the concepts behind Israel's faith is important, it misses the crucial element in theology: the nature of faith itself. To be alive and vital, a theology of the Old Testament must recapture that which was alive and vital to Israel itself:

If, however, we put Israel's picture of her history in the forefront of our theological consideration, we encounter what appropriately is the most essential subject of a theology of the Old Testament, the living word of Jahweh coming on and on to Israel forever, and this is the message uttered by his mighty acts. It was a message so living and actual for each moment that it accompanied her on her journey through time, interpreting itself afresh to every generation, and informing every generation what it had to do.[106]

---

[104]*Ibid.*, 109. The second part of this quote is different from *Theologie* 1 (1st ed.). Compare *Theologie* 1.115 (1st ed.), with *Theologie* 1.121-22 (4th ed.). Von Rad attributes this understanding of poetry to Dilthey.

[105]Von Rad, *Theology* 1.110.

[106]*Ibid.*, 112. This section is not in *Theologie 1* (1st ed.). Compare *Theologie* 1.118 (1st ed.) with *Theologie* 1.125 (4th ed.).

Thus we see in this first volume of the *Old Testament Theology* the elements of actualization coalescing both in theory and in practice. In von Rad's description of his theological method, actualization occupies part of center stage as the hermeneutical device by which Israel kept its faith alive and renewed itself in each subsequent generation. But actualization does not remain mere theory: he consistently applies it throughout his theological exposition to a variety of materials from Israel's history.

No longer is it restricted to an anthropological concept of cultic renewal, nor is it merely an aesthetic device to move people's hearts. Its roots are visible. Both the need to recreate Israel's own understanding of history rather than to impose our modern concept and the use of an empathetic understanding of Israel's thought world as a basis for interpretation stem from Herder's aesthetics. The emphasis upon traditions and their continued re-use proceeds from Gunkel. The indebtedness to contemporary theology in the concept of the word of God is obvious, as is the existential, *hic et nunc*,[107] nature of the confrontation which each new generation faces with this word. However, the synthesis which is actualization is von Rad's own; it is essentially theological but incorporates the insights of historical criticism and the traditio-historical process.

In addition to the clearer understanding of actualization which emerges from our study of this volume, we can sense a development in thought concerning the concept as von Rad revised later editions. Several of the quotes which we have used are missing from the first German edition. As von Rad assessed his work in this volume, he evidently saw a need to clarify the role of actualization in the hermeneutical process. Consequently, he added a number of passages which explained the nature and function of the concept. Rather than altering the thrust of the first edition, these revisions made explicit that which was implicit through the use of the specialized vocabulary associated with actualization.[108]

2

In volume two of *Old Testament Theology* von Rad continues to expand upon the nature and function of actualization. In the first

---

[107]Von Rad, *Theology* 1.199, 394.

[108]See footnotes 100, 104, 106 for specific references.

volume he explained its role in his theological method, but left unanswered many questions about the nature of the mechanism itself. Now, in his section on the prophets, he both discusses these questions directly and consistently applies the concept to the prophetic literature.

In other works von Rad applied actualization to a wide variety of literature. In *The Form-Critical Problem of the Hexateuch* he used the concept to tie the Deuteronomic material closely to the cult, relating it to Mowinckel's idea of cultic drama. In *Genesis* and *Old Testament Theology I* he applies actualization to the J and E documents and to the prophetic writings, materials which have no close cultic ties. He never attempted to explain how one concept could apply equally to these widely disparate materials. Since he regards actualization as originating in the cult, one should not merely assume that it may also be applied to non-cultic materials. In the chapter "Time, History, and Eschatology" von Rad finally clarifies this problem.

He begins his discussion of actualization with a description similar to his initial one in *The Form-Critical Problem of the Hexateuch.*

> The historical acts by which Jahweh founded the community of Israel were absolute.... They were actual (*gegenwärtig*) for each subsequent generation; and this not just in the sense of furnishing the imagination with a vivid present picture *(lebhaften geistigen Vergegenwärtigung)* of past events – no, it was only the community assembled for a festival that by recitation and ritual brought Israel in the full sense of the word into being: in her own person she really and truly entered into the historic situation to which the festival in question was related.[109]

Here he is describing the type of actualization which he discussed in that 1938 monograph and which was absent from his subsequent discussions of the term. It is an actualization which occurs in the cultic festival and involves a re-experiencing of the events being celebrated.[110] He is very careful to distinguish this from an actualization which merely made something real to the imagination – the common meaning of the term which developed from Herder's

---

[109]Von Rad, *Theology* 2.104.

[110]Von Rad acknowledges his debt to Mowinckel for this concept of actualization by footnoting *Psalmen* 2 (*Theology* 2.104).

hermeneutic. Von Rad is talking about a special type of *Vergegenwärtigung* and *Aktualisierung* which goes beyond the normal uses of the words.

This initial statement about actualization differs in one important respect from his earlier description in 1938. The concept is no longer tied to Deuteronomy. Instead, von Rad relates it directly to the cultic festival itself, not to a later literary exposition based upon the festival.

However, Israel moved out of the primitive cultic time sense and achieved a linear sense of history by "historicizing" its cult and connecting the events associated with different festivals into a series of saving events. This developed into the historical sequences we now know as J, E, the Deuteronomistic history, and the Chronicler's history. Von Rad correctly raises the question of the relationship of this linear sense of history to actualization.

His answer is not that actualization died out, but that with the development of a linear sense of time Israel simultaneously had two types of actualization: cultic and chronological.[111] Von Rad does not fully and clearly define what he means by the latter, but he does give some guidelines. Chronological actualization warrants the title because it is still an attempt to contemporize the historical events of Israel's saving history for a later generation. However, now "it was now no longer really possible to regard history as turning back on itself."[112] Instead, a "rational understanding" helps form a picture of that history; and rational, conscious techniques are used to bring about chronological actualization. Deuteronomy reflects the crisis between these two modes of thinking:

> In Deuteronomy the preacher makes it apparent that the generation which he addresses is well aware of the distance which separates it from the one with which the Sinai covenant was originally made. In these circumstances, the covenant,

---

[111]Von Rad, *Theology* 2.108. Chronological actualization did not replace cultic, but the two existed side by side, at least for a time. He attributes this idea to G. Pidoux, "A propos de la notion biblique du temps,"*RTP* 3 (1952) 120-25. In fact, Pidoux states that the two concepts of time existed simultaneously, but he applies actualization only to cultic time (pp. 121-23).

[112]Von Rad, *Theology* 2.108.

contemporaneous *(gleichzeitig)* for earlier generations, now requires to be put on a new basis in order to be valid.[113]

He then quotes Deut 5:2-3 and Deut 29:9-14 to demonstrate the use of "today" as a rationalizing means of actualization. Thus von Rad shifts the position of Deuteronomy from *The Form-Critical Problem of the Hexateuch*. Now it is not an example of cultic actualization, but a crossroads of cultic and chronological, a battleground of two conflicting views of time and actualization. Deuteronomy is still "within the sphere of the cult," but it reflects Israel's new time sense and concept of actualization. Only later do the Chronicler's history and the Deuteronomistic history break with the old cultic actualization and rely totally upon "rational considerations and arguments ... to keep the actuality *(Gegenwärtigkeit)* of the saving events."[114]

Thus, with this expanding role of actualization and redefinition of the place of Deuteronomy, we see that there is no example in the Old Testament of true cultic actualization. The closest that we come is the cultic material in Deuteronomy that has undergone rationalization to fit the new linear time sense which Israel had developed.[115] Therefore, what von Rad is really using in his *Old Testament Theology* is a type of actualization quite removed from the concept laid down by Mowinckel and the anthropological investigations of primitive cults.

In retrospect we can see that this is the concept which was operative for von Rad at least as far back as 1949 in "The City on the Hill" and subsequently applied in *Genesis* and *Old Testament Theology I*. Now we must investigate the concept further in its application to the prophetic literature to determine whether or not this change is justified.

This shift in meaning of actualization is signaled by the use to which von Rad puts the concept in the prophetic literature. The material with which he is dealing is no longer connected with the cult. Therefore, we cannot be talking about actualization in which the events of the cult are made alive to a contemporary audience. No, now the

---

[113]*Ibid.*, 109.

[114]*Ibid.*, 109.

[115]In addition to Deuteronomy one would expect him to refer to the psalmodic material which actualizes the cult. However, he only footnotes Ps 114 as an earlier example of cultic actualization (*Theology* 2.105). He fails to position it clearly in relation to cultic and chronological actualization.

focus is entirely upon traditions. The limited number of traditions (exodus, Sinai, conquest, etc.) are the material which the prophets actualize. In addition, they utilize several traditions not present in Israel's basic creed: Zion, David, and the holy war, for example.

A second important element in the application of this new type of actualization to the prophets is the historical specificity of the message. With cultic actualization one is making vital the events of the cult in a periodic festival. This actualization is the same regardless of external historical events. Indeed, part of the significance of cultic actualization is its performance to preserve the order of creation by emphasizing the sameness and eternal validity of the original creative events. Von Rad speaks of actualization in Deuteronomy responding to an historical need; but the external historical events are secondary to the actualizing of the saving traditions and to the fact that we are dealing with cultic materials. The crisis which produced the book is both a cultic crisis and an historical one. The actualization is presented in the dual cultic/historical framework.

However, in the prophetic literature a different situation pertains. The prophetic message is seen as a response to definite historical movements of the day:

> ... the prophets also show something else that is quite new – a keen and unprecedented awareness of the great historical movements and changes of their own day and generation. Their whole preaching is characterized by an unrivaled ability to adjust itself to new historical phenomena, and by a power of adapting itself to these phenomena.... This correlation between the prophets and world-history is the real key to understanding them correctly, for they placed the new historical acts of God which they saw around them in exactly the same category as the old basic events of the canonical history.[116]

Not only can one not understand the prophetic message apart from the world events surrounding it, but the prophets' actualization of the old traditions is wholly dependent on these events.

> The message of every prophet was exactly directed to meet a specific time, and it contained an offer which was never repeated in precisely the same form as it had with the original speaker.

---

[116]*Ibid.*, 112-13.

... Thus, the message of every prophet was closely bound up with the point in history at which it was delivered, and after this point no message could be repeated exactly in its original sense. This is where creative interpretation begins.[117]

Therefore, every actualization by a prophet of an old tradition was very, very specific. It pertained to one set of historical circumstances, one particular generation. This has two important consequences. First, in order fully to understand a prophetic oracle, we must know the historical situation from which it originates. Second, for a prophet's message to have any validity for later generations of Israel, it must be continually actualized. This is precisely what happened with the prophetic books. The original oracles of the prophets were handed down and reinterpreted by disciples. They added their own words to relate the older prophecy to a new day:

> ... successors took up the themes of Isaiah's message; they added prophecies in the Isaianic style to the old Isaianic texts, and thus kept the old message most vitally alive *(lebendigste)* and made it contemporary *(aktualisieren)* for later generations.... the tradition of this prophet's message was not preserved in archives: it remained a living organism, speaking directly to later generations as it had done to its own, and able even of itself to give birth to new prophecy.[118]

Thus the history of the prophetic books is a history of actualization: the original prophets actualized the old saving traditions; later disciples actualized the earlier materials for their own day.[119]

The third important element in the application of actualization to the prophetic literature is the role of the creative word of God. We have

---

[117]*Ibid.*, 299-300.

[118]*Ibid.*, 167-68. Also see pp. 43-49 where von Rad attributes this understanding of oral tradition of the prophets to Mowinckel and Birkeland.

[119]Von Rad clearly attributes actualization to all the prophets in his introductory section *(Ibid.,* 43-49); but in his exposition of the individual prophets, he refers directly to the concept with widely varying frequency. Actualization plays a major role for Isaiah and Deutero-Isaiah, as well as in his summary of the Babylonian and early Persian period. It appears sporadically in relation to Amos, Hosea, Jeremiah, Ezekiel, and the post-exilic prophets. He frequently uses it as a means for attributing disputed passages to the original prophet: Amos 9:11-12 (p. 138); Jer 23:5-6 (p. 218).

already discussed the concept in relation to *Studies in Deuteronomy*. Von Rad's ideas have not changed significantly since that earlier essay, but he does expand somewhat on them. Now he gives some theoretical background from the history of religions for his concept. It stems from the nature of ancient myth as a creative and guaranteeing force rather than merely an expression of people's understanding of the world. From this grows the idea that for primitive civilizations language itself had a creative power.

> It is well known that in many old and sometimes highly developed cultures language was not restricted simply to the description of objects; in out of the ordinary situations, due to a mysterious power of creation, language could produce either something new, or an intensified form of something already in existence: that is to say, language itself became creative; and this is a possibility which language has never lost, even to this day.[120]

From this von Rad develops the idea that the prophetic word, once uttered, never returns void, but creates its own fulfillment, creates the history of Israel.

> The basic conviction underlying the process of tradition was that, once a prophet's word had been uttered, it could never in any circumstances become void. The time when, and the way by which, it reached fulfillment were Jahweh's concern; man's part was to see that the word was handed on. And we must notice particularly that even the prophecies which had plainly found their historical goal, and had thus clearly been fulfilled, were retained as prophecies which concerned Israel and could always have fresh meaning extracted from them.[121]

In this way the creative word of God became the basis for the actualization of a prophet's words by later generations. Since the specific word is tied down to a specific set of historical circumstances, it must be actualized in order to keep it alive, working in the future, and moving toward its own fulfillment. The fact that it will be fulfilled necessitates actualization. Thus we can see the close interconnection of

---

[120]*Ibid.*, 82. Once again von Rad points to Mowinckel for his theoretical background (also see pp. 83, 87).

[121]*Ibid.*, 45.

the historical specificity of a prophet's message, the creative word of God, and actualization. All of these elements are necessary to make von Rad's scheme of interpretation internally consistent.

In this part of *Old Testament Theology* dealing with the prophetic literature, we can finally see the nature of the mechanism of actualization as it is applied to the Old Testament. The concept has undergone considerable development and alteration since 1938. Most significantly, von Rad has acknowledged that exactly the same mechanism cannot be applied to a cultic festival and to written literature; hence, we now have two related categories: cultic actualization and chronological actualization. The latter is that which is operative in the Old Testament. It is first and foremost a theological mechanism, occasioned by the nature of the creative word of God, which always acts as a promise leading to ever new fulfillments. It alters and adapts old traditions to meet new situations – as opposed to cultic actualization which renews the primeval creative events in the same form as a means of assuring order and stability. Each contemporization responds to a specific historical situation; consequently, each new generation must actualize the older material for its own distinct needs.

3

The final part of von Rad's *Old Testament Theology* is the culmination of his work in actualization: his attempt to relate the Old Testament and the New. He explicitly links this with the earlier parts of his theology:

> ... he [the reader] should not take the last four sections of this volume in isolation. They stand or fall according as what preceded them is valid, in particular what is said about the history of tradition and its continuous re-interpretation *(immer wiederholenden Neuinterpretationen)*.[122]

This all-important relationship is also the focus of two later articles by von Rad, to which we will also refer, "Offene Fragen im

---

[122]*Ibid.*, vii.

Umkreis einer Theologie des Alten Testaments," and "Rückblick und Ausblick."[123]

The major thrust of von Rad's argument on the relation of the Old Testament to the New is that they exhibit the same use of tradition, characterized by actualization. He gives a summary of the Old Testament's use of tradition to demonstrate that "the way in which the Old Testament is absorbed in the New is the logical end of a process initiated by the Old Testament itself."[124] Its active tradition process is characterized by a seemingly arbitrary selectivity in the traditions which are re-used, and by extreme freedom in how they are reinterpreted. Especially in the prophetic literature an entirely fresh, often clashing interpretation is given to the old tradition. This is charismatic in nature. For von Rad this same charismatic freedom appears in the New Testament writers' use of the Old Testament and is an additional characteristic of actualization.[125]

Another link between the Old Testament and the New is the inherent openness of the old traditions to the future. The Old Testament is a succession of promises which have no immediate fulfillment. These promises, moving forward in Israel's history, may find partial fulfillments; but even when they are fulfilled, they are always being altered by actualization for a later time. Thus, they remain unfulfilled or become new and different promises.

> If we seek to extract from the bewildering number of these actualizations *(Aktualisierung)* some characteristic, common, and continuing feature, it is this – in one way or another ... Israel was always placed in the vacuum between an election made manifest in her history, and which had a definite promise attached to it, and a fulfillment of this promise which was looked for in the future.[126]

This future orientation is not a feature forced upon the traditions by these arbitrary actualizations. Rather, the nature of the Old Testament

---

[123]Gerhard von Rad, "Offene Fragen im Umkreis einer Theologie des Alten Testaments," *TLZ* 88 (1963) 401-16, trans. "Postscript," *Theology* 2.410-29; "Rückblick und Ausblick," Postscript to *Theologie* 2.437-47 (4th ed., 1965).

[124]Von Rad, *Theology* 2.231.

[125]*Ibid.,* 324, 327.

[126]*Ibid.,* 414.

materials predisposes them to reinterpretation and prompts free actualization of them. "All presentation of history in the Old Testament is in one form or another inherently open to a future."[127] This binds the two testaments together because the New Testament also participates in this openess.[128] Further, the New Testament presents itself as the fulfillment for which the Old has been striving throughout its history. Jesus Christ is able to sum up all of the promises of a new covenant, a new exodus, and a new David into his own being and present them as completed.[129] Thus, we see that the scheme of promise and fulfillment, which has been a part of von Rad's theology since 1933, is now regarded as a direct result of actualization.

A third major link between the Old Testament and the New is typology. In discussing typology von Rad indirectly responds to the criticisms which "Typological Interpretation of the Old Testament" provoked. He differentiates Biblical typology not merely from literary typology, ancient Near Eastern typology, and allegory, as he did in that article, but also from the religious typology of Calvin and Delitzch. Von Rad's typology is not based upon an "organic view of history," but upon tradition criticism and the selective actualization of discrete traditions.

> ... the bond of unity between the Old Testament and the New is formed by concrete divine acts which appointed salvation and judgment, and does not consist in their common or kindred religious ideas.... There can now be no question of declaring certain persons or objects or institutions as, in their objective and as it were static essence, types. Everything depends on the *events* between Israel and her God.[130]

The result is that von Rad is able to construct a continuous line of typological thinking which extends from the Old Testament through Judaism and Qumran to the New Testament itself, thus solidifying the link.

---

[127]*Ibid.*, 361. Also see p. 422.

[128]*Ibid.*, 361.

[129]*Ibid.*, 327-8, 374ff, 428.

[130]*Ibid.*, 371. Also see pp. 367-69.

In "Offene Fragen im Umkreis einer Theologie des Alten Testaments" von Rad finally makes explicit the relation between typology and actualization: "Unquestionably, the reactualization *(Neuaktualisierung)* of historical saving appointments or events in the eschatological message of the prophets is typical of Jahwism, and is a special form of typological thinking."[131]   This does not mean that actualization is a sub-category of Old Testament typology. Instead, actualization is grouped with all typological/analogical thought – literary, philosophical, mythical. It is the particular kind of typology that is characteristic of the Old Testament. Therefore, all that von Rad has discussed previously as typology (and, consequently, as promise and fulfillment) can be more specifically designated as actualization. When one becomes aware of this point, the overarching nature of actualization for his theology should be abundantly clear.

The relation of the Old Testament to the New raises an important question for actualization. Is the New Testament the final actualization of these saving traditions, or is it merely one more step in a still continuing process? Von Rad apparently wishes to have it both ways. He repeatedly speaks of the New Testament as the final reinterpretation *(letzen Neuinterpretation).*[132]   Christ is the final, full completion of the promises which Israel carried with it throughout its history, which included both the intertestamental period and Qumran. The coming of Jesus Christ is a basic salvific act, comparable with the events of creation, exodus, and conquest in the Old Testament. Therefore, von Rad can refer to his advent not merely as a *Vergegenwärtigung,* but a *Wiederholung,*[133] a term which he has previously avoided. For Mowinckel this referred to the most complete contemporizing of traditions in the cult. Von Rad's use of the term here indicates the fundamental nature of the Christ event. It brought to full reality the partial actualization which preceded it.

Although the Christ event is the final actualization of the Old Testament, it does not prevent us from contemporizing the Biblical materials today. We must employ the same charismatic approach by

---

[131]*Ibid.,* 428.

[132]*Ibid.,* 321, 384; Also see pp. 330, 332, 373, 383, 428.

[133]*Ibid.,* 383.

which the prophets and apostles actualized the old traditions.[134] Both the need to regard Christ as a final contemporizing, yet preserve actualization as a means of interpretation for the present, and the use of *Wiederholung* for the Christ event point to the strain which exists in von Rad's scheme. Can one really speak of a traditio-historical link through actualization when a new salvific event has been introduced?

In discussing the relation of the Old Testament to the New, von Rad has revealed the overarching nature of actualization. It encompasses both typology and promise and fulfillment. The creative word of God is the spiritual force which drives the hermeneutical mechanism. It is revealed as a charismatic procedure which extends to the present day as the way that we may appropriate the Old Testament – and the New – for ourselves.

4

The final question to be discussed in this chapter is the relation of wisdom/apocalyptic to actualization. Von Rad's treatment of the wisdom literature in his *Old Testament Theology* and his attempt to link apocalyptic to wisdom were generally regarded as unsatisfactory. As a result, he returned to these questions in his later work. He thoroughly revised his section on apocalyptic in the fourth German edition of *Theologie des Alten Testaments* (1965), clarifying and defending the close relationship which he discerned between this material and wisdom. Then, in *Wisdom in Israel* (1970), he details his understanding of wisdom literature. Here we are concerned with one question: does his scheme of actualization, so carefully developed for the historical books, the prophets, and the New Testament, carry over to wisdom and apocalyptic?

With regard to the body of wisdom literature (excepting apocalyptic), the answer is a simple no. The reason is equally plain: we are faced with a different conception of history in wisdom literature, one which precludes actualization as its method of interpretation. This is manifest throughout the body of *Wisdom in Israel,* where he completely eschews the vocabulary related to actualization. This avoidance is most evident in his section, "The Doctrine of the Proper

---

[134]*Ibid.,* 337, 409. Also see Gerhard von Rad, "Ancient Word and Living Word," *Int* 15 (1961) 12-13.

Time."[135] He develops wisdom's understanding of time with no mention of actualization or history, a drastic departure from the historical sense of *Old Testament Theology*. Interestingly enough, he also fails to mention a single passage from the apocalyptic materials which he has insistently included in wisdom.

Only in his final excursus, "The Divine Determination of Times,"[136] does he relate wisdom to history and actualization. Here the major emphasis is upon apocalyptic, with only brief mention of other wisdom materials. While he states that Sirach, the Testaments of the Twelve Patriarchs, and Judith all use Israel's historical traditions, these traditions are used in a deterministic sense unrelated to actualization.[137] Only with the Wisdom of Solomon does he directly discuss actualization in relation to a wisdom book. Here he tantalizingly suggests that the "contemporary significance *(Gegenwartsbedeutung)* of history" is still alive. The author, through his interpretation of every detail of Israel's historical tradition, has succeeded in "making it contemporary *(vergegenwärtigen)* with a forcefulness which had not hitherto been granted to Israel." However, this striking change in attitude toward the relation between wisdom and actualization is more apparent than real. He concludes by stating that this attitude toward history may not be true actualization, but timeless didactic truths "which can be detached from history."[138] Therefore, what we encounter here is an ambiguous reference to and attitude toward actualization. Von Rad is quite unclear about whether he is referring to chronological actualization or to a looser literary type – or even whether actualization in any sense occurs in the Wisdom of Solomon. Thus, we may conclude that the bulk of the wisdom material bears little or no relation to the concept of actualization which von Rad finds in the historical, prophetic, and New Testament materials.

However, the situation is not so clear-cut with the apocalyptic literature. While von Rad adamantly defends apocalyptic's relation to and genesis from wisdom, important distinctions remain between the two: his discussions of apocalyptic are never convincingly integrated

---

[135]Gerhard von Rad, *Wisdom in Israel* (Nashville: Abingdon, 1972) 138-43.

[136]*Ibid.*, 263-68.

[137]*Ibid.*, 270.

[138]*Ibid.*, 282-83. The lack of importance of this discussion is indicated by its position as a footnote to an excursus.

with his sections on wisdom;[139] apocalyptic's concept of history is a central concern; actualization is mentioned in relation to apocalyptic in every discussion. Consequently, our most important concern in relation to wisdom literature is not the connection between the bulk of wisdom writing and actualization, but the specific connection between it and apocalyptic.

Although von Rad frequently mentions the concept in relation to apocalyptic, the nature of the actualization being discussed is quite ambiguous. His denial of the development of apocalyptic from the prophetic and historical traditions would apparently preclude the presence of chronological actualization in the former, since a major factor in this denial is the totally different understanding of history in apocalyptic. History is now based on a deterministic view of time. The role of the historical summaries, which were vehicles for actualization in the prophetic and historical materials, is completely altered. These summaries now are placed in the mouth of a man who has lived in the past, making them a prophecy for the future to which God is already privy, rather than a recital of his past saving acts. God knows what will happen; it is immutably decreed and will come about. This understanding is in direct conflict with the old scheme of promise and fulfillment, in which Israel lives in a time of tension between the unexpected promise and the certain but unknown fulfillment.[140]

In addition these past times are no longer envisioned as part of a salvation history: they are periods of unfaithfulness on the part of God's people and periods of suffering and woe for the faithful. There has been a "soteriological depletion of history."[141] Now salvation no longer looks to the past for its analogies, but to the future. The eschaton is the act in history which will bring about salvation – and it is an eschaton that is not analogous to any of Israel's historical traditions, but based on a doctrine of two ages. Another reason for moving away from the old saving history as the basis for redemption is that it is no longer Israel who will be redeemed: instead, only the elect will be. Thus, along with determinism, both a reliance upon the

---

[139]Von Rad, *Theology* 2.301-15; *Theologie* 2.315-37 (4th ed.); *Wisdom,* 271-82. Even in the latter case the discussion is confined to the excursus, with little integration of apocalyptic material into the body of the book.

[140]Von Rad, *Theology* 2.303-05; *Theologie* 2.319-22 (4th ed.); Wisdom, 271-73.

[141]Von Rad, *Wisdom,* 273.

eschaton and a growing individualism combined to shift salvation away from its old historical bases and place it upon new ground. The purpose to which the historical traditions are put has also shifted. No longer are they used as preaching materials, as exhortations which make the people participants in their own history, alive and real to them. The appeal to history is not on this emotional, empathetic level. Now it is on the rational, logical plane. Each incident in history has a moral, a lesson to be learned. It is instructional; it is teaching material. As such it is used "for the correct evaluation of the moment in which one lives."[142]

These drastic changes would seemingly preclude any discussion of actualization in relation to apocalyptic. Von Rad acknowledges that the nature of the material calls for different questions:

> The decisive question which we had to ask of the older conception of history in Israel, namely to what extent it was still able to make God's dealings with Israel topical (*vergegenwärtigen*), can no longer be asked in this way of the apocalyptic historical sketches.[143]

However, in other statements he seems far less certain of the death of actualization. He speaks of it being "on the wane" or of the material losing "much of its contemporary significance (*Gegenwartsbedeutung*)."[144] Furthermore, he applies actualization to apocalyptic materials in his *Old Testament Theology,* in both the first edition and the revised fourth edition. In the former he refers to the apocalyptic writers actualizing written prophecy. In the latter he discusses the final form of various apocalyptic books as being merely the last actualization of a long traditio-historical process.[145]

Obviously, a certain amount of ambiguity surrounds von Rad's application of actualization to apocalyptic. In *Wisdom in Israel* he apparently contrasts the didactic use of history with the type of actualization encountered in prophecy. He is unclear whether this vivid contemporaneity is totally absent or merely on the wane. At best

---

[142]*Ibid.,* 277.

[143]*Ibid.,* 273.

[144]*Ibid.,* 274-77.

[145]Von Rad, *Theology* 2.308; *Theologie* 2.323, 327 (4th ed.).

actualization plays a minor role for apocalyptic. In his *Old Testament Theology* he applies actualization to apocalyptic, but with a considerable shift in meaning. With neither indication nor explanation, he seemingly uses the term in its general literary sense to describe stages in the traditio-historical process. This does not indicate a late overall shift in his use of the term, since he maintains its special sense in relation to the prophetic and historical materials both in the revised edition of *Old Testament Theology* and in *Wisdom in Israel*.[146] Hence, what we encounter in apocalyptic is an ambiguous and multifaceted application of the terms for actualization. However, we may conclude that for von Rad chronological actualization was not a major component for apocalyptic interpretive procedure.

Summary

An extensive summary of the development of actualization in von Rad's thought is unnecessary at this point, since that has been the purpose of the entire chapter. A brief statement of the contours of the concept will adequately prepare us for the continuation of our investigation.

At various points von Rad discusses three types of actualization. We shall refer to one as literary actualization, which is a literary device for making an old image, symbol, or tradition vivid to the imagination. As a rule von Rad contrasts this type with the actualization present in the Bible. However, he apparently allows for the presence of literary actualization in the apocalyptic traditio-historical process at least. The other two major types are cultic and chronological actualization, which are set off from the literary type by the theological significance which they bear and by the extent to which they vivify the old materials. Whether or not cultic actualization is present in the Bible will be discussed later.

Chronological actualization is the type which characterizes both the Old and New Testaments. The distinction between it and other kinds of actualization emerges with reasonably clear contours in *Old Testament Theology II* (although the concept is not devoid of ambiguity and unresolved problems). It is a device which carries the theological import of the traditionary process through which the Biblical materials passed. Its motive force is the creative word of God in history, which

---

146Von Rad, *Wisdom*, 274.

urges Israel to make its promises, traditions, and saving events continually relevant. It is a device which updates and adapts these materials so that each generation not merely understands the past events, but re-experiences them vividly, decisively, in such a way that they "become Israel." Each actualization is valid only for the specific historical situation in which it is enunciated; as the situation changes, the material must be reactualized. Typology and promise and fulfillment are integrally related to actualization; they appear to be the primary means by which the materials are made alive.

Chapter Two

Other Developments in the Concept of Actualization

The development of the concept of actualization by von Rad exerted a profound influence upon Old Testament studies, especially in Germany, but also in Great Britain and the United States. Numerous other scholars adopted the concept and developed it in their own particular manner. The influence of actualization was especially pronounced after the publication of the famous 1952 issue of *Evangelische Theologie* which contained both von Rad's article on typology and Martin Noth's article, "The Re-presentation of the Old Testament in Proclamation." To study the role of actualization outside of von Rad's work, we will begin with that article by Noth and survey important developments up to the present.

Either to discuss every use of actualization in the past quarter-century or to engage in a detailed study of any one scholar's work would result in a perspective that is too broad or too narrow for the purpose of this chapter. In order to cover the various developments in the concept during this period, yet retain depth to our analysis, we will focus this survey upon specific works by eight different scholars. Each work has been chosen because it illuminates a particular facet of actualization which von Rad did not pursue, such as its use in contemporary proclamation, its application to the psalms, or it relevance to exegesis. In this way each segment of the chapter will allow us both to clarify one man's contribution to actualization and to exemplify a significant trend in the growth of the concept.

The Development of Actualization in Germany

The post-World War II period in Germany was one of great theological ferment. The experience of the Confessing Church during the war had aroused a great interest in both the confessional basis for theology and its scriptural foundation. While many different scholars pursued their own hermeneutical methods for making the Bible relevant for contemporary theology, von Rad's emphasis upon the actualization of the ancient credenda had a strikingly direct appeal to the church's stance. Consequently, many important scholars joined him in pursuing this particular method: Martin Noth through his "Re-presentation of the Old Testament in Proclamation," Claus Westermann and Hans Walter Wolff with many articles and books which applied and expanded actualization. Other scholars developed related systems and adapted elements of actualization for their own: Artur Weiser's earlier concept of *Historisierung* was related to actualization, and he used cultic re-presentation in his Psalms commentary;[1] Walther Zimmerli focused upon a more extensive development of a concept of promise and fulfillment similar to von Rad's.[2] Still other scholars followed their own independent roads to a theological understanding of the Old Testament and roundly criticized the route of actualization: Walther Eichrodt retained his systematic approach in which the link to the future remains in conceptual categories;[3] Friedrich Baumgärtel posited an unchanging *Grundverheissung* which needed no re-presentation.[4]

Consequently, while many theological approaches to the Old Testament were being developed and tested in Germany in the fifties and sixties, actualization was of signal importance. Scholars were forced to adopt, adapt, or respond to it. Although many scholars deserve mention in relation to the concept, its development, adaptation, and application can be summarized through a study of three men: Martin Noth, Claus Westermann, and Hans Walter Wolff.

---

[1]In particular see Artur Weiser, *Glaube und Geschichte* (Stuttgart: W. Kohlhammer, 1931); *The Psalms* (Philadelphia: Westminster, 1962).

[2]In particular see Walther Zimmerli, "Promise and Fulfillment," in *Essays on Old Testament Hermeneutics*, 89-122; "Die historische-kritische Bibelwissenschaft und die Verkündigungs Aufgabe der Kirche," *EvT* 23 (1963) 17-31; "'Offenbarung' im Alten Testament," *EvT* 22 (1962) 15-31.

[3]In particular see Walther Eichrodt, "Offenbarung und Geschichte im Alten Testament," *TZ* 4 (1948) 321ff; "Is Typological Exegesis an Appropriate Method?" in *Essays on Old Testament Hermeneutics*, 224-45; "Heilserfahrung und Zeitverständnis im Alten Testament," *TZ* 12 (1956) 104-25.

[4]In particular see Friedrich Baumgärtel, "The Hermeneutical Problem of the Old Testament," in *Essays on Old Testament Hermeneutics*, 134-59.

1

Of all the Old Testament scholars in von Rad's generation, Martin Noth can most readily be assigned a place of equal stature in his impact upon the field. The similarities between the two men extended beyond their age and status, for their approaches to the Old Testament are closely related. In particular, they are both strict adherents to the traditio-historical method, treading the paths blazed by Gunkel and Alt. Additionally, they both see actualization as a primary interpretive category in the Old Testament. Their differences in method and procedure occur within this broad degree of similarity; and, although the differences should not be minimized, they are primarily ones of emphasis and specialization. While von Rad consistently explored the theological aspect of the Old Testament, Noth sought to depict the history of Israel, utilizing the tools of archeology and comparison with other ancient Near Eastern cultures. Neither von Rad nor Noth avoided the other's area of specialization, but their works tend to complement each other rather than to overlap.[5]

With Noth's concentration upon the history of Israel, actualization plays a relatively minor role in most of his work. However, his one direct contribution to the development of the concept was major. In a rare venture into the realm of theology and exegesis, "The Representation of the Old Testament in Proclamation," Noth applied actualization to the contemporary interpretation of the Old Testament for preaching. At its publication in 1952 this was the most comprehensive statement available on the nature of actualization. Although von Rad had been using the concept since 1938, he did not produce such a systematic treatment of it until his *Old Testament Theology* in 1957. Thus, Noth's contribution was a seminal one in defining and applying the term.

This article should not be viewed as an aberration or digression on Noth's part. He consistently demonstrated an interest in and adherence to the concept of actualization in his work. As early as 1940 in *The Laws in the Pentateuch* he showed a concern with the developing idea of actualization. At this point he still retained the traditional vocabulary

---

[5]For more complete descriptions of Noth's work and his relation to von Rad, see Knight, *Rediscovering,* 97-176; Bernhard Anderson, "Martin Noth's Traditio-Historical Approach in the Context of Twentieth-Century Biblical Research," in Martin Noth, *A History of the Pentateuchal Traditions* (Englewood Cliffs: Prentice Hall, 1972) xiii-xxxii.

of Gunkel,[6] as he spoke of the re-establishment of the validity of the law in the various periods of Israel's existence. However, he moved beyond Gunkel's conception of the re-use of old traditions and into the realm of actualization when he spoke of the new vitality *(eine neue ... Lebensform)*[7] of the law. At this point in Noth's work the more historically oriented, theologically neutral vocabulary predominated. The emphasis lay on the re-establishment of the validity of the law, with only an occasional mention of its revitalization as a living, dynamic entity.[8]

Noth's embracing of the concept of actualization becomes clear in *A History of the Pentateuchal Traditions* (1948). He acknowledges his debt to Mowinckel, von Rad, and Pedersen as he applies actualization to the cultic re-enactment of Sinai and the Passover.[9] He does not move beyond Mowinckel or von Rad in his formulation, being content with the category of cultic actualization to describe these events. However, this is a significant step for Noth, for it signals his acceptance of actualization as a mechanism for the transmission and development of Old Testament traditions.

In "God, King, and Nation in the Old Testament" (1950) Noth diverges somewhat from von Rad in his application of actualization. He sees the cultic "remembrances" of Deut 16 and Lev 23 as watered down and rationalized versions of a real actualization.[10] While von Rad views Deuteronomy as a rationalizing, spiritualizing document, he still regards it as a true actualization, not a dilution that has lost its character. Noth's view more closely coincides with Mowinckel's earlier formulation than with von Rad's development of the idea.

While these works indicate a continuing concern for actualization, they break no new ground in relation to the concept. However, "The Re-presentation of the Old Testament in Proclamation" does. Here he

---

[6]Martin Noth, *Die Gesetz im Pentateuch* (Halle: M. Niemeyer, 1940), rpt. in *Gesammelte Studien zum Alten Testament* (Munich: C. Kaiser, 1966) 9-141. Examples of similar terminology are *verändern* (p. 18), *anpassen* (p. 37), *aufnehmen* (pp. 18, 98), and *erneuen* (pp. 98, 100).

[7]*Ibid.*, 48.

[8]Martin Noth, *The Laws in the Pentateuch and Other Essays* (Philadelphia: Fortress, 1967) 8, 48, 79-81.

[9]Noth, *Pentateuchal Traditions,* 60-61, 66-68.

[10]Noth, *Laws,* 166-67.

addresses the problem of how one proclaims the Old Testament today. Interestingly enough, von Rad, for all his theological inclination, never dealt with this issue as specifically as Noth.

Noth is acutely aware of the need to bridge the gap between the historical-critical method and the practical proclamation of the Bible demanded by both systematic and practical theologians. He cannot deny the validity of historical-critical exegesis, because to do so is to deny the nature of the Bible itself. The type of exegesis utilized on a document must grow out of the nature of the document itself. Since the Bible is primarily an historical document, historical exegesis must be the appropriate method. In particular Noth bases Biblical exegesis on the actualization of historical events in the Old Testament.

In line with his earlier discussions of the concept Noth defines the Old Testament phenomenon as cultic actualization. Its genesis lay in the development of Israel's feasts. Rather than relying upon reconstructed rituals in the manner of Mowinckel or von Rad,[11] Noth concentrates on two of the festivals in Israel to which the Old Testament attests directly: Passover and Booths. The historicization of these originally agricultural festivals led to the actualization of "certain elements of past historical events."[12] Noth does not emphasize the element of dramatic performance in cultic actualization, as does Mowinckel. Rather, he sees "narration of the event of God's wonderful act" as the central element of cultic actualization. Although he hesitates to use the reconstructed enthronement and covenant renewal festivals as evidence of actualization, he does utilize the same Old Testament materials which Mowinckel and von Rad employ (Deuteronomy and the enthronement psalms) as prime examples of actualization. While connecting them to the cult, he does not relate them to a specific festival. In the final analysis, the cultic ritual "appears to have consisted primarily of interpretive narration and also of the constantly repeated Word of God as his demand on Israel, accompanied by certain elements of dramatic action."[13]

---

[11]Mowinckel centers much of his analysis upon the New Year's enthronement festival; von Rad reconstructs a covenant renewal festival at Gilgal.

[12]Martin Noth, "The Re-presentation of the Old Testament in Proclamation," in *Essays on Old Testament Hermeneutics* 81.

[13]*Ibid.*, 84.

Noth acknowledges the similarities between actualization in the Israelite cult and that prevalent in the ancient Near East. However, there is an essential distinction between them: Israel contemporizes unique historical events, not timeless myths. This establishes a different basis for Israelite actualization, for it is inextricably linked with its subject, God, acting in history. Thus the basis for actualization becomes the mediation of the tension between the course of time and the timelessness of God: "'Re-presentation' is founded on this – that God and his action are always present, while man in his inevitable temporality cannot grasp this present-ness except by 're-presenting' the action of God over and over again in his worship."[14]

Thus Noth firmly anchors actualization in contemporary theology. He specifically ties it to the Barthian categories of mediateness/immediateness.[15] These are not categories which are inherent in the Old Testament, but are imported from contemporary theology. This would seem to contradict his earlier statement that the nature of exegesis must grow from the text itself. Nevertheless, since Noth's purpose is to bridge the gap between the ancient text and modern exegesis, he must make such a leap. It provides his link to contemporary exegesis and allows him to apply his program to ancient texts. He sees this as exegetically demonstrable.[16] However, what is exegetically demonstrable is the possible presence of actualization in the Old Testament. It does not necessarily follow that one may relate this to modern theological categories.

Nevertheless, having established a theological base for actualization and tied it into contemporary exegesis, Noth draws his conclusions for exegesis. He begins his conclusions with two negations. First, individual human figures may not be used for ethical models or heroes of faith. They are not used thusly in the Bible, nor are they the subjects of actualization. Second, and more important, specific historical situations may not be actualized. The rule of historical exclusivity is in effect and the specific situations of the Old Testament may not be identified with any other specific historical situations. They are unique. Consequently, the only legitimate subject of actualization can be "the saving acts of God himself, to which saving

---

[14]*Ibid.*, 85.

[15]*Ibid.*, 85.

[16]*Ibid.*, 86.

acts belong also the promising and the demanding Word of God, and the punitive judgments of God."[17] Just as these were re-enacted in the old Israelite cult, they must be retold today in proclamation. Noth once again ties the type of proclamation directly to Barth, quoting him as understanding the Old Testament to consist of "news reports" which we must pass on as they are.[18] The nature of the proclamation is determined by historical-critical exegesis, since this is the type of exegesis which can test, discriminate, and translate the data of an earlier historical period in a manner that allows the manifold voices of the Old Testament to speak.[19]

This article is a bold attempt to apply actualization to present proclamation. Noth's general approach to the concept is quite in accord with that of von Rad. Noth takes the more conservative stance in his delineation of the concept. He restricts himself to the category of cultic actualization and avoids the extension and redefinition which von Rad attempts with chronological actualization. He treats the same Biblical data as von Rad and Mowinckel, but restrains himself from reconstructing Israelite festivals in which particular material was re-presented. He is content to regard it as cultic in a general sense. The apparent result is a more limited, precise definition of actualization which he can then apply to exegesis and proclamation.

However, when he approaches exegesis from this limited perspective, he finds the distance between the two categories, ancient and modern, too great to be immediately bridged. This is the problem which later led von Rad to carry the idea of contemporization further, into the concept of chronological actualization, with its emphasis upon the vitality of the word of God. This provided von Rad with a category inherent in the concept of actualization which was also part of contemporary theology. Since Noth eschews this type of development, he must provide another link between actualization and modern exegesis. For this purpose he appropriates Barth's idea of the mediateness/immediateness of history. Thus, the gap is bridged by supplying a modern theological category as the basis for actualization.

A further difference from von Rad occurs in relation to the law of historical exclusivity. Noth sees it as being fully in effect for "the

---

[17]*Ibid.*, 87.

[18]*Ibid.*, 88.

[19]*Ibid.*, 88.

historical narratives of the Old Testament in their entirety."[20] Von Rad, to the contrary, contends that ancient peoples were not aware of that rule and were able to raise historical events, especially those of a saving nature, to the level of the typical.[21] Noth's insistence on this law undermines one of the salient features of actualization, that of the events coming truly alive for the cult participants. Only if historical exclusivity is suspended can one really speak of the time gap dissolving. Noth does not see actualization in these terms, but rather as a bridge between the immediateness of God and the mediateness of human history. Perceived in these terms the need is not to dissolve a time barrier in human history, but to understand the timelessness of God. This leads to a significantly different version of cultic actualization than either von Rad or Mowinckel conceived. Noth understands actualization as restricted to the cult and worship, but with a time barrier remaining.

2

Claus Westermann belongs to the generation of scholars subsequent to von Rad and Noth. Deeply influenced by von Rad, Westermann adapts and applies actualization throughout his work. He not only follows the general traditio-historical program developed by von Rad and others, but specifically sees actualization as a centerpiece in understanding the traditio-historical method. References to the

---

[20]*Ibid.*, 87.

[21]Von Rad, *Theology* 1.110.

concept occur repeatedly in his considerable corpus.[22] The task here is not to examine the similarities between these two scholars but to investigate Westermann's contribution to the development of actualization. Two articles bring this contribution into clear focus: "Vergegenwärtigung der Geschichte in den Psalmen" (1963), and "Was ist eine exegetische Aussage?" (1962).

In "Vergegenwärtigung der Geschichte in den Psalmen" Westermann applies the concept thoroughly to a section of the Old Testament sorely neglected by von Rad. In doing so he specifically rejects cultic actualization as the Biblical mode of interpretation and develops a concept related to but significantly different from von Rad's chronological actualization. After examining several possible examples, Westermann concludes that there is no cultic actualization in the Psalms. All of the examples posited by Weiser in his Psalm commentary specifically refer to the narration of God's saving acts, not their re-enactment through cultic drama.[23] Noth, in his article on re-presentation, also fails to prove the presence of cultic actualization in the Old Testament. Although he sees actualization in Israel as a combination of narrative and cultic re-enactment, he relies primarily upon the narrative aspect.[24] On the basis of this lack of concrete evidence of a cult-dramatic re-presentation of God's saving deeds,

---

[22]For his specific use of actualization, see Claus Westermann, "Das hermeneutische Problem in der Theologie," *Forschung aus Alten Testament; gesammelte Studien* (Munich: C. Kaiser, 1974) 2.68-84, esp. pp. 72-76; *Our Controversial Bible* (Minneapolis: Augsburg, 1969) 5, 12, 42, 114, 116; *Isaiah* 40-66 (Philadelphia: Westminster, 1969) 30; *Creation* (London: SPCK, 1974) 30; *The Praise of God in the Psalms* (Richmond: John Knox, 1965) 82, 101. Other similarities to von Rad related to actualization are also apparent. One is his similar scheme of promise and fulfillment: "Remarks on the Theses of Bultmann and Baumgärtel," *Essays on Old Testament Hermeneutics,* 131, 133; "The Interpretation of the Old Testament," *Essays on Old Testament Hermeneutics,* 48; *Controversial,* 12; *The Old Testament and Jesus Christ* (Minneapolis: Augsburg, n.d.) 77. Another is the relevance of a specific word to a specific hour and situation: *The Basic Forms of Prophetic Speech* (Philadelphia: Westminster, 1967), 99; *Controversial* 195, 117. A third is his devaluation of apocalyptic: "The Way of Promise in the Old Testament," in Bernhard Anderson, ed.,*The Old Testament and Christian Faith* (New York: Herder & Herder, 1969) 220.

[23]Claus Westermann, "Vergegenwärtigung der Geschichte in den Psalmen," in *Zwischenstation. Festschrift für Karl Kupisch zum 60. Geburtstag* (Munich: C. Kaiser, 1963) 260-61.

[24]*Ibid.,* footnote pp. 261-62.

Westermann concludes that only actualization by narration occurs in Israel. For him there is an essential difference between cultic actualization and narrative actualization. In the former the time interval between the original event and its re-presentation in the cult is dissolved and the original event is experienced as present and immediate. The latter bridges that interval without destroying it. This type of actualization places the two events in an historical continuum; it "extends" the earlier history to the present time. This does not mean that the intervening events of history are added to the narration, but that the earlier saving history is seen extending to the present time as a promise yet to be fulfilled. While cultic actualization has a single focal point, narrative actualization must have two foci, since history cannot be constituted in a single event or realized by identity with that event. The continuum of events must be present:

> Gerade das aber ist in der Vergegenwärtigung vergangener Ereignisse allein durch das Wort wesentlich und grundlegend anders [von kultdramatischen Vergegenwärtigung]. Der Zeitabstand zwischen dem einstigen Ereignis und der gegenwärtigen Wiedergabe wird in Erzählen *nicht* gelöscht, er wird *nicht* irrelevant gemacht durch die Vergegenwärtigung im Erzählen. Es bleibt bei zwei Zeitpunkten, zwischen denen die Erzählung bzw. der Bericht die Brükke bildet. Die Erzählung oder der Bericht setzt als Darstellungsform die zwei Zeitpunkte voraus, den des Geschehens und den der Wiedergabe. Die Vergegenwärtigung im Kultdrama ist ein wesentlich anderes Geschehen als die Vergegenwärtigung im Erzählen.[25]

For Westermann narrative actualization characterizes not just the Old Testament, but the New Testament as well, since Jesus is depicted in continuity with both the Old Testament and the early church. He is never absolutized.[26]

As Westermann claims, this view of actualization is radically different from the cult-dramatic re-enactment which Mowinckel and Weiser see in the Old Testament and which von Rad uses as a starting point for his understanding of Old Testament re-presentation. It bears a close resemblance to the chronological actualization that von Rad

---

[25]*Ibid.*, 261.

[26]*Ibid.*, 260-64.

describes for the historical and prophetic literature. However there is one essential difference. Even for chronological actualization von Rad feels that the time interval is dissolved, not merely bridged. Although he qualifies this with his talk of a rationalization in Deuteronomy's presentation, he nevertheless states that the event is made contemporary and that, through the language used, the people feel identity with the earlier events. Westermann's concept draws more from certain aspects of Noth's theory of actualization. He has isolated Noth's emphasis upon narration and eliminated the cultic aspect. His statements about the time barrier remaining in effect make explicit that which Noth leaves implicit. However, Westermann's concept is significantly different in that Noth specifies a cultic setting for actualization while Westermann deals with written materials apart from the cult.

In his presentation of narrative actualization Westermann has touched upon one of the key questions in applying actualization to the Old Testament: if it contains no cultic re-enactment, then how does one define Old Testament contemporization? The primary weakness in his argument is that he merely contrasts narrative and cultic actualization. He fails to discuss the relationship of the two and the possibility of the former developing out of the latter. This discussion is important because the generally accepted premise is still that cult-dramatic re-presentation is characteristic of the ancient Near East. Therefore, if one posits a significantly different phenomenon in Israel, one must demonstrate its development. Von Rad has attempted to do this for chronological actualization, but his argument is not necessarily valid for Westermann's different conception. Nevertheless, he has provided us with an alternative view of actualization. We must now investigate its consequences in the psalms.

He finds three significant points at which history is actualized in the psalms. The first of these is in the psalm type: Lament of the People. In each of these laments there is a section which may be designated "Reference to God's Earlier Saving Deeds." In this section the psalm recapitulates Israel's history by reference to the events of the historical credo. However, the purpose is not to celebrate these events in a liturgy, as von Rad describes the original *Sitz im Leben* of the credo. Here the past events are held up in contrast to the present woes of Israel and God's seeming absence. This actualization in an alternative setting gives a depth dimension to Israel's understanding of history, visualizing both weal and woe.[27]

The actualization of history in the Lament of the People is not exhausted in this section of the psalm. These psalms conclude with a vow of praise. After recapitulating Israel's history and questioning God's present role, the psalms conclude with an affirmation of God in a pledge to continue his praise. As the reference to his saving deeds connects the psalms to the past, the vow of praise lead them into the future with an affirmation that God will indeed continue to act. This demonstrates that actualization occurs not in identity, but in continuity, since the psalms have a clear sense of looking back to the past, seeing it in reference to the present time of trouble, and anticipating God's action in the future. The significance of the vow of praise is clearly expressed in Ps 79:13. The purpose of the vow of praise is not merely to actualize the psalm for that moment, but to make it valid "from generation to generation," to see that God is praised "forever." In this we encounter the core of actualization in Israel:

> Wie sollen Gottes Taten immer wieder vergegenwärtigt werden? In Ps. 79, 13 stehen parallel die beiden Verben "dich preisen" – "deinen Ruhm erzählen." ... Hier ist exakt beschrieben, was ich "berichtendes Lob" nenne: die Weise des Gotteslobes, die sich im Berichten (oder Erzählen) der Heilstaten Gottes vollzieht. Dieses preisende oder rühmende oder lobende Erzählen der grossen Taten Gottes ist die grundlegende Weise des Vergegenwärtigens von Geschichte im alten Israel.[28]

This "declarative praise" is the second point of actualization in the psalms. It originates in the "jubilant outcry" which God's saving actions prompted. These outcries, such as Exod. 15:21, II Sam. 5:20, and Ps. 118:15-16, stand close to the events they celebrate, and their spontaneous expression unites praise of God with the deed which he has performed. They now stand connected to a psalm or to a historical report and help to actualize these later descriptions. However, these direct actualizations have failed to develop into a major psalm category. Westermann feels that the intervening period of time, with its emphasis upon politico-military facts and human participation, have prevented the

---

[27]*Ibid.*, 254-58.

[28]*Ibid.*, 260.

full utilization of this type of actualization. Spontaneous, unconscious contemporization is impossible because of the intervening historical data.

Instead, the third point of actualization of history in the psalms arose: the descriptive praise of God and its later development, the history psalms. These genres are characterized by a narration of Israel's history. This narration describes events in a very general manner in the earlier psalms, changing to an extended and more specific description in the later history psalms. This description resembles the Lament of the People in one important respect: it, too, is addressed to future generations (Ps 78:2-8). However, the contrast which it presents is quite different. The response of the people to God's saving deeds is introduced for the first time. This response is characterized as one of rejection. Thus, these psalms are actualized as a warning to Israel and as a call for its repentence.[29]

The application of Westermann's concept of narrative actualization to the psalms produces quite different results than those we encountered with von Rad. Westermann has cut all ties with cultic actualization implicitly through his failure to discuss any connection between the two and explicitly with his rejection of the identity of the two moments in time. The latter also signals a break with von Rad's chronological actualization. His reasons for these breaks are persuasive. In the introduction to this article he states that he is investigating actualization in the psalms themselves, not in reconstructed institutions which may lie behind the psalms.[30] This virtually necessitates a rejection of cultic actualization, since one cannot expect a written, literary document, even though it stems from an oral tradition in the cult, to preserve the elements of oral, dramatic presentation central to cultic actualization. Westermann not only refuses to indulge in reconstructions, but also questions the data used by others who posit cultic actualization in the psalms. While his specific criticism – that solid linguistic evidence for cultic actualization is lacking – is valid, his overall evaluation at this point is sketchy and open to question. This in turn makes his major conclusion debatable: that Israel's primary mode of actualization in history is narrative, not cultic.[31] He has

---

[29]*Ibid.*, 274.

[30]*Ibid.*, 253.

[31]*Ibid.*, 260-62.

strongly defended that conclusion in relation to Israel's literature, but not in relation to its history. One must look behind the literature and reconstruct institutions to understand that history. Westermann's refusal to engage in reconstruction and his failure to evaluate thoroughly reconstructions of cultic institutions result in an inadequate basis for the broad conclusions which he draws.

His break with von Rad is also well-founded. One of the strengths of von Rad's argument for chronological actualization is the presence of specific linguistic clues in Deuteronomy. Westermann finds no such clues which point to a dissolving of the time barrier in the psalms. The linguistic clues point instead toward narrating, recounting, praising. This not only led to Westermann's positing a different type of actualization, but also is one possible reason for von Rad's neglect of the psalms in his development of the concept.

One other significant divergence from both von Rad and Noth is apparent in Westermann's development of actualization: the emphasis he places upon its validity for future generations.[32] This element is apparent and important in several psalms (see Pss 78 and 79 especially). However, a central aspect of von Rad's concept is that each contemporization is aimed at a specific historical situation, and that the material must be actualized anew by each succeeding generation. The implication of the actualization in the psalms is that they are valid for all generations as they are – Psalm 79 as reiterated praise of God, Psalm 78 as a constant warning to the people of God. This is not easily squared with the psalm being applicable to a specific historical occasion, as von Rad would have it.

The result of this altered perspective on actualization is a diffusion of the term. When it no longer implies identity of a saving event with a later moment in time (at least to the extent that von Rad conceives in the rationalized identity of chronological actualization), it becomes a mere re-use of historical events, a reminder of Israel's past. Westermann describes little more than this when he speaks of Israel's history being in continuity: events such as the exile and return are seen in a continuum with the earlier saving events, separate from them, and not experienced as a living identification with them. Both Mowinckel and von Rad describe a broad, general actualization of this type. It is

---

[32]Noth also makes this point but does not attach the importance to it that Westermann does. See Noth, "Re-presentation," 84.

that which one experiences in poetry, Protestant liturgy, and Platonic ideals. Both explicitly reject this as an adequate description of Biblical thought – not because it does not apply to the Bible, but because it lacks the specificity needed to describe the Bible's uniqueness. In their estimation such a general concept of actualization cannot explain the Bible's continuing grip upon people's lives or the forceful intervention of God and his word upon human society; it is too weak to carry the theological freight which von Rad, in particular, deems a central aspect of Old Testament studies.

Westermann's article "Was ist eine exegetische Aussage?" confirms his attitude toward actualization. It is not merely a part of all exegesis; it is a phenomenon even broader than exegesis. Exegesis has a double impulse: the interest *(Interesse)* that one has in a text, and the consciousness of a distance between the time of the hearer and the time of the fixing of the text. Actualization is the means by which the time interval is bridged. However, exegesis is not necessary to overcome all time intervals. With materials such as the holy writings of a community, a political manifesto, or poetry, the interval may be closed by mere recitation.[33] This is the narrative actualization which Westermann described in the previous article. When a text needs interpretation (such as translation), exegesis enters the picture. Actualization is still the mechanism by which the time interval is overcome. Therefore, any act of interpretation of the Bible, whether it be through liturgy, teaching, proclamation, or historical-critical exegesis, is actualization. Furthermore, any inner-Biblical interpretation is actualization: the addition of psalm titles, superscriptions, the Elihu speeches in Job, the Pauline epistles.[34] As long as there is a fixed text (oral or written) which is interpreted, actualization occurs.

We can readily see that this is the broadest possible definition of actualization. Westermann's use of the concept in the previous article is clearly in keeping with this definition. In "Was ist eine exegetische Aussage?" he has brought actualization into the present and related it to contemporary exegesis, a step that von Rad never took. In so doing, he develops the concept in a strikingly different direction than von Rad did.

---

[33]Claus Westermann, "Was ist eine exegetische Aussage?," *ZTK* 59 (1962) 3.

[34]*Ibid.*, 7.

In making it a useful term in describing the exegetical method, he undercuts its distinctive nature for Biblical interpretation.

3

Thus far we have studied the relation of actualization to contemporary proclamation, its occurrences in the psalms, and its use in exegetical theory. Now we will turn to its application to the Pentateuch. For this we will study the work of Hans Walter Wolff, another student and disciple of von Rad.[35] Of course von Rad himself applied actualization to the Pentateuch in several cases. However, there are some salient differences in Wolff's applications which are instructive for the development of the concept. He treats the Pentateuchal sources in two articles, "The Kerygma of the Yahwist" (1964) and "The Elohistic Fragments of the Pentateuch" (1969), and the Deuteronomist in a related study, "The Kerygma of the Deuteronomic Historical Work" (1961).[36]

The distinctive nature of Wolff's application of actualization centers around the use of what Walter Brueggemann calls his "kerygmatic

---

[35]Wolff treats many of the aspects of actualization in his work. For examples, see Hans Walter Wolff, "Hoseas geistige Heimat," *TLZ* 81 (1956) 245-46; "Hauptprobleme alttestamentliche Prophetie," *EvT* 15 (1955) 227-28; "The Hermeneutics of the Old Testament," *Essays on Old Testament Hermeneutics,* p. 188; "Das Alte Testament und das Probleme der existentialen Interpretation,"*EvT* 23 (1963) 335-37; *The Old Testament -- A Guide to Its Writings* (Philadelphia: Fortress, 1973) 5, 34, 45-46, 55; *Anthropology of the Old Testament* (London: SCM Press, 1974) 86-88. For his treatment of promise and fulfillment, see *Anthropology,* 85, 152; *Old Testament Guide,* 4. For his treatment of the vital word of God which must be preached ever anew, see "Hauptprobleme," 210; "Hermeneutics," 163-64, 169; "The Old Testament in Controversy,"*Int,* 12 (1958) 282-83. Wolff's major borrowing from von Rad is the idea of typological interpretation. For this see especially "Hermeneutics," "Controversy," and "The Understanding of History in the Prophets," in *Essays on Old Testament Hermeneutics,* 344, 346. As we can see from these references, Wolff is involved with a broad range of questions related to actualization: typology, theological exegesis, promise and fulfillment. In these areas he does little to break new ground over the works of von Rad and Westermann. He adds significantly to the development of actualization only in the application of his kerygmatic methodology, which we will discuss in this section.

[36]These essays are collected and translated in Walter Brueggemann and Hans Walter Wolff, *The Vitality of Old Testament Traditions* (Atlanta: John Knox, 1975). We will not discuss Brueggemann's contribution to the book because he merely adapts and applies Wolff's methodology without significant changes.

methodology."[37] This is a method which evolved out of two central aspects of von Rad's work: first, his isolation of the credenda of the Old Testament which carry a kerygmatic intent; second, the idea that Israel continually reinterprets its traditions for each successive generation – an idea that lies at the heart of actualization.

Wolff applies these concepts to the layers of Old Testament tradition, which he views as reinterpretations for specific historical periods. Consequently, his method begins by defining the corpus of material which comprises the document under discussion, whether J, E, or DtrH. In this respect he relies upon the generally accepted results of source criticism. Next, he determines the historical situation in which the document was composed. Then, in the key step of his methodology, he isolates the kerygmatic intent of the document. The intent is a theme which appears frequently in the document in question, particularly at key points of transmission or interpretation. In J, E, and DtrH the theme is summed up in a word or phrase: "all the families of the earth gain a blessing in you"; "the fear of God"; "return." This theme sums up the message which the author wished to convey through the work. It embodies the tradition preached anew.[38] In continuing his method, he applies the kerygma to the entire document and reads sections of the document in its light. Then he relates this kerygma to the historical situation of the writer. In the case of the J document he proceeds one step farther and outlines the subsequent history of the theme in the Old and New Testaments.

Wolff's methodology is a consistent extension and application of von Rad's work. Von Rad seeks the kerygma of the Hexateuch and the historical writings of Israel and finds it in the ancient credo.[39] Wolff seeks the kerygma of smaller units: the documents which compose those writings. One finds that this narrowing of focus, at least in Wolff's application, does not work well. Von Rad's credo, while quite brief, covers a number of historical events, giving him a range of material with which to work. Likewise, the extent of the material related to that kerygma – the Hexateuch, for example – is so great that he feels no compulsion to correlate each and every part. He is content to demonstrate that the credo is the organizing principle of the

---

[37]*Ibid.*, 29-39.

[38]*Ibid.*, 50-52, 55, 63, 65, 69, 99-100.

[39]Von Rad, *Theology* 1.115-16.

Hexateuch. When von Rad focuses upon a single document of the Hexateuch, he does not narrow his kerygma accordingly, but retains the entire credo as the focus of the author's theological message. In his discussions of the Yahwist, he concentrates upon explaining how the writer used the elements of the credo to expand and reinterpret traditional material and how he enlarged upon the basic elements which the credo dictated to him. By dealing with the Hexateuch as a whole, refusing to narrow his kerygmatic focus, and avoiding detailed textual exegesis, von Rad maintains freedom in interpreting the Old Testament – with a resulting vagueness that remains a suggestive and intriguing quality in his work.

But Wolff, in narrowing his scope to the kerygma of a single document, focuses that kerygma in one verse (J), one phrase (E), or even one word (DtrH). As a result he must explain the entire document in relation to that unit. This attempt creates several problems. The first is that both J and E offer little material with which to work. J adds little to the original stories; E is very fragmentary. To extract a kerygma from either one is a dubious proposition, and Wolff's attempt in each case has serious flaws. For example, he admits that the Sinai tradition has little to do with his supposed kerygma in J;[40] yet, according to von Rad, this is a significant addition by J himself to the canonical saving history. In E the kerygma of the "fear of God" is supposed to be related to the threat of syncretism in the Northern Kingdom. But at no point does Wolff refer to a concrete anti-syncretistic attitude. The connection between the document and its historical situation remains very vague and general, a position that is in conflict with the specificity for which Wolff strives in these articles.

Another more serious problem is that isolating one verse as the kerygma of a document results in a theological reductionism. One must interpret the document from an extremely narrow perspective. Gone is the extraordinary diversity and range of the J document. One must look at it through blinders. Although it would be possible to view his kerygmatic intention as one limited perspective among many possibilities, he gives no indication in his articles that this is his intent. The kerygmatic intention sums up the theological message of J, E, and DtrH and governs our theological perspective on the Old

---

[40]Wolff, *Vitality* 61.

Testament.[41] One can well see why von Rad did not narrow his focus to this extent.

Wolff's search not only leads to reductionism, but to a theological absolutizing of the documents. It is no longer the final text or even an easily separable stage of development such as JE which carries theological weight for us. The single, reconstructed (and in the case of E, fragmentary) documents are related to a reconstructed historical situation and then given theological import for the present day. One is no longer dealing theologically with the Old Testament text, but going behind the text to a double set of reconstructions for a theological message. Even Brueggemann considers this a danger in modern interpretation,[42] although he fails to see its clear manifestation in these articles by Wolff. This absolutizing of the documents is not a separate development by Wolff, but is a step inherent in von Rad's methodology. He engages in the same procedure, but both his broader vision and his vagueness prevent such a clear manifestation of the difficulties which it creates. Nor is Wolff the only one who sees the documents as a prime source of theological meaning for today; this is a common trend in applying actualization.[43]

Another problem with Wolff's methodology is his focus on the "kerygmatic intention"[44] of the author. The difficulty or even the admissibility of seeking to determine the author's intention has been thoroughly criticized as the intentional fallacy in American literary criticism.[45] However, this discussion has had little impact upon German scholarship, since the use of the term "intention" is somewhat different.[46] Although some aspects of the intentional fallacy may be

---

[41]*Ibid.*, 66, 81-82.

[42]*Ibid.*, 24-25.

[43]See, for example, Walter Brueggemann, "The Kerygma of the Priestly Writers," *ZAW* 84 (1972) 397-413; Elizabeth Achtemeier, "The Relevance of the Old Testament for Christian Preaching" in *A Light Unto My Path* (Philadelphia: Temple University, 1974), 3-24.

[44]*Verkündigungswille* or *Aussagewille*. See Wolff,*Vitality* 42, 43, 45, 69, 84, 86, 90.

[45]William Wimsatt, "The Intentional Fallacy," in *The Verbal Icon* (New York: Noonday, 1966) 3-18; Eric Hirsch, *Validity in Interpretation* (New Haven: Yale University, 1967).

[46]Hirsch, *Validity*, 217-21.

relevant here, the main problem with Wolff's use of intention is basically different.

It is appropriate to use intention when one is speaking of the manner in which a work functions. In this case it is intent as conveyed by the passage itself that is being projected, not a hypothetical intent of the author being read into the passage. However, this is not the manner in which Wolff uses kerygmatic intent. Intent for him becomes circular. He proclaims that a document has kerygmatic intent and that the intent is related to the historical situation in which the document was composed. With both the J and E documents he begins by postulating the historical situation; only then does he search out the intent of the document – an intent that is compatible with the situation, of course. After finding the kerygmatic intent in a key passage,[47] he traces it throughout the document. This leads us back to the historical situation and a delineation of the message which the document has for its time. The circularity of the argument is clear. With the initial positing of the historical situation and the document's relation to it, one will of course find a message which speaks to the situation. The only way in which such an argument is valid is if the textual evidence from the document points overwhelmingly to the historical situation and to the author's intention. That is certainly not the case with Wolff's articles. In each instance he must explain away key material: the Sinai section for J,[48] the fact that E "recounted much other material simply out of respect for what had been handed down from the past,"[49] and central speeches in DtrH.[50] When this is the case, the kerygmatic intention has clearly become the master of the text, instead of deriving from it.

While Wolff's methodology is closely related to actualization, the nature of that relationship needs to be spelled out. His methodology rests on the assumption that each new generation of Israel reinterprets

---

[47]The passage chosen for J is indeed central; his choices for E and DtrH are debatable.

[48]Wolff, *Vitality* 61.

[49]*Ibid.*, 75. In addition he argues on the basis of E material that is omitted in the combining of J and E and therefore non-existent (p. 77)!

[50]*Ibid.*, 90.

the old traditions for its own time "with compelling power."[51] This reinterpretation does not have a merely historical or literary purpose, but a theological one.[52] As we have seen, these are key characteristics of actualization. The move from here to the idea of kerygmatic intention is a simple one: the purpose of the reinterpretation is not merely theological, but sermonic.[53] The kerygmatic intent refers to the nature of the Old Testament texts as proclaiming a message; they become the ancient equivalent of sermons. As we have seen, von Rad, Noth, and Westermann also adopted this stance. However, it remains an unproven proposition. One can certainly agree with von Rad and Wolff when they claim that the preservation and transmission of Old Testament traditions had a theological motive. However, we do not have to equate theological with sermonic. One may theologize from a number of different perspectives – historical, liturgical, didactic, mystical, philosophical – that are quite removed from the sphere of proclamation. There is no compelling reason to tie the traditio-historical method to this equation.

In this series of articles we have a faithful application of the assumptions of actualization which von Rad laid down. In dealing with smaller units of material and being more specific, Wolff bares many of the dangers inherent in the procedure. He encounters the problems of reductionism, intentionality, and the equation of theology with proclamation. In the final analysis the articles are not satisfying for these reasons, ones which reach beyond their specific application in kerygmatic methodology to the concept of actualization as a whole.

The Development of Actualization in England and America

While the deepest impact of actualization was felt in Germany, the influence of the concept was by no means limited to one country. By

---

[51]*Ibid.*, 63: "idem er die Traditionen mit unableitbaren Vollmacht für seine Zeit interpretiert," in "Das Kerygma des Jahwisten,"*EvT*, 24 (1964) 95; also see *Vitality* 51-52, 64-65, 72, 84, 96-97. Wolff never uses *Vergegenwärtigung* or *Aktualisierung* in these articles, preferring *Neuinterpretation, Aktualität,* and *Kerygma,* terms also used by von Rad.

[52]Wolff, *Vitality* 42, 66, 80, 84.

[53]*Ibid.*, 63, 81, 84, 97-99.

1955 scholars in both England and the United States had begun applying actualization to various areas of Old Testament studies.[54]

In England several men explored the application of actualization to the Old Testament. Although Douglas Jones, Peter Ackroyd, and Norman Porteous explored the concept in one or two articles apiece, they eventually adopted other approaches to relating the Old Testament and theology.[55] Actualization made the greatest impression upon E. W. Nicholson, who adopted von Rad's methodology in a series of studies on Exodus, Deuteronomy, and Jeremiah.[56] However, the total impact of actualization upon British scholarship was not a lasting one. Many factors, including the influence of H. H. Rowley's idealism and analytic philosophy, prevented actualization from gaining a firm foothold in England. However, the most crucial blow was James Barr's devastating criticisms of von Rad's work, which bared severe weaknesses in his system.[57]

In the United States actualization was adopted to a greater or lesser extent by a number of scholars in the fifties and sixties, particularly Brevard Childs, James Mays, and Walter Brueggemann.[58] The road for the acceptance of the concept was opened by the creedal emphasis of the work of G. Ernest Wright, although he never embraced the specifics of von Rad's methodology.[59] Although actualization had a greater and

---

[54]For a more complete history of this period in England and America, see Brevard Childs, *Biblical Theology in Crisis* (Philadelphia: Westminster, 1970) 13-147.

[55]Douglas Jones, "The Traditio of the Oracles of Isaiah of Jerusalem,"*ZAW* 67 (1955) 226-46; Peter Ackroyd, "The Vitality of the Word of God in the Old Testament," *ASTI* 1 (1962) 7-23; Norman Porteous, "Actualization and the Prophetic Criticism of the Cult," in E. Wurthwein and O. Kaiser, eds., *Tradition und Situation* (Göttingen: Vandenhoeck und Ruprecht, 1963), reprinted in *Living the Mystery* (Oxford: Basil Blackwell, 1967) 127-42.

[56]E.W. Nicholson, *Deuteronomy and Tradition* (Philadelphia: Fortress, 1967); *Preaching to the Exiles* (New York: Schocken, 1971); *Exodus and Sinai in History and Tradition* (Richmond: John Knox, 1973).

[57]James Barr, "The Problem of Old Testament Theology and the History of Religion," *CJT* 3 (1957) 141-49; "Revelation Through History in the Old Testament and in Modern Theology," *Int* 17 (1963) 193-205; *Old and New*.

[58]Brevard Childs, "Prophecy and Fulfillment," *Int* 12 (1958) 259-71; *Memory and Tradition in Israel* (London: SCM, 1962); James Mays, "Exegesis as a Theological Discipline," Inaugural Address delivered April 20, 1960, (Richmond: Union Theological Seminary, 1960); Walter Brueggemann, *Tradition for Crisis* (Richmond: John Knox, 1968); *Vitality,* 11-40, 101-26.

[59]G. Ernest Wright, *God Who Acts* (London: SCM, 1952).

more lasting impact in America than in England, the concept faced a number of counter-trends which prevented it from ever gaining the dominance which it exerted in German circles. Roman Catholic theologians never participated in the trend toward actualization. Instead, they continued to work in idealistic terms (John L. McKenzie) or revised the *sensus plenior* (Raymond Brown).[60] James M. Robinson preserved the influence of Bultmannian existentialism which issued forth in the New Hermeneutic, which he presented as the new wave of Biblical interpretation in a series of articles in 1964.[61] Frank Cross and David Noel Freedman regarded the debate between Germanic actualization and Scandinavian myth and ritual as having reached an impasse, one which they resolved by a synthesis utilizing both historical and mythical aspects of Near Eastern thought.[62]

In the midst of these myriad approaches to the Old Testament in both England and America, actualization had its impact. Rather than one person making a singular contribution to the development of the concept, several scholars had an impact in two separate areas of application. Consequently, in this section we will focus upon these two areas: the study of the traditio in the prophetic literature and the questioning of the relationship between actualization and the cult.

1

The nature of the traditio in the prophetic literature became the concern of several English scholars. D. R. Jones began this study with his article "The Traditio of the Oracles of Isaiah of Jerusalem" in 1955. In this work he concentrated on the traditio-historical nature of the transmission. Actualization is certainly present as a force in the transmission process, but it remains very much in the background,

---

[60]See in particular Raymond Brown, "Hermeneutics," *JBC* (1968) 605-23; *Sensus Plenior of Sacred Scripture* (Baltimore: St. Mary's University, 1955); John L. McKenzie, *A Theology of the Old Testament* (Garden City: Doubleday, 1974); *The Two-Edged Sword* (Milwaukee: Bruce, 1956); *Myths and Realities* (Milwaukee: Bruce, 1963).

[61]James M. Robinson, *A New Quest for the Historical Jesus* (London: SCM, 1959); "The New Hermeneutic at Work,"*Int* 18 (1964) 346-59; with John Cobb, eds., *New Frontiers in Theology: The New Hermeneutic* 2 (New York: Harper & Row, 1964).

[62]Frank Cross and David Noel Freedman, "The Song of Miriam," *JNES* 14 (1955) 237-50; Frank Cross, "Yahweh and the God of the Patriarchs,"*HTR* 55 (1962) 225-59; "The Divine Warrior in Israel's Early Cult," in Alexander Altmann, ed., *Biblical Motifs* (Cambridge: Harvard University, 1966) 11-30.

since he is not particularly concerned with the theological ramifications of the traditio.[63] Peter Ackroyd followed this article with "The Vitality of the Word of God in the Old Testament" in 1962. In this article he pursued Jones' ideas further and followed out their theological implications. Later, E. W. Nicholson made a detailed application of these ideas of traditio to the prose portions of Jeremiah in *Preaching to the Exiles* (1970). Although Nicholson's work is significant for its application, it does not advance the theory of actualization over the other two articles.[64] Of these studies, Ackroyd's is the one that best sums up the nature of this trend, since it deals most directly with actualization and its implications.

In "The Vitality of the Word of God in the Old Testament" Ackroyd seeks

> to draw a picture of some of the processes involved in the shaping of the Old Testament material, not by the pens of authors and editors, but by the living application of the recognized word of God – whether in prophecy or psalm, law or story – to the ever new needs of a community sensitive to the vitality of that word.[65]

To draw this picture, he treats the three-fold repetition of a prophecy against Jereboam in I Kings. He concludes that the repetition is not due to quotation or lack of imagination, but to the creative handling of the ever vital word of God.[66] This is a consciously theological motive of the Deuteronomistic historian which reveals some of his methods. Specifically, it shows that he, as the successor to the prophets, used prophecy as a text for sermons at a later date, "... with the prophetic saying not just a text on which to hang a homily, but a living word of God which could not but have meaning in a new situation."[67] The

---

[63]Jones, "Traditio," 227, 230, 243.

[64]Although Nicholson's work shows the greatest influence of von Rad and actualization, he adds little to the development of the concept in any of his work. By faithfully applying the ideas developed by von Rad, Jones, and Ackroyd, he exposes some of the weaknesses of these insights. However, these weaknesses may be discussed more easily in relation to the original work of von Rad and Ackroyd.

[65]Ackroyd, "Vitality," 7.

[66]*Ibid.*, 8-10.

[67]*Ibid.*, 12.

sermonic style which one perceives in the Deuteronomistic history and the later prophets is a development caused by the coalescing of prophecy and wisdom.[68] It is characterized by the exhortatory style derived from wisdom and the "vital apprehension of the historic moment" which leads to the reapplication of older traditions to a new situation. As such it pervades the work of all the creative personalities who helped shape the Old Testament traditions: priests, prophets, disciples, preachers, exegetes, educationists, psalmists.[69]

In this picture of the traditionary process Ackroyd has used the work of Birkeland, Mowinckel, and Jones as a starting point.[70] However he moved beyond them in the theological nature of his formulation. That traditionary process which they present in a relatively neutral light, he imbues with theological motives. The tradition is re-used because it is the word of God. As such it always speaks with power to new situations. We should seek to apprehend it today in a like manner.[71] As we have noted before, there is a distinct neo-orthodox cast to the theological formulation, revolving around the vital word of God and its proclamation.

He places an even heavier emphasis upon the sermonic style than von Rad does in his discussions of Deuteronomy. Several scholars have remarked upon the presence of homiletic material in both Deuteronomy and the Deuteronomistic history, and have used that fact to explain actualization. However, none of the examples that Ackroyd gives are from the homiletic sections of these books. They are part of the more straightforward historical narratives. This is illustrative of his understanding of sermonic style. It is not restricted to specifically exhortatory material in Deuteronomy, the Deuteronomistic history, and the prophets; it is characteristic of all Old Testament materials – wisdom, psalms, stories, etc. In asserting this, Ackroyd is stepping considerably beyond the bounds of his evidence, since he supplies no examples outside the Deuteronomistic history and the prophets. This

---

[68]*Ibid.,* 15-17.

[69]*Ibid.,* 18.

[70]Ackroyd is dependent on Jones and both of them draw from Mowinckel and Birkeland. Von Rad's influence is from *Studies in Deuteronomy* and not directly from his understanding of the prophetic traditio, which he did not explain in detail until *Theology* 2, in 1960. Ackroyd's paper was originally delivered in 1957 at Cambridge.

[71]Ackroyd, "Vitality," 19.

concept of all the Biblical material as proclamation (and consequently as actualization) is an attempt to meet a very real problem. Von Rad and others, with their emphasis upon *Heilsgeschichte,* have excluded many of the disparate materials of the Old Testament from a theologically important position. Ackroyd has attempted to reintegrate them under the rubric of proclamation. Unfortunately, the results are not convincing. The end result is the equation of sermonic style with actualization and its application as a blanket term for the growth of tradition in the Old Testament. Such all-inclusiveness renders both terms meaningless and fails to do justice to the diversity of the Old Testament traditio.

2

The second trend, the questioning of the relationship between actualization and the cult, occurred in both the United States and in England. Brevard Childs' book, *Memory and Tradition in the Old Testament,* opened up that question in 1962 with a study of the Hebrew root זכר and a search for its *Sitz im Leben.* Norman Porteous, relying in part upon Childs' work, continued to investigate the question in "Actualization and the Prophetic Criticism of the Cult" (1963).

One of the most significant features of Childs' book is that he scrutinizes for the first time part of the Old Testament vocabulary associated with actualization. The main portion of the book is a study of the root זכר in its relation to Israel's memory. In the study he finds that most occurrences of זכר do not refer to actualization[72] and that the use of זכר does not warrant constructing a separate Hebrew psychology of memory conducive to actualization, as Johannes Pedersen tried to do.[73] In a few places Childs finds a special theological development of זכר with Israel as its subject. In Deuteronomy זכר has two such usages. In one, Israel's memory makes it "noetically aware of a history

---

[72]Childs, *Memory.* The *hiphil* means "to utter," either in a cultic or juridical context (pp. 11-15); the *qal* with God as its subject is an active but timeless remembering (pp. 31-44) related to the cult; most occurrences of the *qal* with Israel as its subject simply refer to the psychological act of remembering (p. 47); the noun זְכָרוֹן denotes an eternal relationship (pp. 66-70); the noun זֵכֶר is related to the *hiphil* (pp. 70-73).

[73]*Ibid.,* 17-30. Childs concludes that זכר merely has a wider semantic range than the English "remember."

which is ontologically a unity."[74] In the other, participation in Israel's festivals "arouses and incites the memory" which causes Israel to participate in the past decisive events of its tradition. This is actualization.[75] Childs finds similar developments of זכר in Micah, Deutero-Isaiah, Ezekiel, and the individual complaint psalms. The conclusion which he draws from this data is significant. First, there is no specific *Sitz im Leben* for the use of זכר. In particular it is not directly related to the cult, as one would expect for actualization. Instead it seems to function psychologically and refer to an internalization of remembrances.[76] Second, it does not focus on "specific historical events, but on the divine reality who imprinted her history."[77] This, too, is contrary to expectations, since von Rad, Noth, and Westermann all stress the close relationship of actualization and the historical credo of Israel. Through his study of זכר, Childs finds actualization in the Old Testament, but severely limits its scope and challenges many of the previously held assumptions about its nature.

After studying זכר in its various contexts, he turns his attention to the relationship between memory and cult. In not finding a cultic setting for Israel's use of memory, he has raised an interesting problem. If one accepts the presence of cultic actualization in Israel, as Childs does on the basis of the arguments of Mowinckel and Noth, then what is its relationship to actualization through memory? Childs rejects the ideas that זכר may be a late-developing term for cultic actualization or that the two types of actualization developed along parallel lines. Instead he states that the evidence points to the process of actualization undergoing a transformation at times of crisis. All the theological developments of זכר stem from situations in which the participant is cut off from the normal functioning of the cult: in Deuteronomy by secularization and loss of immediacy; in Deutero-Isaiah and Ezekiel by the exile; in the complaint psalms by various troubles. In all these cases the role of the cult in relating the worshippers to their past traditions is internalized and relegated to the active memory of the believers.

---

[74]*Ibid.*, 52.

[75]*Ibid.*, 53.

[76]*Ibid.*, 65.

[77]*Ibid.*, 65.

This leads to a discussion of the nature of actualization in the Old Testament. Childs sees Mowinckel, with his emphasis on mythic immediacy and renewal, and Noth, with his emphasis on the participant being transported back to a once-and-for-all historical event, as having opposite understandings of actualization. Childs feels that both views fail to do justice to the unique nature of Old Testament actualization, which incorporates both the historical nature of the saving events and the immediate experiencing of those events. This is done because the quality of time was changed at the exodus to "redemptive time." Now, through memory, the transfer of time to redemptive time occurs for each new generation. This change in the quality of time preserves the historical nature of the events, yet overcomes the chronological separation which exists, allowing a sense of immediacy to those remembering the redeeming events.[78] This, when properly perceived by the people, calls forth an obedient response to the demands of God's law. Thus, we can understand the Old Testament as "layer upon layer of Israel's reinterpretation of the same period of her history, because each successive generation rewrites the past in terms of her own experience with the God who meets his people through the tradition."[79]

Childs' final formulation of actualization bears a close resemblance to that of von Rad. They have perceived the same central problem: the difficulty of connecting the type of actualization that occurs in the Old Testament with cultic actualization. With the evidence marshalled from his study of זכר, Childs makes the dichotomy crystal clear. Both Childs and von Rad insist on retaining the central aspect of cultic actualization: the sense of immediacy or contemporization which it inspires. Both see the actualization of the Old Testament as a transformation of cultic actualization. For von Rad the transformation occurs as a result of the developing sense of history in Israel with its consequent secularization and rationalization; Childs, as a response to a series of unrelated crises. The basic difference in the two stems from their starting points. Von Rad's concept, beginning with a theological conception and viewpoint, remains external to the people of Israel, focusing on the word of God. Childs' study, stemming from his work on זכר, focuses on the internalization of the concept through memory.

---

[78]*Ibid.,* 83-85.

[79]*Ibid.,* 89.

Several problems exist in Childs' understanding of actualization through memory. It seems questionable that such similar responses would be called forth by such diverse crises. The only unequivocal cutting off from the cult occurs in the crisis of the exile. In particular, the "crisis" which prompted the complaint psalms is both dissimilar and ill-defined. In addition, he fails to relate Micah 6:5, which he discusses in detail, to his crisis theory at all.

However, these are minor points. The major problem is that his conclusions simply do not grow out of his data. His study of זכר brings into question many of the commonly held assumptions about actualization. The lack of a cultic setting for זכר undercuts the argument for cultic actualization in the Old Testament, as Childs recognizes. The paucity of occurrences of זכר in relation to actualization does even more damage to its use as a widespread, even predominate, mode of inner-Biblical exegesis. However, Childs joins company with the other scholars we have studied in seeing this concept as the way in which Israel interpreted its traditions. The evidence from which he works would warrant a much more circumspect approach.

There would seem to be little evidence to support his final understanding of actualization through memory as retaining the cultic sense of immediacy. He states:

> It means more than that later generations wrestled with the meaning of the redemptive events, although this is certainly true. It means more than that the influence of a past event continued to be felt in successive generations.... Rather, there was an immediate encounter, an actual participation in the great acts of redemption.[80]

But if one examines the uses of זכר which he discusses, the influence of and wrestling with the meaning of tradition is precisely what is reflected. This is certainly true for the complaint psalms with their juxtaposition of present sorrows and past triumph, of Deutero-Isaiah and Ezekiel with their call for reflection, and for Deuteronomy with its rationalizing influence. In all these instances the element of rational reflection and psychological wrestling is present, issuing in a response of obedience. To claim a sense of immediacy is to overstep the evidence. Certainly when he bases this immediacy upon the creation of

---

[80]*Ibid.*, 83-84.

redemptive time he is opening himself to James Barr's criticism of a separate concept of Biblical time.[81]

In summary Childs has provided a valuable word study for a key root related to actualization. As a result he calls into question many of the generally held assumptions regarding the concept. However, he then proceeds to overstep his own evidence in the search for a unique Biblical application of actualization.

In "Actualization and the Prophetic Criticism of the Cult" Norman Porteous raises the same questions as Childs from a different angle. He asks why, if actualization of God's saving deeds occurs in the cult, is the prophetic criticism of the cult so strong? His answer is neither to dissociate the prophets from actualization nor to deny actualization in the cult. Instead, he shifts the emphasis of actualization away from the automatic re-enactment of the saving events to the people's obedient response:

> While in worship the transcendent activity of God can be actualized and made relevant to each new generation, which is thus made to realize that God's saving activity is always present and powerful, actualization is never complete until the act of God is matched by the responsive act of man.[82]

While this may seem to be a minor distinction, it is in fact a major shift in meaning for actualization. The origin of the concept lay in a description of the ancient Near Eastern cults, in which it referred to the mechanism of making a mythic event real and alive.[83] Von Rad, Noth, and others have adapted this concept to the Israelite religion where it makes an historical event real and alive. The essence of actualization lies in the act of vivifying, where the people realize the significance of the act and the nature of the demand that is made upon them. However, Porteous' inclusion of an obedient response by the people in the meaning of the term expands actualization beyond the basic meaning of the term, so that it becomes virtually synonymous

---

[81]James Barr, *Biblical Words for Time* (London: SCM, 1962). Childs basically accepts Barr's criticism of Pedersen's concept of a Hebrew psychology of memory in *The Semantics of Biblical Language* (Glasgow: Oxford University, 1961). See Childs, *Memory*, 18-30.

[82]Porteous, "Actualization," 140.

[83]Porteous recognizes and assents to this use of the term, *Ibid.*, 127-28.

with true faith.[84] He has recognized a legitimate problem in the formulation of actualization by Mowinckel and Noth: It is a cultic event and thus isolated from the majority of the Old Testament writings, especially the prophets and wisdom where one deals with the response of the people to ethical demands on secular life. However, his solution is to expand the term into a theological catch-all, which dilutes the meaning of actualization and obscures any distinctiveness which the term might have.

The Influence of Actualization in Recent Scholarship

The early 1960's, with the publication of von Rad's *Old Testament Theology II* (1962) and "Offene Fragen im Umkreis einer Theologie des Alten Testaments" (1963), Childs' *Memory and Tradition in the Old Testament* (1962), Porteous' "Actualization and the Prophetic Criticism of the Cult" (1963), and Westermann's "Vergegenwärtigung der Geschichte in den Psalmen" (1963), saw a virtual end to the development of the theory of actualization. Not surprisingly this cessation coincides closely with James Barr's highly effective criticisms and the rise of the New Hermeneutic. The trend in the United States has been markedly away from actualization with the growth in popularity of Frank Cross' method and the move of such proponents of actualization as Brevard Childs to develop other ways of linking theological concerns with the Old Testament. The shift in thinking in Germany has been far less dramatic, but the rise in popularity of redaction criticism in place of tradition criticism has resulted in substantial alterations in the concept there as well.

However, actualization has continued to play an important role in Old Testament scholarship, primarily through the application of the theory as we have seen it developed. Most of these applications follow the trends which we have studied in this chapter.[85] Another,

---

[84]Porteous refers to Childs' work as one of his sources for this concept (*Ibid.*, 138). However, Porteous carries this much further than Childs does (see Childs, *Memory*, 54).

[85]In addition to the works listed in footnotes 22, 35, 43, 55, 56, and 58, see the following works: Hans Zirker, *Die kultische Vergegenwärtigung in den Psalmen* (Bonn: P. Hanstein, 1964); Joachim Becker, *Israel deutet seine Psalmen* (Stuttgart: Katholisches Bibelwerk, 1966); Joh. Michael Schmidt, "Vergegenwärtigung und Überlieferung," *EvT* 30 (1970) 169-200; Jean-Luc Vesco, "Abraham, actualization, et relectures," *RSPT* 55 (1971) 33-80; F. Dreyfus, "L'Actualisation à l'interieur de la Bible," *RB* 83 (1976) 161-202.

potentially more important, development in actualization has also taken place. It has become so much an integral part of Old Testament studies that various features which comprise it have been separated out and used in methods which are essentially different from the theory of actualization as we have described it. A complete treatment of this influence of actualization would be impossible, since it would involve discussing widely varied methods of Old Testament studies. However, a brief look at the work of two scholars, James Sanders and Odil Hannes Steck, will indicate the nature of this continuing influence of actualization on Old Testament studies.[86]

1

James Sanders' development of canonical criticism owes much to the concept of actualization. Although one can find its influence in his early formulations of canonical criticism,[87] actualization is more prominent in his recent works, such as "Adaptable for Life: The Nature and Function of Canon," and his article "Hermeneutics" in the *Interpreter's Dictionary of the Bible.* Sanders' basic thesis is that the Bible is the book of the Jewish and Christian communities. They shaped it in their common life; its continuing function is to be in dialogue with the heirs of those communities. The early Jews and Christians shaped the scriptures by asking their traditions two questions: who are we and what are we to do, the questions of identity and life style. Those parts of their traditions which continued to provide answers to these questions as new generations asked them came to be regarded as scripture. Re-use was proof of validity and authority and eventually led to canonization. The task of canonical hermeneutics is "determining valid modes of seeking the meaning of a biblical text in

---

[86]Another area in which the influence of actualization is present is comparative midrash. See particularly Renée Bloch, "Midrash," in *DBSup* 5 (1957) 1263-81; Roger le Deáut, "Apropos a Definition of Midrash," *Int* 25 (1971) 259-82. A volume which adapts actualization in several different directions is Douglas Knight, ed., *Tradition and Theology in the Old Testament* (Philadelphia: Fortress, 1977). The chapters by Roger Lapointe, Douglas Knight, Robert Laurin, and Michael Fishbane are of particular interest.

[87]James Sanders, *Torah and Canon* (Philadelphia: Fortress, 1972) pp. xv, xvi, 24, 91-94, 96, 117-21.

its own setting, and then determining a valid mode of expression of that meaning in contemporary settings."[88]

Sanders' debt to actualization emerges in the preceding summary of his task. Actualization grows out of an understanding of the Bible as a book developed by a community which used and re-used traditions. For Sanders "the first consideration of canonical criticism is the phenomenon of repetition.... It is the nature of canon to be 'remembered' or contemporized."[89]   The second consideration is function. Sanders sees the function of canon as answering his two questions of identity and life style.   In answering them, it communicates a power that meets the needs of a community.   In actualization this corresponds to the ability of a Biblical word to speak to a specific historical situation – not just once, but, adapted, to a series of situations.   The combination of these two criteria leads to the definition of the central aspect of canon: its adaptability.   As Sanders states:

> Such material, which met a need in one situation, was apparently able to meet another need in another situation. And that is precisely the kind of tradition that becomes canonical – material that bears repeating in a later moment both because of the need of the later moment and because of the value or power of the material repeated.[90]

It is precisely this combination of adaptability and power that appears as elements of actualization in a slightly different form.   Sanders pays even more direct homage to the concept when he defines the role of memory in canonical hermeneutics:

> But the retelling of that epic story of Israel's origins entailed such intensive identification with those in the past who benefited from God's mighty acts in the story that, in cultic terms, time and space were in that moment of recital transcended.   Those recalling or remembering the story understood themselves *actually* to be the slaves freed from

---

[88]James Sanders, "Hermeneutics," *IDBSup* (1976) 403; also see "Adaptable for Life: The Nature and Function of Canon," in Frank Cross, Werner Lenke, and Patrick Miller, eds., *Magnalia Dei* (New York: Doubleday, 1976) 534, 538.

[89]Sanders, "Adaptable," 534.

[90]*Ibid.*, 542.

Egypt, guided in the desert, and brought into the promised land; that is, the holy story became present reality in them.[91]

Here he draws directly upon the theory of memory and actualization developed by Childs.

The manner in which the influence of actualization permeates Sanders' canonical criticism should be evident by now. However, his endeavor is different from the traditional formulation of actualization in two central respects. First, the theological standpoint is different. In the previous discussions we have noted the consistent neo-orthodox point of view that is stressed: the role of the vital word of God, the emphasis upon proclamation, the inherent power of the traditions. None of that appears in Sanders' work. Instead we encounter an existential point of view: the community struggles with the question of identity; material which is re-used is "historically transcendent";[92] traditions are re-used because they meet the existential needs of the community. These differences are not superficial. In actualization the neo-orthodox elements became part and parcel of the theory. The homiletic nature of the Old Testament materials is quite important. The Old Testament traditions were transmitted and adapted – actualized – primarily through proclamation.[93] In turn proclamation becomes the centerpiece of hermeneutics and exegesis.[94] Sanders changes all that; the terms do not even occur in his work. Instead he takes the idea of contemporization and centers it in the self-questioning of the community. The questing, the internalized groping, the existential need for identity becomes the focus for the transmission of tradition in the Old Testament and for contemporary hermeneutics as well.

Second, Sanders' canonical criticism does not rise from and rely upon form criticism to any great extent. Consequently, both foci of actualization, the coupling of modern historical criticism (at the beginning, form criticism and the nascent discipline of tradition criticism) with neo-orthodox theology, are altered in Sanders' work. While he does not deny the value of form criticism, he minimizes its

---

[91]Sanders, "Hermeneutics," 406.

[92]Sanders, "Adaptable," 542.

[93]See particularly von Rad, Westermann, and Ackroyd. The title of Nicholson's book, *Preaching to the Exiles,* points to this.

[94]See particularly Noth and Westermann.

significance for understanding the transmission of traditions. He points out that von Rad and Noth have come under attack because the credenda with which they work are not ancient in form. He feels that the criticism is correct, but that the question is really misdirected.

> The form of a literary passage cannot possibly answer all the questions necessary concerning it. Indeed, its form may be deceptive, for the ancient speaker or writer may well have intended to pour new wine into an old wineskin, precisely in order to make a point which literary conformity might not have permitted him to make.... one must always ask what function a literary piece served, originally as well as in its subsequent contexts.[95]

By asking the question of function, he avoids the need to tie the tradition down to set forms. He views the two major traditions, the Mosaic and the Davidic, not as credenda, but as stories which can take on varied forms or be used as part of different *Gattungen*. He finds the narrow definition of *Sitz im Leben* to be restrictive and feels that traditions are not passed down conservatively "to fill out a cultic order of service."   Instead they meet a "gut-level existential need."[96] Consequently, the traditions are much more free and flexible to change form, add or eliminate elements, and speak to different situations than they are for those scholars who rely upon form criticism.

We have seen that in canonical criticism Sanders has appropriated several salient features of actualization. In doing so he has stripped away what were constant elements in its exposition: the neo-orthodox theological background and the debt to form criticism. That he has applied salient features to an existential perspective and has had them make sense in that context raises important implications for a basic understanding of actualization, especially in relation to the elements Sanders has eliminated. We will discuss these implications in the next chapter.

2

Odil Hannes Steck was a student of von Rad. Not surprisingly, he has continued the task of tradition criticism which was developed by

---

[95]Sanders, "Adaptable," 536.

[96]*Ibid.*, 538.

von Rad and others. In addition he has retained the use of actualization in his work. However, as one studies his method and its application, significant differences emerge in his use of actualization. Steck has both outlined his method in his book on exegesis and applied it in several studies, the most relevant of which are *Überlieferung und Zeitgeschichte in den Elia-Erzählung* (1968) and "Theological Streams of Tradition" (1977).[97]

In his work on exegesis Steck limits the use of actualization severely, mentioning it only in relation to *Überlieferungsgeschichte* among all the possible types of historical criticism. He further restricts *Überlieferungsgeschichte* to the oral development of a specific text.[98] His statement on the nature of actualization is specific and draws directly on von Rad:

> Das Weiterarbeiten an alten Überlieferungsstücken und ihre jeweils neue Vergegenwärtigung sind im AT eine auffallend häufige Erscheinung. Die Träger solcher Überlieferung gehen offenbar von der Überzeugung aus, dass Texte und Worte auch dann nicht einfach "erledigt" sind, wenn ihr konkreter zeitgeschichtlicher Bezug obsolete geworden ist, dass sie vielmehr Aktualität in sich bergen und in gewandelter Situation "neue Inhalte aus sich zu entlassen imstande" sind.[99]

His conception of the role of actualization contains most of the standard elements and adds little new. However, his application of the concept differs considerably from any that we have seen.

The clearest application occurs in *Überlieferung und Zeitgeschichte in den Elia-Erzählung*. The title, with its juxtaposition of *Überlieferung* and *Zeitgeschichte* is very revealing in regard to Steck's use of *Überlieferungsgeschichte*. For the Elijah narrative he analyzes in detail each layer of the tradition: first the core, then the two major expansions. In relation to each layer he then constructs a *Zeitgeschichte*. By this he means much more than a set of historical

---

[97]Odil Hannes Steck and Hermann Barth, *Exegese des Alten Testaments* (Neukirchen-Vluyn: Neukirchener, 1971); Odil Hannes Steck, *Überlieferung und Zeitgeschichte in den Elia-Erzählung* (Neukirchen-Vluyn: Neukirchener, 1968); "Theological Streams of Tradition," in Knight, *Tradition*, 183-214.

[98]Steck, *Exegese*, 37.

[99]*Ibid.*, 43-44.

events (the *Zeitereignisse*). He specifically includes the social, religious, and political ferment of the times, the intellectual turmoil which might prompt the re-use of an old tradition. Then, as a final step, he brings the two into a direct relationship. He sees the relation as a theological one, as a later generation creates new stories (such as the Horeb pericope) which bring Elijah and the earlier traditions associated with him into contrast with a later age. In so doing, the earlier events become dehistoricized, as Elijah is viewed as a surrogate for Yahweh and the events assume a virtually symbolic meaning for a later age.[100] This theological process is referred to as actualization.[101] However, a term he uses more frequently to describe the process is *Geistesbesuchäftigung*.[102] While his use of the term is vague, it is indicative of a shift in the nature of the hermeneutical connection which Steck perceives between the old and new. It emerges as an intellectual bridge, rather than a living contemporizing – a conscious, studied effort to apply old traditions to new situations.

We can see the differences which emerge in Steck in relation to von Rad. Steck gives a meticulous, detailed dissection of the traditions and sees the expansions as connected to a later *Zeitgeschichte* in a direct one-to-one relationship: the Naboth story to Jehu's rebellion; the Horeb pericope to the Aramaean threat. The relation may be described as actualization but in fact is intellectual, mechanical, and lifeless. Von Rad stresses the charismatic nature of actualization and maintains that in his applications. There is no attempt at a one-to-one correlation between actualizations and historical events. He relates them to a general time period or a general *Sitz im Leben,* but retains a tentative air which suggests that their charismatic nature prevents a close and definite description. That is gone with Steck. His conceptualizations may be basically correct, but they lack the life that pervades von Rad's. Given the theological nature of actualization, this is not a superficial difference. Von Rad's charismatic theology is an integral component of his work, one which leads the reader to react to his work in affirmation or negation of the theology as well as the basic exegetical work. For Steck the theology has become an appendage; it is overwhelmed by the

---

[100]Steck, *Überlieferung* 135-37.

[101]*Ibid.,* 135, 140. Also see Steck, *Exegese,* 43-44.

[102]Steck, *Überlieferung* 85, 125, 135, 144.

Überlieferungsgeschichte and the *Zeitgeschichte*. Actualization is overwhelmed with it.

The other change to which we have alluded lies in the historical nature of the material. For von Rad later actualizations retain their original historicity. The people affirm those original events and participate in them, as well as altering the tradition to relate to their own historical situation. Steck has lost this basic relation to earlier history. His traditions have become dehistoricized, intellectual entities. The person of Elijah, separated from his historical surroundings, has become the vehicle of Yahweh, a surrogate and a symbol.

These changes are the result of a fundamental shift on the part of Steck. He no longer bases his analysis of the Old Testament upon tradition criticism, as von Rad did; he relies upon redaction criticism instead. In this conception the growth of the Old Testament does not result primarily from the reinterpretation of a fluid oral tradition, but from the work of editors upon written collections. While these collections are not regarded as fixed, the editorial process is necessarily regarded as more reflective and intellectual with a consequent loss of charismatic interpretive freedom. While this shift did not originate with actualization, it affects the use of the concept in Steck's theological interpretation. As a student of von Rad, Steck sought to continue his mentor's theological concern for the Old Testament texts even with a different historical-critical basis. However, von Rad's chronological actualization is too dependent upon the charismatic freedom inherent in oral tradition to be transferred to a method which inhibits that freedom. As a result, Steck's theological formulations lack life and appear to be appendages to his analysis. If actualization is to be a viable segment of the redaction-critical process, the concept must be altered to conform to the overall method.

Summary

In this chapter we have studied several scholars who have contributed to the development of actualization. As one would expect, they took the concept in directions which von Rad did not explore, and sometimes developed ideas contrary to his. Perhaps more important than the study of the individual scholars is the recognition that definite trends have emerged in the development of actualization. Noth made a very natural extension of the method to present proclamation.[103] Through Westermann we saw that it is being applied to the psalms, potentially a fruitful area of discussion.[104] Westermann also extended its use to exegetical method, an area in which both Wolff and Steck have contributed.[105] Another trend is its detailed application to the literary strata of the Old Testament, exemplified by Wolff.[106] Ackroyd demonstrated the application of actualization to the prophetic traditio.[107]

In addition to these trends we investigated the influence that actualization exerted on scholars outside of the traditio-historical circle. Sanders and Steck, as examples of this development, have employed elements of actualization in their canon-critical and redaction-critical approaches. These attempts to adapt actualization to a different milieu have met with varied success: Sanders incorporates the concept insightfully from an existentialist perspective; Steck's efforts result in a static and unconvincing theologizing.

Not surprisingly, the various endeavors studied in this chapter have both enriched actualization and revealed deep-seated flaws. While we have begun to evaluate the different perspectives, we have not defined them in relation to each other or to von Rad in any detail. That is the task for the third chapter.

---

[103]Noth, "Re-presentation"; Achtemeier, "Relevance"; Ackroyd, "Vitality"; Nicholson, *Preaching;* Brueggemann, *Vitality.*

[104]Westermann, "Vergegenwärtigung"; Zirker, *Vergegenwärtigung;* Becker, *Israel.*

[105]Westermann, "exegetische Aussage"; Wolff, "Hermeneutics"; Wolff, "existentialen Interpretation"; Steck, *Exegese;* Mays, "Exegesis."

[106]Wolff, *Vitality;* Steck, *Überlieferung;* Schmidt, "Vergegenwärtigung"; Nicholson, *Preaching;* Brueggemann, *Tradition.*

[107]Ackroyd, "Vitality"; Jones, "Traditio"; Nicholson, *Preaching.*

Chapter Three

Actualization Defined and Criticized

Having studied the history and development of chronological actualization, we will now proceed to a systematic investigation and criticism of the constituent parts of the concept. The first step will be a definition of terms. Before we can evaluate actualization, we must set the parameters of the different types of contemporization which we have encountered. Only then can we judge the validity of the application of chronological actualization to the Old Testament.

The major portion of the chapter will be devoted to a criticism of the internal logic of the concept. This investigation encompasses four aspects of that logic, each of which will be considered in a separate section: 1) the claim that chronological actualization is a concept unique to the Bible; 2) the traditio-historical unity which it lends to scripture; 3) the centrality of chronological actualization to Biblical interpretation; 4) the theological-historical equation which has rendered actualization so important to Biblical hermeneutics.

To a great extent this criticism will focus on the degree of consistency with which chronological actualization adheres to its own tenets, especially marking out contradictions and ambiguities. While internal consistency does not stamp a method as valid, it is a first and necessary step in that direction. If actualization is not internally consistent, then one should have serious questions about its general validity. In addition the points of inconsistency in a method can frequently point out areas in which corrections and alterations can make the system itself more valid or lead to the development of a related system based upon the strengths of the old one.

Failure to recognize the internal logic of a method can result in a lack of comprehension not only of the strengths of a method, but also of its true weaknesses as well. While a criticism that is based upon such a total lack of sympathy to the method being studied is not invalid, it is rarely useful. The end result is usually the opposition to two competing and unrelated systems and a statement that one system is *de facto* better than the other. Unfortunately, this is the result of one of the most complete evaluations of von Rad in English, D. G. Spriggs' *Two Old Testament Theologies*. He constantly berates von Rad for making an analysis that is "meaningless," but he rarely comes to grips with the analysis itself.[1]

Another method that is more useful, but somewhat misleading, is the attempt to compare theological methodologies. This leads one to force all the theologies studied into a specific set of categories. This results in a distortion of von Rad's theology and actualization as a whole, since von Rad is making a conscious attempt to break the mold of predetermined categories. His success or failure in this attempt is a question to be answered. The issue is clouded by discussing his theology in general categories set by other theologians. Gerhard Hasel, despite a valiant effort to let von Rad speak for himself, falls into this trap.[2]

Therefore, this investigation, while maintaining a critical stance, will focus on the categories which emerge naturally from actualization itself.[3] This should enable us to appreciate the strengths of the method as well as criticize its weaknesses. This criticism should also help us see beyond actualization to some new bases for doing theology in the Old Testament.

Types of Actualization

In the first two chapters we have seen quite varied definitions of actualization. Each scholar has a particular version. Von Rad has presented the most complete description of its application to Old

---

[1]Spriggs, *Theologies*, 34-59. This section is rife with examples, but pp. 36, 38, 49, 59 are particularly illuminating.

[2]Gerhard Hasel, *Old Testament Theology: Basic Issues in the Current Debate* (Grand Rapids: Eerdmans, 1972); "The Problem of the Center in the Old Testament Theology Debate," *ZAW* 86 (1974) 65-82; "The Problem of History in Old Testament Theology," *AUSS* 8 (1970) 32-35, 41-46.

[3]Fortunately, there are several criticisms of von Rad's work which are able to maintain this perspective: Knight, *Rediscovering*, 97-142; Wolff, *Gerhard von Rad;* Conzelmann, "Fragen"; Honecker, "Verständnis"; Rolf Rendtorff, "Geschichte und Überlieferungen," in *Studien zur Theologie des alttestamentlichen Überlieferungen* (Neukirchen-Vluyn: Neukirchener, 1961) 81-94; Barr,*Old and New*, 65-200.

Testament theology, but no one else has used the terms in exactly the same manner as he. Mowinckel, Noth, and Westermann in particular have significantly different understandings of the concept, while Wolff, Ackroyd, Childs, and Porteous differ to a lesser extent.

Before we can criticize actualization in its application to the Old Testament, we must see how these varied definitions can be grouped together or differentiated. In particular we need to define what constitutes a significant difference in definition. To facilitate our evaluation of actualization, this section will show that three broad categories of actualization may be derived from the material presented in the first two chapters: cultic, chronological, and literary.

1

Cultic actualization is the most easily defined of the three major forms which we have encountered. Its nature and function is a point of general agreement among the proponents of actualization: Mowinckel, von Rad, Noth, Westermann, Childs, Porteous, and Sanders all explicitly acknowledge that it is the basic means of religious communication in the primitive cult. From their discussions of the concept, we may isolate five salient features of cultic actualization.

First, cultic actualization is a re-enactment of the basic, sacred events of a community. These events may be either mythological or historical (in an undefined sense, presumably meaning that the events occurred within time rather than in the *Urzeit*).[4] These events are the constituent events of the community. They define its existence and particularity. Such events might well describe the origin of the community or relate stories concerning its gods.

Second, the re-enactment of these events in the cult is dramatic. The nature of the drama may range from a relatively straightforward portrayal of the sacred deeds (as in many primitive cults) to a highly symbolic actualization (as in the Eastern Orthodox mass). However, the presence of some dramatic form, be it play, symbol, dance, or mime, is an essential element of any cultic re-presentation.[5]

Third, this re-enactment is reality-producing. It does not merely describe these events to the community, but brings them to bear upon

---

[4]Mowinckel, *Psalmen* 2.25, 45; Noth, "Re-presentation," 80-81.

[5]Mowinckel, *Psalmen* 2.25-26.

it in a life-sustaining, reconstituting manner. It provides the power of life which holds back the darkness of chaos, the enmity of foes, the destructiveness of nature. The participant experiences oneness with the god in the ceremony by partaking of the Manna, the divine power. This power forms the basis for the existence of the community.[6]

Fourth, the cultic events must be repeated at regular intervals. The power which they produce is of limited duration. If it is not renewed, then the cosmos breaks down. Therefore, the periodic celebration of the cult is necessary to revive this power and sustain the community.

The fifth and final feature is the most important for our study. Cultic re-enactment involves the identity of two moments in time: the moment in which the sacred event occurred and the moment of celebration. The participants feel that they are experiencing the original sacred event in the festival. There is no sense of "then" and "now," of standing in an historical continuum. While the event (for example, the exodus) may have occurred in time, it did not happen at a "time then" as opposed to a "time now." It is occurring in the celebration, to the celebrant. Because of this lack of an historical continuum, if one speaks of history in relation to cultic actualization, that understanding of history must be severely circumscribed.

The discussion of cultic actualization among the proponents of actualization is somewhat limited. Only Mowinckel describes the phenomenon at length, with Noth, Westermann, and Childs making more limited contributions to our understanding of the phenomenon. Mowinckel makes clear that cultic actualization is based upon independent studies in anthropology and the history of religions.[7] The other scholars are content to draw upon the work of Mowinckel and Pedersen,[8] or to give a non-specific definition of cultic actualization. This demonstrates that cultic actualization is not the primary focus of interest for most of these scholars.

Such a lack of interest can be readily explained by the relationship which they perceive between cultic actualization and the Bible. With the exception of Noth, whom we will discuss in a moment, and Weiser, who is peripheral to a study of actualization, a consensus exists that

---

[6]*Ibid.*, 20-21.

[7]*Ibid.*, 26-35.

[8]cf. Westermann, "Vergegenwärtigung," 253-54, 261-62; Noth, "Re-presentation," 80-82; Childs, *Memory*, 75.

cultic actualization itself does not occur in the Bible. While it is the basis for the actualization one finds in the Old Testament, cultic re-enactment itself merely lies behind the Biblical phenomenon. Even Mowinckel only finds traces in the Bible.[9] The phenomenon of cultic actualization has its true home in the reconstruction of Israel's religion. Only Mowinckel manifests a great concern for the nature of this reconstruction and the role of actualization in the cultic ceremony. The others have a different focus: the nature of actualization in the Old Testament itself. The Biblical writings form the basis for contemporary theological reflection upon the Old Testament, which is the primary concern for the proponents of actualization.

Martin Noth occupies a peculiar position in relation to cultic actualization. He is the one major proponent of actualization who regards cultic re-enactment as the Bible's method of contemporization. In his estimation its presence in the Bible is exegetically demonstrable.[10] However, his use of the same label does not guarantee that what he describes is the same phenomenon. Indeed, some salient differences emerge between Noth's description of cultic actualization and that which we have outlined above, based upon Mowinckel.

First, Noth discusses the actualization of historical events rather than timeless myths. While this distinction is not significant for Mowinckel, it is for Noth because he sees the law of historical exclusivity as being in effect. Consequently, actualization must have some basis other than the cyclic periodicity that prompted the annual re-enactment of the agricultural feasts in the ancient Near East. Noth finds his basis in the immediateness of all history to God. People can grasp this continual present-ness only by actualization in worship.[11] Thus, for Noth the ground of cultic actualization is shifted from the repetition inherent in a cyclical view of time to the interaction of an all-present God with a linear history.

The second difference is a de-emphasis of the dramatic element of the cult. While Noth does not deny its presence in Israelite worship, he

---

[9]There is fairly general agreement on what traces of cultic actualization do exist in the Old Testament: there is unanimous agreement on the rituals related to Passover and the Feast of Booths and on certain passages in Deut; von Rad adds the material associated with his reconstructed covenant renewal festival; Mowinckel concentrates in the psalms and on his reconstructed enthronement festival.

[10]Noth, "Re-presentation," 85-86.

[11]*Ibid.*, 85.

places much more weight upon the narrative element. Israel retold God's saving acts and repeated his demands of obedience as the primary element of the cult. Indeed, this fits with Mowinckel's description of actualization in the Old Testament. However, he did not see this narrative retelling as a true cultic actualization, but merely as a residue of actualization remaining in a religion based upon law.[12]

The most important question to put to Noth's view of actualization is its effect upon the relation of the two moments in time, the original enactment of the event and its re-enactment in the cult. Do the two moments become identical or remain separate in the eyes of the participants? Unfortunately, he does not answer the question directly and conclusively. However, his mention of historical exclusivity, his description of the events passed down as "news reports," and his de-emphasis of the dramatic element lead us to conclude that he is not discussing identity of moments in time in a true cultic sense. Instead, he describes the identification of the believer with the event, the awareness and appreciation of its import and power for the life of the community. However, such identification is not identity, since there is no mention of the dissolving of the time barrier.

We may conclude that Noth's use of actualization, although designated as cultic re-enactment, is in fact substantially different from the generally accepted definition given above. These differences are great enough that we must continue to search for a proper classification for Noth's concept of actualization.

2

At the opposite pole from cultic actualization lies a broadly based phenomenon which we shall call literary actualization. This phenomenon includes such diverse manifestations as Herder's sense of contemporization, Gunkel's ideas on the transmission of oral tradition, and Westermann's understanding of actualization. Despite the apparent differences in these concepts, we shall see that the similar origins, characteristics, and applications warrant their inclusion in the same category.

In essence literary actualization is the manner in which any new age grapples with older materials or traditions. When a new age

---

[12]Mowinckel, *Psalmen* 2.36-38.

recognizes that an historical gap exists between itself and an earlier period, it must attempt to span that gap in order to appropriate the earlier literature, art, or religion for the later time. That attempt at a bridge is literary actualization. One might also speak of a cultural gap, although that is less relevant to our concerns here. When one is faced with a foreign literary work, a translation is necessary if that work is to be made accessible to a wide audience. When interpreting a foreign work of art, knowledge of the principles of that culture's art is necessary for the fullest appreciation and interpretation. In this sense any art of interpretation or translation may be termed actualization. We have chosen to call this phenomenon literary actualization in light of its origins and its particular relationship to Biblical actualization.

The origin of this concept of actualization lies in Herder's aesthetic (primarily literary) theory. He recognized the need to discriminate between historical epochs and refused to judge previous periods (in particular the Greek and Roman periods and Hebrew culture) by his contemporary Germanic standards. One must ascertain the spirit of that particular age and communicate that spirit to the contemporary world as a standard of evaluation and appreciation.[13] This concept of interpretation subsequently became a basic principle in hermeneutics.[14] It appears both as an essential element in Westermann's exegetical theory and in limited application by Mowinckel and von Rad.[15]

An understanding of the nature of literary actualization is important because Westermann and von Rad apply the same terms, *Vergegenwärtigung* and *Aktualisierung,* to both literary and cultic actualization. While the other men we have studied do not clearly use the same terms for two different phenomena, we must be aware of the distinction in order to understand which concept they are employing. We may describe literary actualization in terms of four salient features.

First, literary actualization perceives a difference between two moments in time. Indeed, this consciousness of a distance *(Bewusstsein des Abstandes)* between the original work and the time and place of the interpreter prompts the actualization. Two poles are clearly

---

[13]Herder, *Spirit,* 2.182, 184, 228.

[14]For a brief description of this element in the thought of Hegel, Schleiermacher, and Dilthey, see Frei,*Eclipse,* 287-295.

[15]Westermann, "exegetische Aussage," 3-4; Mowinckel, *Psalmen,* 2.34-35; von Rad, *Theology,* 2.105; *Hexateuch,* 28.

present and the task of the interpreter is to relate them.[16] This is in direct contrast to cultic actualization, in which the distance is dissolved and one experiences identity between the two moments.

This awareness of a distance produces a dialectical movement between the two poles. The interpreters first immerse themselves in the spirit of the other time. They seek to become a part of that time to the greatest extent possible and to understand the original meaning of a text both intellectually and empathetically. Then the exegetes return to their own time and express their deeply felt understanding of the text in a manner that makes it relevant for people of their own time. Thus, they produce a dialectic and participate in both periods.[17]

Second, literary actualization is directly related to the historical situation. In a conscious exegetical endeavor the interpreters are aware that the original text partakes of its historical period and is shaped by it. Likewise, their interpretation must be governed by their own historical and cultural milieu, since it is impossible to be divorced from the language and intellectual trends of the age. However, this relationship to the historical situation remains even in unconscious exegesis. Gunkel applied this concept to the Old Testament by showing that old traditions gradually change and take on the spirit of a new age.[18] The historicization of folk heroes and myths is a further example of this transformation by a later age. This relationship to an historical situation is also antithetical to cultic actualization. The essence of the cult is the dissolution of time and history and the participation in an a-historical *Urzeit*.

Third, literary actualization is applied primarily to written materials. Mowinckel applies *Vergegenwärtigung* to written poetry, reserving *Wiederholung* for reference to cultic re-enactment. Von Rad distinguished actualization as a literary device from the cult-related actualization of Deuteronomy.[19] In his work on the psalms Westermann highlights this characteristic by treating the psalms in their present (i.e., written) form rather than reaching behind them to

---

[16]Westermann, "exegetische Aussage," 3-4.

[17]Herder, *Philosophy*, 181-83; Westermann, "exegetische Aussage," 3-4.

[18]Gunkel, *Legends*, 95, 98-103.

[19]Von Rad, *Theology*, 2.105; *Hexateuch*, 28.

reconstructed institutions.[20]   As Gunkel's application of literary actualization to oral tradition shows, the concept is not limited to written materials. Rather, this is a general boundary which describes its primary application, especially in relation to the Old Testament. Its distinction from cultic actualization in this regard is quite complete. The milieu of written material for the former has little overlap with the milieu of dramatic presentation for the latter. However, the boundaries are less strictly observed between literary and chronological actualization. We shall study the consequences of this overlap presently.

Fourth, literary actualization is not reality-producing as is cultic re-enactment. The effective use of literary actualization should lead both interpreter and participant to feel something of an older time, to experience in part a past age. However, this does not supercede an awareness of the present time. The participant may see the past age as real, but it does not become a reality in the power-producing sense of cultic actualization.[21]

We have seen that there is general agreement among the men whom we have studied that literary actualization, vaguely defined, is a valid category for understanding non-Biblical materials. Herder, Gunkel, Mowinckel, von Rad and Westermann all explicitly acknowledge its use. In addition Gunkel and Westermann see it as an inner-Biblical category of actualization. Westermann, describing it as narrative actualization, sees it as the mode of contemporization in the psalms, to the exclusion of cultic re-enactment.

In addition to these clear examples of the use of literary actualization, one wonders whether or not von Rad also uses it as an inner-Biblical category. We have already noted that his use of actualization in relation to the Qumran community and to wisdom/apocalyptic diverge considerably from chronological actualization.[22]   A possible explanation for these inconsistencies is that von Rad is utilizing a broader concept of actualization more in line with literary actualization in these instances. Unfortunately, he says so

---

[20]Westermann, "Vergegenwärtigung," 254.

[21]Herder, quoted in Frei, *Eclipse,* 193-94; Mowinckel, *Psalmen,* 2.34-35; Westermann, "exegetische Aussage," 3-4; von Rad, "Typological," 17-18.

[22]Von Rad, *Theology,* 2.308; *Theologie,* 2.323-27 (4th ed.); *Wisdom,* 270-76, 282-83.

little about the actualization of these materials that a definite answer is impossible. The types of materials with which he is dealing certainly bear the characteristics of literary actualization: they contain an awareness of an historical distance, and they are written materials. However, whether this is a conscious distinction on the part of von Rad or merely inconsistency is unclear.

In conclusion we may state that few similarities exist between cultic and literary actualization. We have seen that they differ in all of their salient features. In addition they apply to a totally different milieu and have different origins. In effect they are two quite different phenomena to which the same general term has frequently been applied.

3

Cultic re-enactment, based upon evidence from ancient Near Eastern and contemporary primitive religions, and literary actualization, founded in aesthetic theory and applicable to any body of literature, are concepts which stand apart from the Bible, both in their origin and in their primary usage. While both may be applied to the Bible, most proponents of Biblical actualization view these categories as insufficient to cope with the unique nature of scripture. Consequently, they have developed a new category to describe the dynamics of inner-Biblical actualization. Unfortunately, no consensus ever emerged on a rubric for this distinct category, leading to the confusion which has surrounded its application. In order to distinguish the biblical phenomenon clearly from cultic and literary actualization, we will refer to it as chronological actualization. This designation appears only once, in von Rad's *Old Testament Theology*,[23] but it accurately encapsulates the category utilized by von Rad, Noth, Wolff, Porteous, Childs, and many other scholars who follow in their footsteps. The element which unites all of their conceptions is Israel's concern for history in dealing with its traditions. This sense of history is the seminal element which sets Israel's use of actualization apart from the cultic actualization of its neighbors and the modern understanding of aesthetic contemporization.

At this point we will merely outline the salient features of chronological actualization which we have garnered from the historical studies of the first two chapters. This will enable us to contrast this concept with the alternative categories of cultic and literary

---

[23]Von Rad, *Theology*, 2.108.

actualization. We will reserve our critique of this category for the remainder of this chapter.

The first essential characteristic is its relation to the two moments in time, the time of the original event and the present time. Cultic and literary actualization take opposite viewpoints on this: the former visualizes an identity of the two moments, the latter a consciousness of the distance between the two moments. While it would seem to be impossible to take a position between these two, that is precisely what chronological actualization seeks to do. Childs states this most succinctly:

> ... we are suggesting that neither the mythical nor the historical analysis of the process of actualization are adequate to describe the Biblical category. This appears to be a concept which shares features of both yet exhibits a unique character of its own.[24]

Although Israel had a true sense of history which gave its saving events a once-for-all, irreversible character, its actualization of the tradition enabled it to experience "an immediate encounter, an actual participation in the great acts of redemption" through the medium of redemptive time.[25] Thus, Israel was able to experience identity of the two moments in time, yet maintain the historicality of its revelation.

Von Rad's stance on the element of identity is more ambiguous than Childs'. While he can state that the idea of contemporaneity – in the strict cultic sense of the word – is not a part of chronological actualization, and that the generation of Deuteronomy "is well aware of the distance which separates it from the one with which the Sinai covenant was originally made,"[26] he can also maintain that Israel "truly entered into the historic situation to which the festival in question was related,"[27] and that the rule of historical exclusivity was suspended in

---

[24]Childs, *Memory*, 83. His distinction between mythic and historical is based upon the characteristic we are discussing here: the presence or lack of identity between the two moments in time.

[25]*Ibid.*,84.

[26]Von Rad, *Theology*, 2.109.

[27]*Ibid.*, 104; also see von Rad, *Hexateuch*, 28-29.

Old Testament actualization.[28] Actualization which is a "living force," extending far beyond a mere rhetorical device, is a characteristic of Old Testament material that is both late and not cult-related.[29] Von Rad's ambivalence and ambiguity undoubtedly stem from his desire to differentiate chronological actualization from cultic re-enactment, but simultaneously to retain a sense of identity of the two moments in time that is far deeper than that of literary contemporization. As a result, we may affirm that a strong sense of identity, although one that falls short of the full contemporaneity experienced in the cult, is a central element for von Rad's understanding of chronological actualization.

Noth's understanding of contemporization is also difficult to pin down. He refers to his understanding as cultic actualization, yet insists upon invoking the uniqueness of historical events, which is characteristic of literary actualization. This ambiguity may best be explained in the same way as the statements of Childs and von Rad cited above: it is an attempt to create a unique Biblical category which partakes of both cultic and literary actualization. This is confirmed by his understanding of re-presentation as the human attempt to grasp the eternal present-ness of God and by his discussion of Deuteronomy where "the later generations of Israel ... were expected to listen to the law just as if they themselves – and not their ancestors – were standing at Mount Horeb."[30]

A second characteristic of chronological actualization is its relationship to the historical situation. This relationship is much closer to literary than to cultic actualization. While cultic re-enactment dissolves history into timelessness, literary actualization grows out of its own historical milieu. Chronological actualization agrees with the latter in this regard; it does not merely repeat the old traditions but changes and adapts them according to the spirit of the new age. However, chronological actualization goes a step beyond this. It does not merely grow out of a particular historical situation, but the actualization is so formulated that it speaks to that historical situation. Each contemporization carries a message to its own particular historical hour.[31] This is generally associated with the idea that Biblical

---

[28]Von Rad, *Theology*, 1.110.

[29]Von Rad, *Theology*, 2.46-47, 167, 299.

[30]Noth, "Re-presentation," 82; also see p. 85.

[31] von Rad, *Theology*, 2.129-30, 175, 267-68, 299.

passages or documents arise in response to a crisis and thus respond specifically to that crisis situation.[32] This characteristic is associated with the whole complex of ideas involved in a kerygmatic theology.[33] Theological interpretation, of course, is the primary focus of chronological actualization. This theological interest, and especially the kerygmatic focus of the theology, is absent from the alternative categories of actualization, rendering them inadequate for Old Testament hermeneutics.

A third characteristic which grows out of this relationship to the historical situation is the limited validity of chronological actualization. Since it responds to a crisis in a particular way, with particular words, that response is valid only for that time. The words do not *remain* valid for succeeding ages, but *become* valid when a later generation adapts them for their specific needs. This concept of limited validity also applies to cultic and literary actualization, but for different reasons. In cultic re-enactment the actualization loses its sustaining power and, consequently, must be repeated to renew that power. In literary actualization interpretations must change because time, customs, and the cultural milieu alter. This is quite similar to chronological actualization, differing primarily in the sense of urgency in the latter, precipitated by the crisis atmosphere.

Fourth, chronological actualization is primarily applied to oral traditions rather than to written documents. However, this is at least a semi-permeable boundary. Von Rad has no hesitation in equating New Testament actualization with that encountered in the prophets, even though the New Testament handles the Old in written form. This equation is a characteristic which von Rad regards as significant, since it more easily accounts for the adaptation of traditions by the New Testament and makes their vividness more understandable. He repeatedly contrasts this characteristic with the "mere rhetorical device" of literary actualization.[34] Literary actualization, likewise, moves across this boundary, as evidenced by Gunkel's application of it to oral

---

[32]Childs, *Memory*, 76-80; von Rad, *Theology*, 2.109, 129-30; *Genesis*, 28-29; "The Beginnings of Historical Writing in Ancient Israel," in *Essays*, 170, 203-04; Brueggemann and Wolff, *Vitality*, 32-34, 80-82, 84, 99-100.

[33]Von Rad, *Theology*, 1.108-09, 115-16, 125-28; *Theology*, 2.411-16; "Typological," 27-29, 32, 36-39; Noth, "Re-presentation," 84-86; Brueggemann and Wolff, *Vitality*, 29-39, 42, 45-46, 66, 84, 99-100.

[34]Von Rad, *Hexateuch*, 28; *Theology*, 2.104, 299.

tradition. Given the fluidity of the situation, one question to be raised in the subsequent analysis is the validity of this distinction between the two types of actualization.

This delineation of the categories of actualization sets the definitions and characteristics necessary for an evaluation of the concept as applied to the Bible. While the scholars we have studied admit the validity of cultic and literary actualization, the consensus is that both categories are inadequate to describe Biblical actualization, the former because it lacks a true sense of history, the latter because it is applicable to any work of literature and consequently fails to account for the unique response of people to the message of scripture. The response to this problem is the creation of chronological actualization, a concept which incorporates the best aspects of both cultic and literary contemporization and emphasizes the uniqueness of the Bible. In the remainder of the chapter we shall see how this concept is applied to the Old Testament and whether or not such an amalgam of characteristics is a tenable mixture.

Chronological Actualization as a Unique Concept

While von Rad developed the concept of chronological actualization specifically to describe the Old Testament's method of contemporizing old traditions, neither he nor the other scholars utilizing the concept operated in a vacuum. An important aspect of their work was to set Biblical actualization apart both from the Near Eastern environment that preceded and surrounded it and from the subsequent exegesis of the church (both the pre-critical and historical-critical phases). This task revolved around three issues: 1) the connection between cultic re-enactment in the ancient Near East and chronological actualization, both in comparison and contrast; 2) Israel's unique sense of history which set it apart from its environment; 3) Israel's unique sense of time which focuses upon the distinction between redemptive time and our modern concepts.

1

A central element in establishing the uniqueness of chronological actualization lies in its relationship to the cultic re-enactment of the ancient Near East. The connection was not merely one of contrast, but of development from cultic to chronological contemporization. Von

Rad, along with Mowinckel and most other Biblical scholars, made the assumption that cultic re-enactment was the form of contemporization generally present in the ancient Near East. Demonstrating a link between cultic and Biblical actualization permits both the establishing of a link between the Old Testament and its environment and the retention of elements of cultic actualization in Biblical contemporization. Development from the former to the latter allows for both comparison and contrast. The most important factor in this relationship is the element of identity. This vivid reimagining of and participation in the sacred events of a people is a presumed characteristic of the latter. Development allows for the presence of identity in chronological actualization, even though it is a distinct category from cultic. Identity, in turn, provides the Old Testament with its distinctiveness from mere literary actualization. Consequently, the development from cultic to chronological actualization helps establish the uniqueness of the Biblical concept from both its environment and mere literary theory. Proving this relationship became an important endeavor for the proponents of actualization, with von Rad and Noth presenting the most complete arguments on the subject.[35]

Von Rad's argument is posited on historical/theological grounds. As the traditions of the Old Testament are gradually liberated from the sphere of the cult and a true historical sense comes into being, a shift in the nature of actualization occurs. No longer is it dominated by the cyclical sense of repetition and regeneration, the need for the periodic re-establishment of the basis of creation. Now a linear sense of history is developing from the sequentializing of God's saving deeds.[36] Central to this new understanding of history is the creative word of God, which presses forward into the future, reinterpreting old saving promises for a new age.[37] Chronological actualization is tied to both of these elements: the linear sense of history and the creative word of God. Consequently, in von Rad's view chronological actualization developed out of cultic, and the basis for the sense of contemporaneity is the word

---

[35] Wolff, Ackroyd, and Porteous all affirm the connection implicitly or explicitly. Only Westermann dissents and defines Biblical actualization in a manner which rules out such a connection. Childs, while affirming the connection, offers some of the strongest arguments against it.

[36] Von Rad, *Theology*, 2.107-10.

[37] *Ibid.*, 95.

of God which presses into the future, rather than a cyclical sense of repetition.

However, in his specific discussions of the development of Biblical contemporaneity, von Rad leaves some unexplained ambiguities. These center on the book of Deuteronomy, either upon its connection to cultic actualization or upon its relationship to the rest of the Biblical material. In *The Form-Critical Problem of the Hexateuch* von Rad discusses the contemporization present in Deuteronomy and ties it closely to cultic re-enactment, claiming the same sense of immediacy for both phenomena.[38] This description is repeated and developed in each volume of *Old Testament Theology*.[39] In this later formulation Deuteronomy is depicted as reflecting a crisis in actualization with a resulting rationalization and spiritualization. The book becomes von Rad's primary example of the link between the cultic actualization of the Near East and Biblical actualization. Deuteronomy can function as a link because it consists of material which originated in the cult and retains a vital sense of immediacy, but now also reflects a concept of linear history.

Von Rad leaves unanswered some very important questions concerning Deuteronomy's relationship to the development of actualization. First, the type of actualization which occurs in Deuteronomy is unclear. Is it the chronological actualization which we find in the rest of the Old Testament or an intermediate form between that and cultic re-enactment? The extent of the change precipitated by the Deuteronomic crisis is unclear: the sense of contemporaneity present in cultic actualization was shattered in the shift to chronological, yet Deuteronomy still retains the power to make events contemporaneous.[40] Von Rad never explains how materials can pass through such a crisis and retain a high degree of vitality.

Second, he fails to deal adequately with the shift from oral re-enactment in the cult to the written form of Deuteronomy. The proven setting for a sense of identity and participatory immediacy is the oral-dramatic performance in a religious ceremony. The form of Deuteronomy is far removed from this milieu: it is not even the direct preaching activity of material once associated with the cult, but the

---

[38]*Ibid.*, 28-29.

[39]See particularly von Rad, *Theology*, 2.102-12.

[40]*Ibid.*, 108-109.

collected and reworked residue of such activity presented in written form. While we will discuss more fully the implications of this shift at a later time, we can see that the distance between the cult and Deuteronomy is so great that one cannot assume that the same type of actualization occurred in both.

Third, von Rad leaves unanswered questions about the connection of Deuteronomy to contemporization in the rest of the Old Testament. An integral part of chronological actualization in the Deuteronomistic history and the prophets is the creative word of God, which provides both the basis and the impetus for that revitalizing of the tradition. However, the creative word of God is never applied to actualization in Deuteronomy. All the discussions of actualization in Deuteronomy are tied to its development from cultic re-enactment and its distinctiveness from literary contemporization. Actualization in the Deuteronomistic history and the prophets is closely linked to the creative word of God and the consequent sense of history as promise and fulfillment.[41] As a result, the connection between cultic contemporization and von Rad's fullest expression of chronological actualization in the Deuteronomistic history and the prophets is not one of historical development. Instead, he relies upon analogy to establish a relationship: he describes the two types of actualization, notes the similarities in structure and function, and concludes that chronological actualization arose from cultic re-enactment and preserves its sense of identity of two moments in time. While one should not dismiss such an analogical relationship out of hand, it does not provide the solid evidential base for such a connection

---

[41] Von Rad's concept of the creative word of God appears originally as a separate category from actualization. When it first appears in "The Deuteronomic Theology of History in I and II Kings" (in *Essays*, 205-21) in 1947, it is not linked to actualization. The concept appears in essentially the same form in the first edition of *Theologie* 1 in 1957. There it is clearly separated from the discussion of actualization: the latter is linked closely with the poetic materials derived from the cult, encountered primarily in the Hexateuch (*Theology*, 1.106-15; *Theologie*, 1.112-20 1st ed.), while the creative word of God is connected with the historiographic materials (*Theology*, 1.334-46). Only with *Theology* 2 (1960) and *Theologie* 1 (4th ed.), (1962), are the creative word of God and actualization unmistakably connected. In the former the connection is not given in relation to the history of actualization, but as a statement that the prophetic word incorporates both (*Theology* 2.80-98). In the latter von Rad connects the two concepts through an addendum to this previous discussion of actualization: *Theology* 1.112; compare *Theologie*, 1.118 (1st ed.), with *Theologie*, 1.125 (4th ed.). Consequently von Rad's linking of actualization and the creative word of God is another example, along with typology, of his efforts to unite all of his previously developed interpretive categories under the rubric of actualization.

as von Rad would wish from a consistent application of the traditio-historical method.

Therefore, we may conclude that von Rad's evidence for a connection between cultic re-enactment and chronological actualization is open to question. While he has demonstrated the possibility of a relationship between actualization in Deuteronomy and the near Eastern religious milieu, the exact nature of that connection remains ambiguous. Although von Rad's analogical argument is sufficient to posit some type of actualization in the Deuteronomistic history and the prophets, more evidence is needed for a direct connection between these traditions and cultic re-enactment to claim the presence of the element of identity in chronological actualization.

Noth's discussion of the relation of cultic and Biblical actualization in "The Re-presentation of the Old Testament in Proclamation," although differing in particulars from von Rad's, has the same general strengths and weaknesses. By concentrating upon the historical reconstructions of Israelite festivals rather than the Biblical literature itself, he is able to demonstrate a general relationship between cultic re-enactment and actualization in Israel. This part of his argument is more persuasive than von Rad's, since von Rad endeavors to unveil actualization in the literature itself, not merely in Israel's religious ceremonies. However, Noth's attempt to explain the uniqueness of Biblical actualization is less successful. He proposes explicitly theological categories drawn from Barthian neo-orthodoxy as the mechanism in Old Testament actualization which replaces the cyclical periodicity of cultic re-enactment. For Noth actualization is precipitated by the need of the community to apprehend the immediateness of God while enmeshed in the mediateness of an historical existence.[42] This importation of a modern theological category violates one of Noth's own exegetical criteria: that the nature of the exegesis must grow out of the subject matter.[43] Certainly the imposition of such a category provides an inadequate link between cultic and Biblical actualization. Consequently, Noth presents a persuasive case for a connection between the Near Eastern milieu and the presence of actualization in Israel's religious festivals, but he fails to demonstrate convincingly that such

---

[42]Noth quotes Barth in deriving these categories: "Re-presentation," 85, 87.

[43]*Ibid.*, 80.

central elements as identity were retained in the transition of Israel's oral traditions to written, literary material separated from the cultic milieu.

Serious criticism of the relation of cultic to chronological actualization arises from two proponents of the concept. Childs, through his word study of זכר casts serious doubt upon the presence of such a relationship. After conducting a form-critical investigation of the passages in which זכר occurs, he concludes that none of them exhibits evidence of a cultic *Sitz im Leben,* even in those passages which include the actualization of old traditions.[44] If there were a connection between cultic and chronological actualization, we would expect to find at least traces of a cultic milieu in the actualized material. Childs, conducting the type of detailed study which could provide a sound basis for such a connection, is able to find none.

Westermann raises a further challenge to this relationship. He explicitly refutes the presence of cultic actualization in the psalms, a portion of the Old Testament closely related to the cult.[45] He goes a step further by denying that chronological actualization is present. His concept of narrative actualization, with its denial of the element of identity, is associated, rather, with literary contemporization. Westermann's criticism cuts deep, for it, like Childs', is based upon a close study of texts instead of general schemes of development. His challenge does not merely deny the connection between the two types of actualization, but questions the uniqueness of Old Testament contemporization by linking its characteristics to a more general literary type.

In summary, we have found that the central point of concern in relating cultic and chronological actualization – the presence of identity in both – is an unproven assumption. Von Rad presents the most impressive case, which in the final analysis rests upon an analogical connection between the two types of actualization. In light of the unresolved ambiguities in his analysis and the strong reservations of Childs and Westermann based upon detailed textual studies, the connection which von Rad proposes is insufficient evidence upon which to posit the presence of identity in Biblical actualization. What von Rad and Noth are able to demonstrate is that a general relationship exists between cultic re-enactment in the ancient Near East and

---

[44]Childs, *Memory,* 74-76.

[45]Westermann, "Vergegenwärtigung," 260-262.

actualization in Israel's religious festivals. Whether or not the actualization experienced in these reconstructed festivals, even in altered form, survived the separation of the traditions from the cult and their subsequent committal to writing is a question to be pursued in the course of this analysis.

2

The second element in establishing the uniqueness of chronological actualization is Israel's concept of history. In the case of the connection between cultic and chronological actualization, von Rad and Noth sought to establish a developmental relationship. With Israel's concept of history, however, they postulated a negative connection to the cultural milieu: although this sense of history originated in the historicization of Israel's cult, it became a unique bearer of Yahweh's revelation, distinct from any Near Eastern counterparts. The central elements in this concept of history were that God was depicted as active in historical events, that the creative word of God was the force which impelled this history into the future, and that history was a succession of promises and fulfillments ever open to the future. The two latter elements link Israel's sense of history inextricably to chronological actualization. The uniqueness of these two interrelated concepts sets Israel apart from its cultural milieu, which is dominated by a cyclical view of history based upon gods operating in the realm of nature.

However, Harmut Gese and Bertil Albrektson have cast serious doubt both upon the uniqueness of Israel's use of history and upon its development from an historicized cult. Through a thorough study of Mesopotamian and Hittite historiography they have undercut the idea of a cyclical sense of history in the ancient Near East,[46] and discovered several elements by which Israelite and Near Eastern history writing are related, such as the action of the gods to influence the course of history,[47] purposiveness in divine events,[48] history as the milieu of

---

[46]Harmut Gese, "The Idea of History in the Ancient Near East and the Old Testament," *JTC* 1 (1965) 55; Bertil Albrektson, *History and the Gods* (Lund: C.W.K. Gleerup, 1967) 94-95. Also see Spriggs,*Theologies,* 44-49.

[47]Albrektson, *History,* 24-41.

[48]*Ibid.,* 68-97.

revelation,[49] history as a series of acts and their consequences,[50] and the divine word active in history.[51]

The final factor is the most significant in relation to chronological actualization. One of the unique elements in the concept is the presence of the divine word in history, which, since it never becomes void, leads ever into the future. However, Albrektson has demonstrated that this understanding of the divine word is also present in Mesopotamian historiography. The establishing of boundaries, victories in battle, the king s prosperous reign, the punishment of guilty officials are all attributed to the power of a god's word. While some examples reflect the formal inquiry for a god's will (word) through an oracle, other examples clearly demonstrate the active, unexpected intrusion of a god's word upon history.[52] There is even one example of the combination of divine prediction and subsequent fulfillment which is reminiscent of the Deuteronomist's pattern of promise and fulfillment.[53] While one example does not serve to equate prediction and fulfillment in Mesopotamia with the highly complex pattern developed in Israel, it does illustrate the similarities between the ideas of history in Israel and Mesopotamia. The difference in the two conceptions is one of degree, not kind. The role of the divine word, the concept of prophecy and fulfillment, and the other elements present in Israel's history writing are also visible in Mesopotamian historiography. Israel has applied them to a monotheistic religion, developed them into different constellations, and produced historical works of a superior literary quality. Israel's sense of history is distinctive, but not unique.

Perhaps the most important aspect of this similarity in historical sense between Israel and the Near Eastern milieu is the light which it sheds upon the connection between chronological actualization and the cult. Von Rad, Noth, and Childs all posit a development of chronological actualization out of the historicized cult, spurred by the emerging sense of history. This development is held in opposition to the cult-bound cyclical history of Mesopotamia. Both Albrektson and

---

[49]*Ibid.*, 98-114.

[50]*Ibid.*, 61-64; Gese, "History," 54, 56-58.

[51] Albrektson, *History*, 53-67.

[52]*Ibid.*, 55-61.

[53]*Ibid.*, 64.

Gese question this idea of development, since the elements which coalesced into Israel's historical sense were already present in the general cultural setting and cyclical history was not present in the ancient Near East. Instead, they consider Israel to be a people who made a late appearance in the history of the Near East. Consequently, the Semitic world of which Israel was a part had already developed several complementary and conflicting views of history. These views were presupposed as part of Israel's general cultural heritage.[54]

While cultic life was the source of some elements of Mesopotamian historiography (the development of the historical inscription from the dedicatory inscription, for example),[55] other areas of culture, such as omen science and didactic literature also played significant roles.[56] The Near East has developed other modes of history writing as well, including autobiography and history-as-consequence.[57] The uniqueness of Israel's concept of history has been upheld only because of a faulty comparison between the Old Testament and ancient Near Eastern documents. The comparison has been limited to Near Eastern cultic documents; if the Old Testament had been related to the full range of Near Eastern historiography, then the points of similarity would have emerged.[58]

How, then, can we account for the historical element in Israelite cult-related texts, an element which is of minor importance or missing altogether in most other Near Eastern cultic material? Both Albrektson and Gese recognize this element as distinctive in Israel, although the distinctiveness is a matter of relative importance, not a difference in concept.[59] While a developmental scheme such as that devised by von Rad, Noth, and Childs is a possibility, the presence of established history writing prior to the origin of Israel's cult lessens that possibility. A reverse influence is as likely an alternative. Yahweh's saving act at the exodus was recognized from the beginning as occurring in history, as opposed to being a primeval event. This occurrence,

---

[54]*Ibid.*, 67; Gese, "History," 61.

[55]Gese, "History," 51-52.

[56]*Ibid.*, 53-56, 58.

[57]*Ibid.*, 56-57, 59-60.

[58]Albrektson, *History*, 66, 116.

[59]*Ibid.*, 115-17; Gese, "History," 61-64.

regarded as historical, was incorporated into the cult because it became constitutive for Israel's religious life. The assumption of the exodus tradition into the cult resulted in a (partial) dehistoricizing of the event in the cultic context.[60] However, this dehistoricization did not necessarily affect the understanding of the exodus event in the historiographic tradition: the recognition of its historicity preceded its cultic use. Consequently, cultic actualization remains in its own realm, the festival worship services, and Biblical historiography retains its separate identity with a minimum influence from the cult.

Such a theory is difficult, if not impossible, to prove. We can merely demonstrate that the available evidence may be interpreted in a manner contrary to that used to establish a unique sense of history in Israel. This theory of separate developments of cultic actualization and Biblical historiography unveils a Near Eastern background for both and accounts for evidence neglected by the supposition that the latter developed from the former.

In summary, we have demonstrated that both the uniqueness of the Biblical concept of history and the development of Israel's historiography from the cult are questionable assumptions. Consequently, the concept of chronological actualization, which is related to both these assumptions is further undermined. If the creative word of God, central to both chronological actualization and Israelite historiography is an active element in history writing throughout the ancient Near East, then it no longer contributes to the uniqueness of chronological actualization. Our further questioning of the developmental connection between cultic and chronological actualization renders it even less likely that identity plays a role in the latter.

3

The third element utilized by von Rad to establish the distinctiveness of the Old Testament is Israel's unique view of time. Although this view is integrally related to its concept of history, von Rad employs it to highlight a different area of Israel's distinctiveness: whereas its concept of history sets it apart from the Near Eastern environment, the understanding of time distinguishes it from our modern temporal experience. While this is not an absolute distinction

---

[60]Albrektson, *History*, 116-17.

in von Rad's exposition, since the two elements function together to create a time-history scheme that is utterly unique, it does accurately represent the dual thrust of his overall argument.

The centerpiece of Israel's sense of time is its inability to "think of time in the abstract, time divorced from specific events."[61] Hebrew has no word for time as such, but can only specify a period of time with the word עֵת. Each period of time is designated by its specific content (war, peace, day, night, etc.). The organizing factor for Israel's sense of time is the cultic festival:

> The rhythm of festal and non-festal times gave their own lives their rhythm in time. Indeed, one might even go a stage further and describe the time of cultic festival as the one and only "time" in the full sense of the word, for it alone was time furnished with content in the truest sense of the term.[62]

Even when Israel historicized its cult, its sense of time remained basically the same. Its linear sense of history did not resemble our own, since it consisted of a set of saving "times" placed in sequence. Even in this sequentiality each event retained its discrete nature as a period of God's saving activity.[63]

This concept of time is closely tied to chronological actualization. Since the periods of time incorporated into an historical sequence were all God's saving events, they retained at least some of the redemptive, contemporary quality of the cult from which they originated. For example, through the evocative use of "today," "we," and other special words in Deuteronomy, the Sinai covenant is vivified and the people enter into the quality of redemptive time.[64]

This concept of time, and especially von Rad's formulation of it, is influenced by the idea of a "Hebrew mentality," which enjoyed great

---

[61]Von Rad, *Theology*, 2.100.

[62]*Ibid.*, 102.

[63]Von Rad's terminology relating time and history is highly ambiguous. While he is willing to refer to a linear concept of history (*Theology*, 2.106, 108), he denies the possibility of a linear concept of time (p. 100). That he regards the absence of linear time as a characteristic of the entirety of the Old Testament is clear from his supporting examples of the Deuteronomistic history and Ecclesiastes (pp. 99-101).

[64]Childs expresses this special quality of redemptive time most clearly: *Memory*, 83-85. Also see von Rad, *Theology*, 2.108-09; Noth, "Re-presentation," 82-83.

currency in the late 1940's and the early 1950's. Central to this mentality, which is particularly contrasted to Greek (hence, modern Western) thought, is a unique sense of time. The most thorough exposition of the nature of Hebrew time appears in John Marsh's *The Fulness of Time* (1952). He takes great pains to distinguish between chronological time *(chronos)*, which is characteristic of Greek and modern thought, and realistic time *(kairos)*, which is characteristic of both the Old and New Testaments. As with von Rad, *kairos* is distinguished as a "time being filled with its own specific content by God, and so demanding a response."[65] Realistic time is further characterized by the governing force of the creative word of God, which, having entered time, has a "quasi-objective, independent and dynamic existence of its own until it reaches fulfillment."[66] Since the special periods of God's grace are always present with the people of Israel in realistic time, no chronological time barrier exists for them and events such as the exodus are readily actualized throughout Israel's history. Contemporaneity is a natural consequence of this special understanding of time.[67]

James Barr has thoroughly undermined this concept of a separate Hebrew mentality. His criticisms reach far beyond the construct of a unique sense of time and center upon the direct psychologizing and theologizing upon lexical data which is characteristic of Johannes Pedersen, Thorlief Boman, James Marsh, and Kittel's word-book.[68] In his specific criticism of a unique Hebrew sense of time, Barr demonstrates that the opposition between *kairos* and *chronos* established by Marsh is false. In fact, chronological time played a major role for Israel; the distinctions drawn between the two words may be accounted for by syntactical differences, not a unique time sense.[69]

While von Rad and Childs avoided the blatant excesses of the "Hebrew mentality," such as arguing directly from lexical stock and establishing an entirely different thought world, the connections between the two time constructs are evident. Von Rad stresses the

---

[65]John Marsh, *The Fulness of Time* (London: Nisbet, 1952), 22.

[66]*Ibid.*, 23, 67, 87.

[67]*Ibid.*, 64; Thorlief Boman, *Hebrew Thought Compared with Greek* (London: SCM, 1960) 147-49.

[68]Barr, *Semantics.*

[69]Barr, *Time,* 21-49. For his brief criticism of von Rad, see p. 32.

absence of chronological time in Israel and the force of the creative word of God, while Childs describes a special quality for redemptive time which admits the experience of contemporaneity.[70] Their separate Hebrew time sense, constructed in relation to actualization, is open to many of the same criticisms as that of Marsh and Boman. Barr has established that neither lexical nor syntactical evidence points to a separate time sense in either the Old or New Testaments and that the Hebrews did utilize chronological time. While we will not go into detail here, our study of Deut 5:1-3 in the next chapter will demonstrate that the use of "today" and "we" in Deuteronomy, which von Rad uses as textual evidence for chronological actualization, is an example of different rhetorical levels of language, not a unique time concept. Finally, we have already demonstrated that Childs' conclusions on the nature of redemptive time in actualization run counter to the evidence which he presents in his word study.

As a result, we must conclude that the Biblical evidence for a unique Hebrew concept of time is exceedingly weak. While one may speak of a sense of redemptive time or the experience of contemporaneity as a general theological or religious concept (as Kierkegaard does, for example),[71] such references do not establish it as a unique Biblical category; indeed, they argue against the specifically Biblical notion. Therefore, the Biblical sense of time does not help establish the uniqueness of chronological actualization. It does not set the Old Testament apart from either its cultural milieu or from contemporary thought in a manner that is theologically relevant.

4

We have examined the major elements in the attempt to define chronological actualization as the Bible's unique perception of God's saving activity. The proponents of this concept sought to set the Old and New Testaments apart from both the Near Eastern cultural milieu and modern thought patterns by establishing the presence of the element of identity and unique patterns of history and time as central to Biblical actualization. However, both external criticism and logical

---

[70]Childs takes Barr's criticisms in *Semantics* quite seriously, as Barr notes in *Time*, 178.

[71]Boman refers to Kierkegaard as a proponent of contemporaneity in modern Christianity in *Hebrew Thought*, 148.

inconsistencies have cast doubt upon the presence of any of these elements in the Bible. Consequently, we must conclude that the uniqueness of chronological actualization remains an unproven assumption.

The Traditio-Historical Unity of the Bible

A central issue in all Old Testament theologies is the relation of the two testaments. Since these theologies have been written from a Christian perspective, such a connection is necessary to link the Old Testament into Christian theology and exegesis. Most criticisms of von Rad have this relationship as a central concern.[72] However, the issue really should be reworded when applied to actualization. Since the Old Testament has no center and therefore no conceptual unity, one cannot readily bring the Old and New Testaments into a conceptual relationship. For actualization the unity of the Old Testament is methodological, based on repeated re-use of traditional materials. Its connection to the New Testament must be viewed in relation to this pattern and discussed in the larger context of the total traditio-historical unity of the scriptures.

The proponents of actualization conceive of the unity of scripture as based upon a continuing series of witnesses, beginning with the earliest traditions of Israel, extending through God's revelation of Jesus Christ, and reaching to the present day. Only von Rad delineates a comprehensive chain of witnesses. Most of the other men we have studied concentrate on one part of the chain or on one connecting link. In the final analysis none of them contradicts von Rad,[73] whose traditio-historical train may be summarized thusly:

| primitive | ⇒ | J,E,D | ⇒ | DtrH | ⇒ | New | ⇒ | contemporary |
| cult | | | | prophets | | Testament | | preaching |

---

[72]See, for example, Honecker, "Verständinis," 155-58; Eichrodt, "Problem," 513-20; Barr, *Old and New;* Knight, *Rediscovering,* 136-40; Hasel, *Theology,* 105-28.

[73]We have used the work of Childs and Westermann to contest von Rad on certain points. However, both men ultimately agree with him. Westermann denies the presence of cultic and chronological actualization in the psalms. However, he does not link this study to von Rad's chain of witnesses. His works which explore the links in the chain generally agree with von Rad. See Westermann, *Jesus Christ; Controversial;* "Way of Promise."

1

Since we have already examined the connection between cultic actualization and the chronological actualization of Deuteronomy, we do not need to repeat that material here. We found the arguments for a substantive connection between the two to be unconvincing. While there must be a traditio-historical connection between Israel's cultic life and the written documents of J, E, and D, the developmental relationship described by von Rad is only one possibility – and one which is based on questionable assumptions at that.

We focused our earlier discussion mainly on Deuteronomy, since von Rad uses it most directly in his discussions of the relationship between cultic and chronological actualization. However, he includes the J and E materials in these discussions as a sidelight and regards them as exhibiting the same general characteristics as Deuteronomy: they are originally cultic materials which have been cut off from their function in the festivals, secularized, and repeatedly re-used to bear Israel's traditions of promise into the future.[74] Consequently, they exhibit the same type of actualization as Deuteronomy, which is either chronological actualization or a form intermediate between that and cultic re-enactment. Von Rad regards this complex of traditions as that most closely related to the cult in the Old testament and, therefore, retaining some characteristics of primitive cultic re-enactment.

2

The second link in the traditio-historical chain is between J, E, and D on the one hand and the Deuteronomistic history and the prophets on the other. Since von Rad concentrates upon the connection between Deuteronomy and the Deuteronomistic history, we will discuss this aspect first. That the two sets of material are related is indisputable; the question is whether or not chronological actualization adequately describes that relationship.

Deuteronomy and the Deuteronomistic history together provide von Rad with the key elements for describing chronological actualization. While Deuteronomy is his central example for the vivid reimagining of tradition through the identity of two moments in time, the Deuteronomistic history provides the clearest exposition of the role of

---

[74]Von Rad, *Hexateuch,* 50-73; *Genesis,* 27-42; *Theology,* 1.38-39, 124-25; *Theology,* 2.99-112.

the creative word of God and promise and fulfillment. Von Rad interprets this relationship developmentally: Deuteronomy depicts a crisis in actualization in which cultic material is rationalized and spiritualized; this new spirit then blossoms into chronological actualization in the Deuteronomistic history.

However, this relationship is more implicit than explicit, deducible from the descriptions of actualization given for the two sets of material. Von Rad's explicit descriptions of the connection between Deuteronomy and the Deuteronomistic history view Deuteronomy as a "status confessionis," and as "almost already canonical."[75] Deuteronomy sets the standards by which the historian makes historical judgments, with the reign of each king being rigidly evaluated by these criteria. Von Rad also depicts the historian as working with source documents in scholarly fashion.[76] Such a relationship is not the vivid reimagining described for J, E, and D. The studied, rigid evaluation of each king and each prophecy is counter to the charismatic eclecticism proposed for chronological actualization. Instead, the Deuteronomistic history and many of von Rad's terms for its relationship to Deuteronomy depict a carefully constructed, written document replete with patterns of almost scribal exactitude. While the history may well have grown out of the need of a particular generation, its authors give no indication that they regard either Deuteronomy or their history to be of passing relevance. Instead, Deuteronomy appears as a standard good for all time and their own work as a lasting evaluation of Israel's history.

Given the disparate nature of the materials in Deuteronomy and the Deuteronomistic history, a connection through the medium of chronological actualization would be surprising. Deuteronomy is the residue of preaching activity. It has retained a degree of rhetorical vitality that allows von Rad to argue for the vivid reimagining of chronological actualization. However, the Deuteronomist applied many of the standards of Deuteronomy to quite different material: the history of the kingship. Such material entails a change in approach. The author is now dealing with source documents and sequential events. He chooses to apply Deuteronomy's standards through intricately wrought patterns of promise and fulfillment, apostasy and judgment. This type

---

[75]Von Rad, *Theology*, 1.336, 341.

[76]*Ibid.*, 335.

of re-use of traditional material is quite different from chronological actualization.

The nature of the Deuteronomistic history also raises questions about the connection between it and the prophets. Von Rad links them through their similar attitudes towards the creative word of God and promise and fulfillment.[77] While the basic concepts may be similar, their application diverges significantly. The scheme of promise and fulfillment in the Deuteronomistic history is a prime example of the authors' studied style. Each prophecy is given a corresponding fulfillment at some point in the course of the history. Even if the nature of the fulfillment does not quite meet the original terms of the prophecy, the traditional material is twisted enough to produce a reasonable correspondence.[78] In the prophets we encounter a different situation. Here we find the free handling of tradition that is a central characteristic of chronological actualization. While promise and fulfillment are operative, the prophets are not concerned with detailed treatments of fulfillments or with correspondences for each and every prophecy. An atmosphere of charismatic, eclectic treatment of tradition exists. Consequently, the link which von Rad has posited between the Deuteronomistic history and the prophets is not a methodological one of similar types of actualization, but a conceptual one relating to promise and fulfillment and the creative word of God. While he regards both of these as elements in his overall scheme of actualization, they function so differently in the two sets of material under consideration that they act as conceptual, not methodological connections.

In summary, we have discovered a break not just in the links between the groups of Old Testament materials, but in the groupings themselves which von Rad proposes. While one may legitimately speak of a traditio-historical connection between the Deuteronomistic history and the prophets, the link must be defined apart from

---

[77]Von Rad, *Theology,* 2.94-95, 242, 268; Ackroyd gives a much more complete description of this relationship in "Vitality," 7-12, 18-20.

[78]Von Rad and Ackroyd see such discrepancies between prophecy and fulfillment as the ability of the creative word of God to seek its own fulfillment, not bounded by literalness. It is equally plausible to regard this as a need on the part of the historian to find a reasonably accurate fulfillment within the traditional materials to complete a painstakingly careful scheme. The overall picture in reading Kings is one of a historian bound by the materials and a rigid concept of the word of God, not of the charismatic freedom on the prophets.

chronological actualization. It lies instead in the concepts and traditions shared by the two sets of material.

3

Before we move on to the third link in von Rad's traditio-historical scheme and link the Old and New Testaments, we must consider one further issue related to the literature of the Old Testament. This problem is the material which actualization has omitted in its chain of witnesses: the psalms, wisdom, and apocalyptic. The psalms should provide major evidence for actualization since they are cult-related. However, von Rad and Noth use them only as secondary evidentiary references and never locate them in a developmental scheme for actualization, while Wolff and Porteous avoid them completely. Only Westermann, Weiser, and Childs tackle them directly. Westermann and Weiser find different kinds of actualization in the psalms, but they do not really relate them to the rest of the Old Testament. Thus, this exceedingly important segment of the Old Testament remains outside of any pattern of traditio-historical continuity.

Most proponents of actualization avoid wisdom completely. Von Rad, aware of his failure to integrate the wisdom materials into his theology, deals with them again in *Wisdom in Israel*. As illuminating as his analysis is, it clearly fails to place these traditions in the continuum which we are discussing. Ackroyd perceives the dilemma and seeks to integrate wisdom (as well as the psalms) into actualization. Unfortunately, his reliance upon the sermonic form as a rubric to join these disparate traditions distorts the nature of the material and fails totally. Consequently, wisdom, too, remains apart from any unity established by actualization.

Probably the most significant omission is the failure of von Rad to incorporate apocalyptic into his continuum. Even his reassessment of apocalyptic in the fourth edition of *Old Testament Theology II* and *Wisdom in Israel* maintains its primary relation to wisdom. While the nature of actualization in apocalyptic is never fully described, it clearly does not correspond to chronological actualization. Apocalyptic's understanding of history and tradition is quite different from the prophets' and stands apart from the great chain of witnesses summarized in the credo. As a result, it assumes a secondary role in the Old Testament.

Even if von Rad's traditio-historical continuum proved valid, his neglect of the psalms, wisdom, and apocalyptic literature is a serious problem. He attempts to provide a sense of unity through tradition criticism and actualization. Unfortunately, at best the unity attained relegates large sections of the Old Testament to secondary status. Without a thorough appraisal of this material on an equal basis, a theology of the Old Testament remains incomplete.

4

The third link in von Rad's traditio-historical chain is the most important, since it provides the continuity between the two testaments, rendering the Old Testament relevant for Christian theology. Von Rad's selectivity in his use of Old Testament materials is most apparent in his discussion of this connection: he rejects apocalyptic but accepts prophecy as a link between the testaments.

The most serious consequence of von Rad's general neglect of apocalyptic is his rejection of it as an element in the central traditio-historical continuum. By making a direct connection between the prophets and the New Testament, he skips over the intertestamental period entirely. In fact the New Testament rests upon this period literarily, historically, and religiously. While a traditio-historical link does exist between the prophets and the New Testament, the prophetic traditions utilized are filtered through the eschatological hopes and heightened Messianism of intertestamental times. To overlook this period is to eliminate a key link in traditio-historical development. Such a move falsely places the two testaments in a direct relationship which distorts the New Testament's appropriation of the Old – and enhances the boldness of the New's reinterpretations, since intervening developments are not discussed. Consequently, von Rad's neglect of apocalyptic constitutes a major weakness in his third traditio-historical link.

In his development of chronological actualization in the Old Testament von Rad joins the Deuteronomistic history and the prophets together as demonstrating the same characteristics of contemporization. However, in discussing the third link in his chain, he connects only the prophets and the New Testament. This move heightens the split which we noted in the previous section: the Deuteronomistic history forms a link with Deuteronomy; the prophets form a link with the New

Testament; the grouping of the history and the prophets is quite artificial.

As a result, having rejected the intertestamental literature and neglected the Deuteronomistic history, von Rad traces three primary connections between prophecy and the New Testament: promise and fulfillment, typology, and the charismatic-eclectic nature of their actualization. Von Rad's use of the concepts of promise and fulfillment and typology has already been thoroughly criticized. James Barr has given one of the most complete analyses of von Rad's use of the New Testament and especially of the role of typology.[79]   Of particular relevance to our study is his questioning of the history-centeredness of New Testament typology. He demonstrates that the concern of New Testament typology with history is based upon subject matter rather than method.[80]   The nature of the Old Testament material and the particular use to which the New Testament writers wish to put it result in a preponderance of examples of historical typology. However, there are several examples of non-historical typology in the New Testament as well as many non-typological, non-historical uses of the Old Testament.[81]   He concludes that there is no evidence of a particular method of historical typology in the New Testament as opposed to other kinds of typology present then or developed since. In the final analysis, while typology and promise and fulfillment are links between the Old and New Testaments, they are only two links among many and do not offer special support to von Rad's scheme of history-centered actualization.

The point of contact between the testaments which has not been thoroughly explored is the charismatic-eclectic nature of the re-use of traditions which one finds in both the prophets and the New Testament. A problem immediately arises which von Rad notes and then promptly dismisses: the fixation of the Old Testament in writing. He states in connection with this problem:

---

[79]Barr, *Old and New*, esp. pp. 103-48. Although Barr concentrates on typology in this section, his analysis of promise and fulfillment (pp. 118-26) shows that the same arguments hold for it as well.

[80]*Ibid.*, 110. The connection which we made earlier in relation to DtrH and the prophets makes Barr's argument even stronger: von Rad's whole theological enterprise is based upon links in methodology, not in subject matter.

[81]*Ibid.*, 108, 115.

... the difference is not a radical one, however, but affects the "formal" aspect more than anything else, since, where a document is concerned, the process of hermeneutics and interpretation must of course bring definite requirements along with it ("proof from scripture," etc.)[82]

However, von Rad has disregarded the degree of change involved in the transition from the Old Testament to the New. It includes not merely the fixation of the Old Testament in writing, but also the simultaneous process of canonization. The New Testament confronts a written document that is authoritative for the religious communities involved. It is regarded as eternally valid, "good for all generations." The New Testament can even state that neither jot nor tittle shall pass away (Matt 5:18). This is considerably more than a "formal" change; it is a methodological one involving the manner in which the traditions – now written documents – are re-used.

One clear and constant characteristic of chronological actualization is that the old traditions are not merely re-used, but reworded. There is a freedom of expression which allows the old events, patterns, and ideas to be described in different ways at different times. Such freedom is possible because of the close proximity of the Old Testament traditions to the stage of oral transmission and because of their precanonical status. While these traditions were endowed with authority and faithfully transmitted, the tradents felt no compulsion for a word-by-word fidelity.

Two examples of hermeneutical techniques from the New Testament highlight the distinction in methodology. First, there is an emphasis upon quotation from the Old Testament rather than rewording of a passage. The freedom to change the words of a tradition no longer exists. While the application of a Davidic promise to Jesus may be considered charismatic-eclectic, the method of application is not. Such quotations are precise and studied. Indeed, the application of such a promise to a Messianic figure is much less random than von Rad implies if one considers the intertestamental background of the New Testament.

A second hermeneutical technique is the argument from linguistic detail. For example, in Gal 3:16 Paul argues from the singular "seed"

---

[82]Von Rad, *Theology*, 2.328.

of Gen. 3:15 as opposed to the plural "seeds." Similarly, the gospels argue from the repetition of the word "lord" in Ps. 110:1 (see Mark 12:35; Matt 22:44; Luke 20:41f).[83] Once again the precise, studied argument betrays a method much more aligned with rabbinical exegesis than chronological actualization.

Von Rad has demonstrated that the New Testament writers re-use the Old Testament materials through their reapplication of old traditions to new situations. However, the force of that re-use is quite different from that encountered in chronological actualization. The Old Testament's status as a written, canonical document greatly restricts any vivid reimagining of the old events. There is no sense of identity or contemporaneity with the Old Testament events and figures. Indeed, the emphasis is quite different. The New Testament projects an image of a new happening that stands at a remove from the Old Testament traditions. Quotations and allusions are drawn not so much from the Old Testament credenda as from the Davidic promises and other, less significant incidents. One can certainly speak of a sense of continuity between the two testaments, since the New Testament writers continually invoke the Old Testament to explicate the figure of Christ. However, this invocation lacks the sense of contemporaneity characteristic of chronological actualization. As a result, although all three elements discussed by Von Rad do indeed connect the two testaments, they do not provide a methodological connection through chronological actualization.

One final problem presents an obstacle for von Rad's method of relating the two testaments: the nature of the Christ event. While it is true that the New Testament writers regarded this event as being in continuity with the Old Testament saving events, they also viewed it as a new, unprecedented saving act that exceeded the limits of tradition. Von Rad is aware of this understanding of the Christ event and grapples with the problem which it presents. His interpretation of the prophets as spokesmen who declare the old bases of salvation as null and void is a preparation for the new events of the New Testament. However, he still maintains essential ties between the prophets and the rest of the Old Testament. He is able to describe their actualizations of the old traditions in the same terms as the other Old Testament contemporizations. Furthermore, they describe no new saving event

---

[83]Barr, *Old and New*, 114.

calling for drastically new language; they rely upon a non-specific new exodus, new David, new covenant, etc. When von Rad moves to the New Testament, he is unable to maintain his consistent terminology. He must use language which highlights the Christ event, calling it a final actualization *(letzte Neuinterpretation)* and a *Wiederholung* (referring to a basic, primitive repetition of a saving event).[84] Through these phrases he affirms that the Christ event is unique and final, standing at the end of a chain of tradition.

However, this creates a dilemma for von Rad. A consistent train of traditio-historical continuity such as he tries to create undermines this uniqueness. A new, fundamental saving event cannot be handled adequately by the actualization of old traditions. The old concepts can be used (as they undoubtedly are) to explain the new mystery only in part. The Christ event stands on the level of the original exodus and the original covenant at Sinai, not on the level of their later actualizations. Israel never experienced another giving of the covenant of such an unprecedented nature, but referred to other covenants in terms of the first, either in comparison or contrast. Even the return from the exile in Babylon, both in its expectation and in its reality, was not significant enough to create a new typology; rather than being unique, it was regarded as a second expression of the exodus. But one must use new terms for the unique event of the Christ; the Davidic promise can characterize it but not encompass it. Von Rad acknowledges this with his use of *Wiederholung*. However, this also weakens his final traditio-historical link. His scheme of actualization is inadequate to explain the difference, the newness, the uniqueness of Christ. He makes an attempt to maintain a solid link to the Old Testament through actualization and yet retain the uniqueness of the Christ event. Unfortunately, his method is inadequate to the task.

Thus, we must conclude that this link in the chain of traditio-historical continuity is flawed on both historical and theological grounds. As expressed by von Rad it neglects its closest historical relative, the intertestamental period. Further, it overlooks the fixation and canonization of the Old Testament. Finally, it undermines the traditional Christian interpretation of the Christ event as unique, a view that von Rad himself espouses but fails to support adequately.

---

[84]Von Rad, *Theology*, 2.321, 332, 383-84; *Theologie*, 2.332, 343, 397-98 (1st ed.).

5

The final and somewhat debatable link in the chain of traditio-historical continuity is the relation of Biblical actualization to contemporary exegesis and preaching. Does the same scheme of actualization continue after the New Testament, or does the Christ-event signal the close of a traditio-historical era? Von Rad remains curiously silent on this issue. In all his programmatic statements up to and including his *Old Testament Theology*, he never discusses directly the relationship between the Bible and modern exegesis. This lack in itself may indicate his stance; his view of the New Testament as a final reinterpretation suggests a break between Biblical actualization and modern exegesis. However, such infrequent hints form a inadequate basis for any solid conclusions.

He provides more substantial evidence in his lecture "About Exegesis and Preaching" and in his article "Ancient Word and Living Word." While the references to actualization in both of these sources is incomplete and disappointingly vague, he offers some enlightenment at least. In the former his description of the nature of contemporary preaching is quite reminiscent of actualization, especially when he states that the best sermons are those in which "the texts themselves actually speak."[85] Further reminders occur when he states the need for the preacher to bring the author to the congregation (quoting Schleiermacher) and when he regards a critical paraphrase of the text (itself a type of actualization) as "the crown of any interpretation."[86] However, at no point does von Rad discuss the relation of exegesis to actualization or indicate clearly that the elements of chronological actualization are present in contemporary preaching.

In "Ancient Word and Living Word," which is subtitled "The Preaching of Deuteronomy and Our Preaching," von Rad relates the book more to the New Testament than to contemporary proclamation. He concentrates on establishing the message of Deuteronomy as a prefigurement of the New Testament through such themes as the free gift of God's election, promise and fulfillment, mediatory suffering, and the presence of paraclesis.[87] Von Rad applies this understanding of the

---

[85]Von Rad, "About Exegesis and Preaching" in *Biblical Interpretations in Preaching* (Nashville: Abingdon, 1977) 17.

[86]*Ibid.*, 15, 13.

[87]Von Rad, "Ancient Word," 6-12.

Old Testament viewed in light of the Christ-event only briefly to modern proclamation, but he does indicate the presence of some type of actualization in our preaching. Deuteronomy is pertinent to us only when it is interpreted anew *(neu zu deuten)*. The continual reinterpretation which occurs in the book is a model for the freedom for revitalization which the word of God has for each new age.[88] Therefore, while von Rad remains vague on this point and eschews the technical vocabulary of actualization, we can safely state that he regarded contemporization in some form as present in the preaching of the Biblical word.

Noth and Westermann are much more direct about this issue. Noth explicitly links contemporary proclamation to Old Testament actualization and states that true preaching must use the Biblical method of narrative restatement of God's saving acts. Westermann, through a more complex analysis, arrives at much the same conclusion. However, his concept of actualization is considerably different than Noth's cultic/chronological variety. Westermann's narrative actualization, descriptively presented in his study of the psalms and applied to proclamation in his article on exegesis, allows for a sense of distance between the original tradition and the present day. In addition he affirms a sense of history for this type of actualization in the worship of various Christian sects: actualization through liturgy in the Eastern Orthodox church; actualization through instruction in the Roman Catholic church; actualization through proclamation in the Protestant church. Actualization through proclamation most closely reflects Biblical actualization.[89]

However, one factor sets contemporary proclamation and exegesis apart from Biblical actualization in the work of all these men. None of them affirms a continuous history of exegesis between the Bible and modern times; there is no sign of a traditio-historical continuum such as von Rad develops for the Bible itself. With the exception of Westermann's brief mention of actualization in worship, one would have to conclude that the history of Christian exegesis is unimportant for actualization. Their traditio-historical connection is directly between the Bible and modern proclamation. Noth states this explicitly; one may infer it from the methodologies of von Rad, Westermann, and

---

[88]*Ibid.,* 12-13.

[89]Westermann, "exegetische Aussage," 6-7.

Wolff. Thus, in the final analysis the proponents of actualization affirm that chronological actualization ended with the closing of the New Testament. The contemporary task is to revive that exegetical tradition, dormant in the history of Christian exegesis.

6

In summary, we conclude that each step of the traditio-historical continuum proposed by von Rad is seriously flawed. No proponent of actualization has been able to demonstrate a unity of method or concept for the Bible through the application of chronological actualization. No necessary connection exists between cultic actualization and the Bible's re-use of traditions, casting doubt upon the uniqueness of the Biblical phenomenon. The Bible itself appears not as a totality, but as a set of discrete units (J, E, D, the Deuteronomistic history, the prophets, the New Testament) which reinterpret traditions by significantly different methods. Furthermore, large blocks of material (the psalms, wisdom, apocalyptic) are only secondarily related to the traditio-historical continuum. Finally, the connection between the overall design of chronological actualization and contemporary theology is flawed by a neglect of the history of Christian exegesis. We must conclude that chronological actualization by itself is unable to provide the necessary sense of unity for a Christian interpretation of the Old Testament.

The Centrality of Actualization

A major concern for von Rad and other proponents of actualization is to demonstrate that chronological actualization is a central method for Old Testament interpretation. The two topics which we have already discussed, the uniqueness of Biblical actualization and the traditio-historical unity which it provides for scripture, are used to bolster the claim for centrality. The presence of the element of identity and the development of unique concepts of time and history set the Bible apart from both its Near Eastern cultural milieu and our modern, philosophically based concepts. Chronological actualization is intimately related to identity, time, and history; consequently, an understanding of this concept is central to an empathetic interpretation of the Bible. Chronological actualization is also the connective tissue for the traditio-historical unity of the Bible. As such, it is essential to any comprehensive theological interpretation. We have demonstrated that the underlying arguments for uniqueness and continuity are questionable. Consequently, to use these elements as the basis for establishing the centrality of chronological actualization is to step beyond the available evidence.

Proponents of actualization posit a third reason for their claim of centrality: chronological actualization is the most important type of inner-Biblical exegesis. This element is necessary in order to meet Noth's criterion that any exegesis must grow out of its subject matter.[90] The evidence for the inner-Biblical nature of actualization focuses on three types of material: passages used to describe the development and nature of the concept; discussions of the importance of actualization to particular types of Old Testament literature; the application of the concept to different passages.

A quite select number of Biblical passages form the major arguments about the development and nature of chronological actualization. Since its origin lies in the cult, these passages center around some of the supposedly cult-related material in the Old Testament: the descriptions of the feasts of Passover and Booths (Exod 12:1-27; Lev 23:42-43; Deut 16:3; 31:10-13);[91] Deuteronomy's use of "today" and "we" (especially Deut 5:2-3; 6:20-25; 26:5-9; 26:16-19; 29:4-14).[92]

Other discussions center on the importance of actualization to particular types of Old Testament literature. One particular focus of concern is the prophetic literature. Von Rad discussed this area twice, both times drawing his examples almost exclusively from Isaiah 1-39.[93] We also find discussions of the nature of prophetic actualization which draw from a wider range of passages by Jones, Ackroyd, Nicholson, and Childs.[94] An equally important concern is the presence of actualization in the Deuteronomistic history. The discussions concerning this section of the Old Testament, which we find in von

---

[90]Noth, "Re-presentation," 80.

[91]*Ibid.*, 81-83; von Rad, *Theology*, 2.104-05; Childs, *Memory*, 54-55.

[92]Noth, "Re-presentation," 82-83; von Rad, *Theology*, 2.108-10; *Hexateuch*, 28-29; *Theology*, 1.192-93, 225-26, 253; Childs, *Memory*, 52-54; Ackroyd, "Vitality," 12.

[93]Von Rad, *Theology*, 2.43-44, 167-69.

[94]Jones, "Traditio," 227, 230, 243; Ackroyd, "Vitality," 12-15, 18-19; Nicholson, *Preaching*, 1-18; Childs, *Memory*, 56-59. We also find discussions of prophetic actualization by Mowinckel in *Prophecy and Tradition* and Birkeland in *Traditionswesen*.

Rad, Wolff, and Ackroyd, center not so much on specific passages as on the overall pattern of prophecy and fulfillment, the theology of history, and the creative word of God.[95] A third area of major concern for von Rad is the New Testament, which he relates directly to the prophetic literature.[96] Although there is a great deal of discussion about the presence of actualization in the psalms, only Childs presents a detailed argument for chronological actualization; the others investigating the psalms (Westermann, Weiser, and Zirker) find different kinds of actualization.[97]

While these discussions provide the primary theoretical basis for the centrality of actualization to the Bible, they are a small proportion of the actual uses of actualization by its proponents. Far more numerous are the applications of actualization to various Old Testament passages. It is through these that we ascertain the pervasive nature of the concept. Particularly in the work of von Rad, but in the work of other scholars as well, we find actualization applied to J, E, and P, the Chronicler, the psalms, apocalyptic, the Qumran writings, and wisdom literature in addition to the sections of the Bible we have already discussed.[98]

The proponents of chronological actualization have marshalled an impressive array of evidence to demonstrate that the phenomenon lies at the heart of inner-Biblical exegesis. However, a careful examination of the material presented cautions against any sweeping conclusions. We have discussed the nature of the arguments presented concerning the first two types of material (the development of actualization and its importance to different types of Biblical literature) in the two previous sections and found the evidence inconclusive at best. The third category is the application of chronological actualization to different Biblical passages. This category does little to describe the nature of the inner-Biblical exegesis present; it merely relates the passages to actualization and relies upon previous discussions to illuminate its nature.

---

[95]Von Rad, *Theology*, 1.304, 343-44; *Theology*, 2.74; "Deuteronomic Theology"; Ackroyd, "Vitality," 7-12; Wolff, *Vitality*, 83-100.

[96]Von Rad, *Theology*, 2.327-29.

[97]Childs, *Memory*, 60-65; Westermann, "Vergegenwärtigung"; Weiser, *Psalms*, 23-52; Zirker, *Vergegenwärtigung*.

[98]The works which do most in applying actualization to various parts of the Bible are as follows: von Rad, *Theology*, 1 and 2; Wolff, *Vitality*; Ackroyd, "Vitality"; Childs, *Memory*. The citations in the first two chapters give specific references.

Furthermore, large areas of Biblical literature have been neglected in the discussion and application of chronological actualization. While we encounter scattered references to actualization in discussions of the psalms, wisdom, and apocalyptic, many of these point to a concept considerably at odds with chronological actualization.

Therefore, we must conclude that the centrality of chronological actualization to the Bible has not been convincingly demonstrated. What the proponents of this concept have succeeded in proving is that the re-use of older traditions by a later age is a central feature of inner-Biblical interpretation. However, the evidence indicates that such re-use can take varied forms and is not necessarily characteristic of all sections of the Old Testament. Chronological actualization is an inadequate category to encompass even the bulk of the myriad methods of inner-Biblical exegesis.

We should note in passing that the attempt by the proponents of actualization to establish the centrality of chronological actualization is their response to a question frequently posed to Old Testament theology: what is the center of the Old Testament? Whereas most theologies have focused upon a unifying concept, von Rad shifted the ground for the debate.[99] The Old Testament has no central concept, but a central method. Actualization is the connecting thread which acts as the basis for theological reinterpretation and allows the Old Testament to speak in its manifold voices.

The Theological-Historical Equation

The primary purpose of actualization – and the major problem of any contemporary Old Testament theology – is to relate the historical-critical method to the theological dimension of the Old Testament. In

[99]For a summary of this question see Hasel, *Theology*, 77-103, "Problem of the Center." Hasel places the center of von Rad's theology in the Deuteronomistic concept of history. I disagree with him for two reasons. First, as Hasel acknowledges, von Rad denies that there is a center for the Old Testament and does so correctly if one looks to a concept or a particular book as Hasel does. It is only in the unorthodox sense of a method that one can find a center in von Rad's theology. Second, by Hasel's own criteria he misses the most influential book for von Rad. Deuteronomy, not the Deuteronomistic history, is the key for him. His defense of a rationalized actualization centers on Deuteronomy from *Hexateuch* through *Studies in Deuteronomy* to both volumes of *Theology*. The Deuteronomistic history is secondary both in time ("Deuteronomic Theology" did not appear until 1947) and in its role (that article is appended to *Studies in Deuteronomy;* the Deuteronomistic history is relegated to a decidedly secondary role in *Theology*).

this section we will examine both sides of the equation in relation to the Old Testament materials. First, we will focus upon the nature of the theology which grows out of the application of actualization to the Old Testament. Then, we will investigate the relationship of actualization to the historical-critical method.

1

Since actualization reveals the theological nature of the Bible by illuminating the continuing methodological connections between segments of scripture, we should not expect concrete concepts, such as the covenant or God as Lord, to be the center of this theology. However, certain rubrics, certain recurring categories, are necessary to order and illuminate the theological nature of actualization. Chief among these are the vital/creative word of God, promise and fulfillment, typology, salvation history, and kerygma/kerygmatic intention (with its attendant emphasis upon the sermonic form and proclamation).

We have already studied these categories in relation to the growth and development of actualization. We have noted the general lineaments of each rubric and seen the particular emphasis that each has in its connection to the concept. We will not repeat this analysis in this section, but will instead concentrate upon two facets of the theology of actualization. First, having compiled all these rubrics, we will look for connections among them and try to discern an overall picture of the theological thrust underlying actualization. Second, we will probe the legitimacy of this theological enterprise by asking whether or not these rubrics are the natural and necessary results of actualization.

All of the rubrics which carry the theological impact of actualization have a familiar ring. The vital/creative word of God, kerygma/kerygmatic intention, and proclamation/sermonic form are all closely associated and form a strong link to twentieth century Protestant theology. We have already mentioned the direct influence of Barth in Noth's theological categories and Kierkegaard's possible impact upon von Rad's idea of contemporaneity.[100] However, the relationship

---

[100]Noth quotes and footnotes Barth both for his understanding of actualization as the mediateness/immediateness of history and for the nature of proclamation as passing on news reports ("Re-presentation," 85-88). Porteous acknowledges Barth as his source for the idea of connecting actualization and obedience in *Living*, 2-3, 170-71.

between contemporary Protestant thought and the theological dimension of actualization is far more pervasive than an occasional quotation or footnote. Nor can it be traced to the direct influence of one person. These categories formed the theological atmosphere in which von Rad and his colleagues worked. Given their theological interest in the Old Testament, the question which they pursued quickly became how to make the Old Testament relevant to these categories. While they made a decision to work within the present Protestant scheme, their emphasis was quite different from that of the dogmatic theologians: they applied these categories to the traditionary process which they regarded as central to the formation of the Old Testament.[101] Now that we have established the source and milieu of the theological rubrics which dominate actualization, we can investigate what accommodations were necessary on the part of both the theological concepts involved and the interpretation of the Old Testament in establishing this relationship. We will particularly note any strains and tensions which arise from this marriage.

Contemporaneity appears as a significant element in modern Protestant thought. However, the use of this category by von Rad and his colleagues is quite different from that of dogmatic theologians. The proponents of actualization emphasize the human, historical side of contemporization: it is depicted as an effort by Israel and the early Christians to bridge the gap between their historical existence and the reality of their old traditions of faith in God. As opposed to this human endeavor, systematic theologians emphasize contemporaneity as an act of God, bringing his followers into relation to him:

> Fulfilled time takes the place of our non-genuine and improper time as genuine and proper time.... It is therefore not an edifying trick of thought, but the assimilation of nourishment absolutely indispensible to our life, when Holy Scripture and the proclamation of its message call and transpose us from our own time into that time, namely, into the time of Jesus Christ. There and only there, in contemporaneousness *(Gleichzeitigkeit)*

---

[101]The decision to pursue these particular concerns involved the rejection of other avenues of approach. Theologically, they chose the regnant Protestant emphases over Roman Catholic ones, a choice reflected in the minimal impact of actualization upon Roman Catholic Old Testament research. It further involved the rejection or adaptation of the other Old Testament-theology connections outlined in the introduction to this study.

with Christ mediated to the church by the witness of the prophets and apostles, do we really possess time.[102]

Further emphasis lies upon the direct connection between the present-day believer and the person of Christ – neither with the traditions that surround him nor with the continuum of tradition begun in the Old Testament. The experience of contemporaneity is a non-historical one:

> ... every man can be contemporary only with the age in which he lives – and then with one thing more: with Christ's life on earth; for Christ's life on earth, sacred history, stands for itself alone outside history.... for what true Christians there are in each generation are contemporary with Christ, have nothing to do with Christians of former generations, but everything to do with the contemporary Christ. His earthly life accompanies the race, and accompanies every generations in particular, as the eternal history; His earthly life possesses the eternal contemporaneousness.[103]

While we could multiply examples to demonstrate the various formulations of contemporaneity in modern theology, these two are sufficient to illustrate the total, essentially non-historical identification experienced by the believer with the life of Christ. Without suggesting a direct influence, we cannot help but notice the similarity with the element of identity in chronological actualization. Significant differences occur when identity is applied to the Old Testament traditionary process, however. While the dogmatic theologians found its genesis in the immediate action of God and related it directly to Jesus Christ, the proponents of actualization sought a human origin in cultic re-enactment and applied it to the continuing traditio-historical spectrum.

---

[102]Karl Barth, *Church Dogmatics* (Edinburgh: T&T Clark, 1936), 66. In speaking of contemporaneity Barth tends to use *gleichzeitig/Gleichzeitigkeit: Die kirchliche Dogmatik* (Zollikon: evangelischen Buchhandlung, 1938), 1/1.106, 119; *Dogmatik*, 1/2.55, 66. He uses *Vergegenwärtigung* only on occasion (*Dogmatik*, 1/1.111; 1/2.45, 53). The concept of contemporization is present in his work as early as the second edition of *The Epistle to the Romans* (1921), where he states that "the walls which separate the sixteenth century from the first become transparent" (*The Epistle to the Romans* [London: Oxford University, 1933] 7).

[103]Kierkegaard, *Training*, 68.

A further point of contact between Protestant theology and actualization appears in the quotes above: a selective emphasis in the stream of witnesses to God's revelation. The prophets and apostles are elevated to a primary position, Jesus Christ is the centerpiece, and a direct connection is made to contemporary proclamation. These elements encapsulate the selective emphasis in von Rad's traditio-historical continuum (with the significant exception of Deuteronomy and the Deuteronomistic history). This similarity may be traced to the prominent role of proclamation in both dogmatic theology and actualization. Barth, for example, states that the Bible is "the deposit of proclamation made in the past by the mouths of men," and is the beginning of an event for which modern preaching is the continuation.[104] His selective emphasis in the Bible reflects the material which he regards as the most closely tied to modern proclamation. Von Rad (with Deuteronomy and the Deuteronomistic history) and Wolff (with the Yahwist and the Elohist) posit these sections as central to the Old Testament message because they are the residues of preaching activity and reflect a kerygmatic intention. Even the same gaps occur in the two schemes, with modern Protestant thought eschewing both apocalyptic and church tradition as part of the stream of witnesses.[105]

However, the basis for this stream of witnesses is quite different for modern theology and actualization. For example, Barth makes his direct connection between the two testaments because no relation of historical cause and effect governs revelation in either the Old or New Testament. Instead, the revelation of the word of God in either one is a matter of pure miracle.[106] The church can do nothing but accept this miracle, which it does by affirming the canon of scripture. This affirmation puts the word of God in a unique relationship with contemporary proclamation, placing the canon above both written and oral church tradition and permitting selective emphasis upon segments of scripture as the spirit moves.

---

[104]Barth, *Dogmatik*, 1/1.114. Also see *Dogmatik*, 1/2.111; "The Authority and Significance of the Bible," in *God Here and Now* (New York: Harper & Row, 1964) 47; *Evangelical Theology* (New York: Holt, Reinhart, Winston, 1963) 26-29; "Biblical Questions, Insights, and Vistas," in *The Word of God and the Word of Man* (n.p.: Pilgrim, 1928) 65.

[105]For example, see Barth, *Dogmatik*, 1/2.114-16; 1/2.72; "Authority," 49-50.

[106]Barth, *Dogmatik*, 1/2.102.

While actualization expands the chain of witnesses in the Old Testament, it retains the same selective emphases and omissions as Protestant dogmatic theology. However, the basis for actualization is not purely theological; it is traditio-historical as well. Consequently, the suspension of historical cause and effect is not applicable to actualization. Therefore, a gap such as the omission of the role of apocalyptic and the intertestamental period, which may be admissible in a dogmatic framework, becomes a serious flaw when one includes an historical basis for analysis. Therefore, we may conclude that when these particular Protestant emphases are applied to the role of tradition in the development of the Old Testament, one result is puzzling omissions and flawed argumentation for a selective chain of witnesses.

Another group of theological ideas which play an important role for actualization centers around the concepts of promise and fulfillment, typology, and *Heilsgeschichte*. These ideas were prominent in the Reformation and experienced a recrudescence in the *Heilsgeschichte* school exemplified by Johann Christian Konrad von Hofmann that continued to exert influence until von Rad's time. While these categories were part of the general theological atmosphere of twentieth century Protestant thought, they were especially important in the realm of Biblical theology.[107] Von Rad, in particular, draws upon these rubrics in his theology. His treatment of these elements is quite enlightening for his theological method. Whereas previous systems applying these categories to the Old Testament were at the most only obliquely concerned with secular history, von Rad has drawn direct connections between promise and fulfillment, typology, *Heilsgeschichte,* and the historical-critical method. The Old Testament promises are seen primarily in their historical setting and in relation to the actual or expected Old Testament fulfillment. Then, secondarily, they continue to live in history and become ever new promises receiving ever new fulfillments, the culmination of which is the New Testament. Even this continuing life of the promises is grounded in secular history, since the traditions are re-used to meet the needs of Israel in concrete historical situations. Consequently, von Rad's adaptation of these categories is to move them out of the symbolic,

---

[107]See particularly Johann Christian Konrad von Hofmann,*Weissagung und Erfülung* (Nordlinger: C. Beck, 1841); *Interpreting the Bible* (Minneapolis: Augsburg, 1959). As an example of the use of similar categories in dogmatic theology, see Barth, *Dogmatik,* 1/2.70-121.

systematic realm and to ground them firmly in the traditionary process of the Old Testament.[108]

We may draw two conclusions concerning the theological program which emerges from actualization. First, the connection which the proponents of actualization draw between theology and the Old Testament is a response to the theological climate of the times. All of the theological categories which emerge from the application of actualization to the Bible are part of the general atmosphere of twentieth century Protestant theology. The novelty of actualization lies not in the theological categories which it employs, but in its applying them to the Old Testament. Von Rad and his colleagues were able to take the categories which expressed the pressing religious issues of their time and discover corollaries for them in the traditionary process in the Bible. The rebirth of confessional theology juxtaposed to von Rad's credenda, the emphasis upon proclamation in both dogmatics and the Bible, the role of the Word of God paralleled by the creative word of promise and fulfillment, the mutual focus upon kerygma and kerygmatic intention – all these connections produced a sense of vitality in the theological program of actualization that no other method of Old Testament interpretation could match.

Second, the correlation between dogmatic theology and Old Testament studies produced significant strains and tensions in the method of actualization. The shift of these categories from theology to the Bible involved important changes. In actualization they are applied to the traditionary process and tied closely to historical methods. One strain arose in relation to the presence of identity in chronological actualization. We found that the inclusion of this element in actualization is based upon a questionable connection between cultic and chronological actualization. Neither historical evidence nor textual studies lend significant support to the contention that identity occurs in the Old Testament, yet most proponents of actualization posit its presence. The reason for their insistence is quite possibly a theological one which does not rest upon textual evidence. Dogmatic theologians describe the Christian's relationship to the time and life of Christ as one of complete identity – but as an a-historical phenomenon. Therefore, the shift of the theological understanding of identity to the realm of

---

[108] For von Rad's criticism of previous systems of promise and fulfillment and typology, see *Theology*, 2.362-74.

actualization, which is intimately connected to history, produces an unresolved tension in the method.

A second strain arises in relation to the selective emphases in the traditio-historical continuum associated with actualization. We find similar emphases in the Protestant chain of witnesses to the proclamation of God's word – again accompanied by a suspension of historical cause and effect. A similar emphasis upon proclamation in actualization, however, leaves serious gaps in the historical development of the Biblical traditions. Selectivity which can be defended on dogmatic grounds produces developmental gaps when applied to the historically related method of actualization.

A third strain occurs when von Rad and Noth turn to the old categories of typology and promise and fulfillment to describe the theological content of the Old Testament. This, too, is an attempt to adapt non-historical categories to an historically related method. The distinction which von Rad and Noth draw between historical typology and other types of typology and allegory is thoroughly and successfully criticized by Barr as being an inadequate description of the hermeneutical processes of the Bible.

In summary, we can conclude that the theological nature of actualization is primarily a response to the religious needs and emphases of its times. A measure of the method's success rests upon its ability to correlate elements from contemporary dogmatic theology with the traditio-historical development of the Bible. However, as successful as this endeavor was, it produced serious strains and inconsistencies in actualization when the theological correlation overrode the historical criteria which also functioned in giving actualization a firm base in Old Testament critical studies.

2

Having studied the theological nature of actualization, we will now examine the historical foundations of the enterprise more carefully as we turn to the other end of the theological-historical equation. Of course higher criticism is a general term encompassing many possible approaches to the Biblical literature. We will concentrate our analysis upon the two areas of greatest influence upon and interaction with actualization: form criticism and tradition criticism.

The emphasis upon form criticism which we find in most proponents of actualization grew from the influence of Gunkel, Gressmann, and Alt, the founders of the field.[109] While their influence upon von Rad and others was immense, we should note that one of these form-critical pioneers entertained the theological interest and emphasis that we have encountered in actualization. Form criticism has left its mark upon actualization in several ways. The most obvious is the strict form-critical methodology which is particularly evident in the work of von Rad, Wolff, and Noth in the Pentateuch, Westermann on the psalms and prophets, and Childs in his word study of זכר. Less obvious are the more general methodological imprints of form criticism. One of the central form-critical characteristics is the search for a concrete *Sitz-im-Leben* for each pericope. Even when form criticism is not employed, this has left two manifestations in actualization: the desire to pinpoint the historical situation of a passage and the search for the cultic origin of Old Testament material (and thus a connection to cultic actualization). A second characteristic of the form-critical method which has facilitated actualization is the breaking of a text into its constituent parts. This provides discrete units and genres whose re-use through actualization is more easily traced. The smaller units also provide entities for which a distinct kerygma is easily ascertained. In these ways form criticism, as a prior higher-critical methodology, paved the way for the development of actualization.

In contrast, actualization and tradition criticism have developed hand in hand. Both stem from Gunkel's insight that old traditions gradually change and are imbued with the spirit of a new age. Thus, one can trace the development of specific traditions as they are altered and re-used by succeeding generations. Gunkel himself applied this insight only within the bounds of form criticism. He traced the development of integrated units such as the Jacob and Joseph cycles and demonstrated how these cycles altered the original sagas in later use. However, he did not undertake the study of the growth and re-use of

---

[109]In addition to their other formative roles in relation to actualization, Gunkel and Mowinckel were pioneers of form criticism. See in particular Gunkel, "Fundamental Problems"; *Genesis* (Göttingen: Vandenhoeck & Ruprecht, 1901); *Einleitung in die Psalmen* (Göttingen: Vandenhoeck & Ruprecht, 1933); Mowinckel, *Prophecy and Tradition*. Also see Albrecht Alt, "The Origins of Israelite Law," in *Essays on Old Testament History and Religion* (Garden City: Doubleday, 1968) 101-72; Gene Tucker, *Form Criticism of the Old Testament* (Philadelphia: Fortress, 1971); Kraus, *Geschichte*, 301-34.

discrete traditions in the whole of the Old Testament. Von Rad, with *The Form-Critical Problem of the Hexateuch,* and Noth, with *A History of the Pentateuchal Traditions,* began to develop the full parameters of the discipline by tracing the use of creedal traditions throughout the Hexateuch. The former work also witnessed the genesis of actualization. Thus, of all the critical disciplines, tradition criticism is most closely linked to actualization. Indeed, it is reasonable to state that tradition criticism is based upon a broad understanding of actualization as the attempt by a later age to come to terms with an earlier oral or written heritage by adaptation, translation, and re-use.[110] However, this delineation of actualization resembles literary contemporization far more closely than it does von Rad's more restrictive definition of chronological actualization.

The purpose of this section, then, is to see what consequences the links to form and tradition criticism have for actualization. A great deal of criticism has been directed at von Rad's understanding of the connection between history in the Old Testament and contemporary historical methodology. He has been thoroughly criticized for basing his theology on a concept of history which does not rest on historical facts. As such his concept of history is an alien one to the modern mind and cannot form a sound basis for a modern theology. The debate has raged for many years, but its general lineaments may be traced in two series of articles: first, Conzelmann's attack in "Fragen an Gerhard von Rad" and von Rad's reply, "Antwort auf Conzelmann's Fragen"; and second, Eichrodt's "The Problem of Old Testament Theology" and von Rad's more general reply, "Offene Fragen im Umkreis einer Theologie des Alten Testaments."[111] One point emerges from the debate which will have some significance in our discussion: as the debate progresses, von Rad moves much closer to affirming an historical basis in the contemporary sense of the word for the Old Testament saving events.

---

[110]Knight sees this understanding of actualization as a general basis for tradition criticism: *Rediscovering,* 5-6; *Tradition,* 167.

[111]Conzelmann, "Fragen," 13-15; Gerhard von Rad, "Antwort auf Conzelmann's Fragen," *EvT* 24 (1964) 388-94; Eichrodt, "Problem"; von Rad, "Offene Fragen."

Since this question of a faith-history dichotomy is oft-discussed[112] and impinges only indirectly upon actualization, I do not wish to rehash it here. Instead, I wish to shift the ground of the question to an equally important area. The relation of faith to history, which involves only a small portion of the use of modern historical techniques by the proponents of actualization, is only part of a larger question: what is the impact of the use of modern historical methods, through form and tradition criticism, upon the theological interpretation of the Old Testament? This is the question I wish to address now.

As his critics claim, von Rad does not assert that the events of the *Heilsgeschichte* are historically valid. He is content with the statement that they stem from and are related to historical occurrences. However, despite von Rad's hesitancy to ascribe a modern historical base for Israel's saving events, he freely uses historical-critical methods to reconstruct the institutions, celebrations, and events which underlie the Old Testament traditions. This application of modern historical methodology has serious consequences for the description of Biblical actualization which emerges. We will briefly consider two applications of historical reconstruction to help us understand the nature of these consequences.

The first application is to the relationship between Israel's cultic institutions and actualization. Since the Old Testament does not give a detailed description of such institutions and celebrations, historical reconstruction is useful in reaching the fullest possible understanding of Israel's cultic milieu. However, reconstructions can be more or less feasible, depending upon the strength of the evidence presented and the manner in which the reconstruction is applied. Martin Noth is quite circumspect in his reconstructions. He posits the presence of cultic actualization in Israel on the basis of festivals mentioned in the Old Testament (Passover and Booths) and on passages which are connected with those festivals and have linguistic clues which may point to

---

[112]In addition to the articles above, see Honecker, "Verständnis"; Rendtorff, *Geschichte;* Theodorus Vriezen, "Geloof, openbaring, en geschiedenis in de nieuwste Oud-Testamentische Theologie," *Kerk en Theologie,* 16 (1956) 97-113, 210-218; J.A. Soggin, "Geschichte, Historie, und Heilsgeschichte im Alten Testament," *TLZ* 89 (1964) 721-36.

actualization.[113] The adaptation of cultic actualization to the religion of Israel (the historicizing of the festivals and the reliance upon narration rather than dramatic re-enactment) is based upon the same textual evidence. As a result, Noth makes a strong case for the presence of cultic actualization in Israel, and for residual traces of its influence in the Old Testament. The difficulties with his procedure lie not with the historical reconstruction itself, but in his broad application of it as the basis for both inner-Biblical and contemporary exegesis. After producing a guarded and circumspect reconstruction, he oversteps the bounds of his evidence in his sweeping application of actualization in the cult.

Von Rad's reconstruction of the cult presents another problem. For him the nature of actualization in the Old Testament is closely connected with a quite tenuous historical reconstruction: the covenant renewal festival.[114] This festival, which von Rad regards as Israel's central religious rite, is not mentioned in either the Old Testament or in later Jewish writings. Such a lack strains the credulity and brings into serious question the existence of the festival at all. Furthermore, von Rad uses numerous texts from the Old Testament which are not specifically cultic in nature to describe and delineate the religious rites involved. Virtually ignoring the psalmodic material, which is most closely related to the cult, von Rad focuses his attention upon the Hexateuch. Indeed, most of his evidence comes not from the cult-related sections of P, but from the Yahwist and Deuteronomy. Whether or not these two sources are closely related to the cult is a matter of discussion, however. Deuteronomy in particular invites many interpretations, only some of which are cultic. Even those scholars who hold most strongly to the cultic origin of the book argue that its present form is quite far removed from the actual cultic performance because of its long history of oral transmission, its current written form, and the considerable expansions it has undergone. In summary, von Rad has reconstructed as a central religious institution of Israel a festival which is never mentioned in the Bible, based upon evidence far

---

[113]Noth, "Re-presentation," 80-84. For another example of Noth's hesitance to reconstruct festivals (in contrast to Mowinckel and von Rad), see *The History of Israel* (New York: Harper & Row, 1960) 97-109.

[114]See particularly von Rad, *Hexateuch*, 26-40; *Studies in Deuteronomy*, 11-24; *Theology*, 1.15-35, 219-20.

removed from the cultic sphere. The tenuous nature of this reconstruction is evident.

This questionable procedure has serious ramifications for actualization. The nature of Deuteronomy is explained in relation to this reconstructed festival; at the same time, the book is central for von Rad's understanding of contemporization. Since Deuteronomy is derived from the rites of a cultic festival, it is connected to cultic re-enactment. In its present, rationalized form the book is linked to a later time in Israel's history and reflects the crisis which produced chronological actualization. Consequently, the connection between the cultic and chronological actualization, which is quite important for von Rad's developmental scheme, rests not upon direct textual evidence, but upon a reconstructed historical setting. When this reconstruction comes under attack, the criticism necessarily extends to actualization.

The second application of historical reconstruction demonstrates the extent of the procedure in relation to actualization. Historical reconstruction is not limited to institutions and celebrations; it also encompasses the historical situation of a particular pericope or document. We can cite numerous examples of this application: Wolff traces the historical situation of J, E, and the Deuteronomistic history; von Rad seeks the events behind the pronouncements of the prophets; Noth reconstructs the setting behind the Deuteronomistic history. We have already discussed the chief problem with this use of historical reconstruction: the circularity of the argument. One posits a particular historical situation for a passage, finds a message in the passage which fits that situation, then uses the message to prove the historical situation. This procedure has serious consequences for actualization, because the historical reconstruction is used to impart theological significance to the pericope: the kerygmatic intention of the author is viewed in relation to the historical situation and is the basis for the actualization of the old traditions.

From these two applications we can understand the primary difficulty in the use of historical reconstruction in actualization. Actualization seeks to base the theological message of the Old Testament upon what the Old Testament itself says. However, with the use of historical reconstruction the message is based not so much on the text as on the reconstructed institutions, festivals, and situations which lie behind the text. Von Rad's claims for chronological actualization are seriously weakened if his highly debatable covenant renewal festival is false; Wolff's kerygma for the E document hinges upon a fragmentary and dubious link to an historical situation. If a different historical situation is posited for E, the document's theological message could be considerably altered. One example of this difference emerges in a comparison between Artur Weiser and Claus Westermann on the psalms. Weiser chooses to base his analysis of the psalms upon Israel's reconstructed festivals. In so doing he finds numerous examples of cultic actualization.[115] Westermann does not base his work on such reconstructions, but concentrates on the text itself. As a result he finds no linguistic evidence for cultic re-enactment in the psalms, but posits another, quite different variety of actualization.[116] This leads to significantly different interpretations of the psalms.

The relationship among historical reconstruction, form criticism, and actualization is complex. Both Weiser and Westermann apply form criticism to actualization in the psalms. Yet, Westermann eschews historical reconstruction, with a strong resultant impact upon his studies. Nevertheless, in order to understand the history of Israel, one needs to reach behind the Old Testament text and describe institutions and situations. Indeed, many times a convincing historical argument can bring new light to a problematic text. So the major question here is not the validity of historical reconstruction *per se*. Rather, it is the relationship of historical reconstruction and theology: can the former be allowed to govern the theological meaning of a text?

Obviously, many Old Testament scholars believe so, for this is the focus of their attacks upon von Rad. They claim that he has not based his theology upon historical facts, but upon faith-centered interpretations of possible events. Most of them overlook the fact that his interpretations, as well as those of other proponents of actualization, are in the final analysis the result of modern historical methods, for they are based upon historical reconstructions which influence and sometimes determine the theological message of a passage.

Before we resolve this question, we need to study a second, related issue that arises out of the contact between actualization and the historical-critical method: that of historical specificity. This issue is more closely linked to tradition criticism than to form criticism. It

---

[115]Weiser, *Psalms*, 23-35.

[116]Westermann, "Vergegenwärtigung," 260-62.

rests upon Gunkel's insight that traditions slowly change with the times and that the expression of a particular tradition at a particular time is governed by the needs and interests of that historical period.[117] Tradition criticism took this insight and developed it into the idea of the continual re-use of traditions. Von Rad extends this idea to say that one cannot fully understand a particular passage unless one knows its historical situation.[118]

However, actualization takes this insight one step further. Any particular Old Testament passage does not merely arise from a specific historical situation, but speaks to that situation. Here we have a close interrelation of a general tradition-critical insight and the kerygmatic theology usually associated with actualization. Every Old Testament passage is religious in nature and therefore must have a message to proclaim. This message is so specific that it is valid only for that particular generation; each new generation must actualize the traditions for itself in a message that fits its own time.[119]

Contributing to this view of historical specificity is an idea originating in both form and tradition criticism: the theory that each reworking of Old Testament traditions is a response to a crisis in Israel's history. Crisis is loosely defined as political (the exile, for example), intellectual (the stimulating atmosphere of the Solomonic court) or religious (the cult's encounter with secularization). However, despite the disparate nature of the crises, each causes a spiritual turmoil that forces Israel to rethink its traditions and issues in a new actualization of the old materials. The theory has the further benefit of making it easy to pinpoint the historical situation of a particular passage. The crises and key events in Israel's history are much better known than the slow intermediate periods. Thus, we find that scholars tie most Old Testament passages and documents to a relatively few key events in Israel's long history. Their favorites are the Solomonic period for earlier material and the exile for later passages. Indeed, many passages can be legitimately dated to a specific period. However, at some point the crisis theory becomes a self-fulfilling prophecy. If one

---

[117]Gunkel, *Legends*, 88-122. This insight applied to history in general dates back to Herder, who saw the need to treat each historical period in its specificity rather than to judge all periods by modern criteria: *Philosophy*, 181-83.

[118]This idea permeates his understanding of the prophetic re-use of tradition. See particularly von Rad's *Theology*, 2.35, 48-49, 80.

[119]*Ibid.*

expects each passage to be responding to a crisis, then surely an appropriate crisis can be found. This in turn influences the interpretation of the passage, since it is seen in light of the crisis. The result is the same circularity of argumentation that we encountered with historical reconstruction.

Perhaps Gunkel's original statement of the manner in which old traditions are re-used is the most appropriate cautionary remark for the crisis theory: "Slowly and hesitantly, always at a certain distance behind, the legends follow the general changes in conditions, some more, others less."[120] Undoubtedly, many Old Testament passages are an immediate response to a specific historical situation. This is especially true in the work of the prophets, with their eyes focused on the contemporary political situation. However, Gunkel's considerably different focus is also valid. Old traditions change slowly; cults are by nature conservative. Thus, to associate material with the cult (for example, Deuteronomy and the J document), and then to link the same material to a specific crisis (as von Rad and Wolff do) is quite risky. It is an equally tenable theory that many Old Testament passages respond to a general change in conditions or arise from periods of quiet reflection in Israel's history. However, this alternative theory, while it is quite amenable to tradition criticism, undercuts the particular theological application of actualization. Kerygmatic intention and proclamation are necessarily tied to a theory of crises; it is unlikely that they would be responses to gradual change and quiet reflection.

Von Rad is much more circumspect in his use of the crisis theory than are some other proponents of actualization. Wolff, Ackroyd, Childs, and Steck, for varying reasons, are much more inclined to tie their analyses of material to particular historical crises than is von Rad. However, the most likely reason for this is the greater specificity of their work. Von Rad, dealing in sweeping terms with large bodies of material, remains on a more general and consequently more vague level. The application of the crisis theory by these other men is a natural consequence of von Rad's method.

A further consequence of historical specificity is the limitation of the validity of the text. An oracle is theologically valid for only one time – its original situation. Any re-use of the text entails a further reinterpretation. However, this runs counter to the canonical process at

---

[120]Gunkel, *Legends,* 99.

work in the Old Testament. In the later history psalms Westermann finds within actualization a trend to reinterpret material "for all generations," rather than one specific time. Von Rad recognizes that parts of Deuteronomy acted as a standard for later generations. The standards of Deuteronomy were not rewritten, but simply applied by later ages.[121] Numerous examples of the canonization process in the Old Testament have been traced by various schools of Old Testament interpretation.[122] What we need to note in connection with actualization is that the canonization process, which concluded with the fixation of both the number of books and the texts of those books for the Old and New Testaments, regards the Biblical material as eternally valid, good for all generations. This is directly contrary to the concept of historical specificity. While one cannot deny that historical specificity did function in the Old Testament, especially in relation to the prophetic oracles, one cannot deny that the counter-trend of canonization was also present. As Westermann has shown, its focus "for all generations" can also be regarded as a type of actualization, although of a considerably different nature than chronological actualization.

A further result of both historical reconstruction and historical specificity as they are applied in form and tradition criticism (as well as in source criticism) is the atomization of the text. Both reconstruction and specificity focus our attention on the original situation of a passage in isolation. Indeed, reconstruction may force us back behind the passage as we now have it to an Ur-text considerably different than the final form. The textual connections to the surrounding passages are minimized or overlooked all together. The two most obvious examples connected with actualization are the isolation of the original words of a prophet and the division of the Pentateuch into sources. In both cases the texts as we have them are not only fragmented, but new entities are also constructed. These new entities carry a different message than the final text. The numerous attempts to explore the theology of the

---

[121]Von Rad, *Theology*, 1.335-36, 339-41.

[122]For example, see Brevard Childs, "The Old Testament as Scripture of the Church," *CTM*, 43 (1972) 709-22; "The Canonical Shape of the Prophetic Literature," *Int*, 33 (1978) 46-55; Sanders, *Torah;* Bloch, "Midrash"; Le Deáut, "Midrash"; Isaac Seeligmann, "Voraussetzungen der Midraschexegese,"*VTSup*, 1 (1953) 150-81; Burke Long and George Coats, eds., *Canon and Authority* (Philadelphia: Fortress, 1977); Knight,*Tradition*, 261-300.

Yahwist is a good example of this.[123] Von Rad's reduction of Isaiah's message to the themes of Zion and David is another.[124] Of course, there is value in understanding the process by which the Pentateuch was constructed, or in reconstructing the message of a prophet. The questionable aspect of this endeavor comes in the link which actualization makes with theology, imparting theological value to the reconstructed entity. Neither the J document nor Isaiah's words exist now except as hypothetical reconstructions. They have not been treated as theological entities in the history of Jewish or Christian exegesis until the modern historical-critical period. The primary context in which these words now rest is not in relation to other J passages or Isaianic oracles, but in relation to passages from other documents or secondary prophetic additions. Many times the two are so inextricably linked that they cannot be separated without doing great violence to the final text.

Von Rad and other proponents of actualization claim to have rescued the secondary material in the prophets from obscurity and returned it to a place of theological validity.[125] Compared to Wellhausen's scornful dismissal of non-genuine words, they have. However, all that actualization has done is to create more layers of interpretation in the prophetic literature to go along with the original layer. At no point have they pressed far enough to restore the relation of primary and secondary materials or to consider a prophetic book as a book. In summary, actualization has made no real attempt to defend the imparting of theological validity to reconstructed documents and atomized texts. It assumes that since this reconstruction and atomization is a legitimate result of the historical-critical method that theological validity follows naturally.

Gerhard von Rad and the other proponents of actualization are accomplished practitioners of modern historical-critical techniques. Their work, consistently grounded in form and tradition criticism, includes some of the most astute and discriminating applications of that

---

[123]In addition to von Rad, *Genesis*, 13-43, *Theology*, 1.105-305, and Wolff, *Vitality*, 41-66, see Peter Ellis, *The Yahwist, The Bible's First Theologian* (Notre Dame: Fides, 1968); Lothar Ruppert, "Der Jahwist -- Künder der Heilsgeschichte," in *Wort und Botschaft* (ed. Josef Schreiner; Würzburg: Echter, 1967) 88-107.

[124]Von Rad, *Theology*, 2.147-75.

[125]*Ibid.*, 46-49, 168; Ackroyd, "Vitality," 18-19.

art in contemporary Old Testament scholarship. Yet von Rad's method is attacked for departing from the historical orthodoxy of our day with its focus upon the "critically assured minimum" as the basis for all Old Testament interpretation, be it historical, theological, or practical. These attacks reveal a limited understanding of his work in relation to historical criticism. Von Rad's acceptance of historical reconstruction, specificity, and atomization as basic ingredients in his interpretation demonstrates that he remains solidly in agreement with modern critical theory. While his move toward a theological evaluation of Israel's faith-centered interpretations of God's saving acts is a deviation that should be criticized and investigated, we must keep in mind that von Rad still relies upon an historical-critical view of Israel's history and religion for his understanding of these events. The hermeneutical procedures of actualization rest upon modern critical methods in the final analysis.

3

Actualization posits an ideal theological-historical equation for the Old Testament: an historical-critical investigation (legitimate because the Bible is historically based) operating upon the Old Testament traditions reveals the faith-centered theological categories of the traditionary process itself; these theological categories derived from the Old Testament are in turn related to our contemporary setting through retelling. That the actuality of the method falls short of this ideal comes as no surprise. We ask too much of both the Old Testament and our modern methods of research to expect either a ready corollary of theological categories or an easy application of modern historical techniques, much less both simultaneously. We have discovered that both ends of the theological-historical equation strain the fabric of actualization. The theological categories generated by actualization reflect the contemporary scene too closely, produce tensions with the historical methodology employed, and distort and limit the full theological range of the Old Testament. The traditio-historical method too often results in circular arguments, tenuous reconstructions, and fragmentation of the text, which make the critical method the master of the text and determinitive for its interpretation. While actualization aspires to an excellent ideal and partially meets those goals by focusing more upon the text than most Old Testament theological enterprises, in the final analysis the method is too weak to carry the weight of the tensions, omissions, and distortions of the modern methodologies which it uses to operate on the Old Testament. The goal of an inner-Biblical base for a theological-historical interpretation of the Old Testament is yet to be achieved.

Summary

This chapter has demonstrated that the method of chronological actualization falls short of its espoused goals because of its internal weaknesses and inconsistencies. The three most important lapses in the method are its inability to demonstrate the uniqueness of Biblical contemporization, the unity of scripture necessary for an overall theological interpretation, or the centrality of chronological actualization. The elements which von Rad considered unique in chronological actualization – the element of identity and a special sense of time and history – are unproven assumptions. His particular application of the traditio-historical method results in distorted emphases and major omissions that undermine any sense of unity. Lacking both uniqueness and unity, the Old Testament appears as discrete sets of disparate material, some utilizing elements of contemporization, others employing different interpretive methods, rather than chronological actualization functioning as a central, overarching interpretative method. With these evident difficulties, we must search for another basis for the theological interpretation of the Old Testament.

What, then, has actualization been able to demonstrate about the Old Testament and the possibilities of theological interpretation? While the questions which we have raised undermine the presence of chronological actualization in the Bible, they do not question the basic insights gained into the re-use of old traditions. Actualization has firmly established that the Pentateuch, the Deuteronomistic history, and the prophetic corpus have this re-use at the core of their interpretive procedures. This re-use may lack the unique characteristics of chronological actualization, but its general lineaments fit the category of literary contemporization. Therefore, we would like to suggest that a type (or types) of contemporization related to literary actualization does occur in significant portions of the Old Testament. In the next chapter we will expand upon this suggestion and begin to seek ways in which it may contribute to the interpretation of the Old Testament, both theologically and non-theologically.

Chapter Four

Towards a Redefinition of Actualization

In the previous chapter we considered the problems with the internal logic of chronological actualization. This final chapter will approach the concept from a different angle. We will study three Old Testament passages as illustrative examples relating to actualization. Each discussion will first focus upon one of the problems with chronological actualization which we encountered in chapter three. This approach will provide a firm, specific example to flesh out the general discussion of the previous chapter and demonstrate how the application of chronological actualization can lead to a distorted interpretation of a passage. Then, we will present some alternative suggestions on interpreting each passage. These alternatives will give us some direction in redefining actualization in a way that more closely reflects the handling and interpretation of tradition in the Old Testament than does chronological actualization.

These studies will be illustrative and suggestive rather than comprehensive and definitive. A complete redefinition of actualization would require numerous, detailed studies of the type von Rad produced in developing the concept originally. That task is clearly beyond the scope of this study. What we can accomplish in this chapter is to put forth some suggestions about the direction of that redefinition.

Our concern is to view each passage in relation to actualization, not in relation to the totality of Biblical scholarship. Consequently, the discussion will focus upon the use of the passage by the proponents of actualization and upon alternative suggestions. Other secondary exegetical references will be introduced only when they relate directly to the discussion at hand.

Deuteronomy 5:1-3:
The Problem of the Hebrew Concept of Time

We have already noted that an important part of the concept of chronological actualization is the special nature of time for the Hebrews. For the proponents of the concept, "redemptive time" incorporates the qualities of the immediate presentness of cultic time and the sense of progression of chronological time. The Biblical evidence for this special time sense rests primarily upon references in Deuteronomy. The use of הַיּוֹם ("today"), הַיּוֹם הַזֶּה ("this day"), and the first person plural pronoun (especially in such extended constructions as Deut 5:1-5 and 29:10-14) demonstrate that the author was concerned with making these sermons vitally alive, immediately present for his audience.[1] His total absorption in this task results in the presence of redemptive time. This concept of time is determinative for the nature of actualization in the Old Testament.

However, as well as criticizing redemptive time on theological grounds, we may question its presence in the Old Testament on exegetical grounds. Nowhere in the discussions of actualization are the passages used as evidence treated in context.[2] The words and phrases concerning time are discussed in isolation, apart from the function of the passage as a whole. More thorough redaction-critical and form-critical studies, performed by Norbert Lohfink and Simon DeVries,[3] have resulted in significantly different conclusions about these words and phrases.

We will examine one of these passages, Deut 5:1-3,[4] from an alternative point of view, focusing upon the nature and function of the language used in the passage in the context of Deuteronomy. This approach does not contradict the previous redaction-critical and form-

---

[1]Von Rad, *Hexateuch*, 28; *Studies in Deuteronomy*, 70; *Theology*, 1.231; *Theology*, 2.108-10; *Deuteronomy*, 20-30.

[2]Von Rad places them in context in *Deuteronomy*. However, actualization plays a minor role in the commentary and is not mentioned at all in his exposition of the specific passages.

[3]Norbert Lohfink, *Das Hauptgebot* (Rome: Pontificio Institutio Biblico, 1963); Simon DeVries, *Yesterday, Today, and Tomorrow* (Grand Rapids: Eerdmans, 1975).

[4]While verses 1-3 are not the limits of the form-critical unit, these verses contain all the time references in the passage as well as the significant rhetorical phrases. The rationale for omitting verses 4-5 will emerge more clearly in the course of the study.

critical work; indeed, it draws from the studies of both Lohfink and DeVries. However, questioning the functioning of the language itself is more closely linked to the idea of redemptive time than is a pure redaction or form-critical approach. Specifically, we shall ask whether or not the nature of the rhetoric in Deut 5:1-3 can account for the admittedly unusual and convoluted time constructs in this passage without resorting to a separate Hebrew time sense.

This question of the rhetorical function of language is one for which von Rad has evinced concern. He demonstrates his concern most obviously in describing Deut 5-11 as paraenetic and homiletical. However, he fails to expand upon this allusion even in his detailed exposition in *Deuteronomy*. He is content to regard the language of these chapters as the repetitive residuum of preaching activity without pursuing the implications of such a statement.

More important to von Rad is the delineation of the subsections of the book and the study of their traditio-historical roots and theological message. While he admits that the book must be understood finally as a unity, his exegesis concentrates on the picture of Deuteronomy as a "mosaic of innumerable, extremely varied pieces of traditional material."[5] This concentration upon the small units has considerable exegetical value. At the same time it produces blind spots which lie at the heart of von Rad's analysis of Deuteronomy and the nature of actualization. Although he recognizes a remarkably uniform use of language in Deuteronomy, his concentration upon small units allows him to abstract the book's concern about time from the total language picture and use these words in isolation as a basis for actualization. He further identifies extremely small units of two to four verses as sermons. While one may have a rounded homiletical unit of such brevity, it is surely misleading to regard this as a sermon. This may seem like an overly fine point of criticism, but such an attitude has serious consequences. Designating these brief passages as the basic homiletical units prevents von Rad from analyzing the effect of language in Deuteronomy in the broader context of the collected rhetorical or literary units of the book. This results in the vague references to paraenetic/homiletical material.

The context in which the words concerning time occur consists of three concentric circles. The innermost circle is the surrounding words

---

[5]Von Rad, *Deuteronomy*, 12-13.

and phrases of Deut 5:1-3. The primary question addressed to this context concerns how the words of time interact with the remaining words and phrases to form a rhetorical entity. The middle circle is the whole of the central paraenetic section of Deuteronomy, chapters 5-11.[6] The words and phrases of the opening pericope echo and re-echo in the succeeding chapters. The nature of this repetition and its positioning in chapters 5-11 shed further light on the nature of the Deuteronomic rhetoric. The outer circle is the whole of Deuteronomy. To examine this context is beyond the scope of this brief study. For our purposes the context of chapters 5-11 is sufficient to generalize about the whole book.

We may move freely from one circle to the next because of the general agreement among commentators on the unity of language in Deuteronomy. Although chapters 5-11 are composed of disparate units and there is even a question concerning the unity of 5:1-5,[7] we may regard these chapters as a collected and organized body of homiletical material. Repetition of words, phrases, and syntactical constructions is a basic feature of the entire book.

Deut 5:1-5 occupies a pivotal position in these chapters, since it serves both as the beginning of Moses' second speech to the people of Israel and as an introduction to the decalogue in 5:6-22. As one might expect in such a prominent location, these verses (especially 5:1-3) are a gold mine of Deuteronomic exhortatory phraseology. The speech begins with the summons שְׁמַע יִשְׂרָאֵל ("Hear, O Israel"), the imperative followed by the vocative. The referent for this opening phrase is the commandment of God (the חֻקִּים and the מִשְׁפָּטִים). Thus, Moses' address begins with a ringing call to obedience in standard Deuteronomic phraseology. More significant than the words themselves is the function which the command to hear/obey serves in this opening verse and in the rest of the central paraenesis. The call is repeated in the imperative in 6:4 and 9:1; other forms of the verb "to hear" (שׁמע) used in the same sense occur in 6:3, 8:20, 9:23, and

---

[6]We are following the generally accepted division of the book into chapters 1-4 as the opening historical retrospective (generally regarded as a later addition), 5-11 as the central paraenesis, 12-26 as the main body of laws, 27-34 as the concluding sections (many of a later date). For detailed expositions see: Martin Noth, *Überlieferungsgeschichtlichen Studien* (1941; rpt. Tübingen: M. Niemeyer, 1967); von Rad, *Deuteronomy;* Lohfink, *Hauptgebot,* 3-9; DeVries, *Yesterday,* 164-86.

[7]Lohfink, *Hauptgebot,* 145-8; DeVries, *Yesterday,* 173-4.

11:13,27,28.[8] With the exception of 9:23 all of these appearances of שמע are at significant junctures in the text.

The double occurrence in 6:3-4 is especially instructive. In 6:3 וְשָׁמַעְתָּ serves a dual purpose. First, it harkens back to 5:1 and marks the conclusion of the opening exhortation with a chiastic call to obedience. While the imperative is not employed in this verse, the verb carries imperative force, especially when coupled with the following vocative, "O, Israel." Second, שמע acts as a bridge to the next section, which opens in 6:4 with the same "Hear, O Israel" as 5:1. Here the referent is not the general sweep of the commandments, but one specific statute and its exposition. Thus, while carrying the same exhortatory force as 5:1, the phrase in 6:4 clearly refers to a more limited section.

A similar conclusion/bridge/introduction occurs in 8:20 and 9:1. In 8:20 תִשְׁמְעוּן in a non-emphatic position closes out the exhortation. The sense here is the opposite of that encountered previously. Its referent, the voice of Yahweh, carries the same sense as the commandments, but the negative particle is attached and the verse refers to the disobedience of Israel. The verb also acts as a bridge, since in 9:1 we again encounter שְׁמַע יִשְׂרָאֵל, introducing another exhortatory section.

The verb שמע does not mark all of the transitions in chapters 5-11. The emphatic use which we have been considering is almost wholly absent in chapters 7-8.[9] (It is noteworthy that most of the strongly exhortatory phraseology which we will consider is also missing in these chapters.) The one significant transition which lacks שמע is 10:12, where the concluding exhortation for these chapters begins. However, although the imperative verb is lacking, the vocative is present and the exhortatory note is carried forward by a rhetorical question. The force of the exhortation increases as this concluding section progresses. The increased tempo includes three occurrences of שמע. While none of them is in the imperative, 11:13 is strengthened and emphasized by the infinitive absolute. Then, at the beginning of the final pericope, 11:26-32, there is a double occurrence of the verb,

---

[8] A similar use of the imperative in Deuteronomy occurs outside chapters 5-11 only in 4:1, 20:3, and 27:9. Other forms of the verb conveying the same sense of obedience are frequent.

[9] The only occurrence of שמע in these chapters is תִשְׁמְעוּן in 7:12.

first in the positive sense of obedience, then emphasized by repetition in the negative.

In summary, we find that the writer uses the verb שמע, frequently in the imperative and accompanied by the vocative, at each major point of exhortation in Deut 5-11: the opening and close of the first exhortation of 5:1-6:3; the opening of the second exhortation in 6:4; and the concluding exhortation of the section, 10:12-11:32 (which is introduced by the vocative alone). In addition the combination is used to signal a lesser transition between chapters eight and nine.

Lohfink regards these as structural signals and catchwords.[10] They certainly function in this way, but their significance transcends the mere catchword. They act as structural signals because they occur at rhetorical high points in the material. At key points in the passage they elevate and intensify the language to a level beyond that of mere narrative or recitation of the law. Phrases such as "Hear, O Israel" justify the description of Deuteronomy as exhortatory, since they impart to the language that which characterizes exhortation: an intensity beyond the everyday. Thus, the use of the phrase to open 5:1-3 is appropriate and consistent with the use of language in the whole of Deut 5-11.

Following this opening call ot obedience is the clause אֲשֶׁר אָנֹכִי דֹּבֵר בְּאָזְנֵיכֶם הַיּוֹם ("that I am speaking in your hearing today"). Lohfink refers to this as a promulgation formula, defined as a relative clause introduced by אֲשֶׁר which modifies one or more of the synonyms for commandment.[11] The formula frequently follows such words and identifies the commandment, usually by naming the speaker and stating the fact of proclamation.[12] An additional reference to the time of proclamation is often added with the appearance of הַיּוֹם.[13]

The promulgation formula is of no great rhetorical interest in and of itself; the words themselves do not excite or raise the level of the language. However, through repetition and altered wording the writer

---

[10]Lohfink, *Hauptgebot,* 66-67.

[11]Lohfink, *Hauptgebot,* 59-63, 297-98. Also see DeVries,*Yesterday,* 186, and "The Development of the Deuteronomic Promulgation Formula,"*Bib* 55 (1974) 301-16.

[12]Lohfink, *Hauptgebot,* 297-98. In Deut 4:45-28:68 the speaker is in most instances either Yahweh (10 times stated; 5 times implied) or אָנֹכִי (27 times); the most common verb is some form of צוה (45 times out of 50).

[13]הַיּוֹםappears in 21 of the 50 cases.

employs the formula rhetorically. The clause in 5:1 is unique in its wording with neither דָּבָר nor בְּאָזְנֵיכֶם employed elsewhere in a paraenetic setting of the formula.[14] Rhetorically, בְּאָזְנֵיכֶם strengthens the opening שְׁמַע and reinforces the face-to-face encounter of Yahweh and the people at the proclamation of the decalogue mentioned in 5:4. The unique wording further stresses the importance of 5:1 as a central verse to the entire address.

The significance of the formula is strengthened by the presence of הַיּוֹם in this particular occurrence. This sets Moses' speech squarely in the present and focuses it upon the audience at hand. With its presence in the very first verse of the speech, there can be no doubt on the listeners' part that they are subjects of what is to follow. We will pursue the significance of the time reference further in connection with verse three, since הַיּוֹם is reiterated there and the use of the promulgation formula is the question presently at hand.

Both the repetition of the formula and the clustering of the repetitions contribute to its rhetorical significance. Although the phrase is related to commandments and laws, its occurrences are clustered in the paraenetic sections of Deuteronomy. Of the eighty occurrences of the formula, fifty-one are in the highly rhetorical contexts of chapters 4-11 and 28-30. Even within the central paraenesis the formula is prevalent in the portions which we have already discussed as intensely exhortatory: Deut 5:1-6:20 and 10:12-11:32 have nineteen of the twenty-five occurrences in chapters 5-11.[15]

Of particular interest in relation to 5:1 are two clusters of the formula. Deut 5:31-6:3 has five repetitions in the space of six verses. Thus, the formula stated once in the opening verse of the speech helps build the homily to a climax through its repetitions, some from the mouth of God, others from Moses. A similar process occurs in the

---

[14]The verb דבר appears in 4:45 in a superscription in the third person. It is probably influenced by the form of 5:1.

[15]A general breakdown on the distribution of the promulgation formula is as follows: chapters 1-3, 4 times; chapters 4:1-44, 10 times; chapters 4:45-11:32, 25 times; chapters 12-27, 19 times; chapters 28-30, 16 times; chapters 31-34, 4 times. Lohfink's list of formulas for 4:45-28:68 (*Hauptgebot*, 297-98) includes some very loose examples, in which the relative clause does not modify one of the synonyms for commandment. If we apply a more strict definition, the total number of occurrences is reduced to 65, of which 47 occur in the homiletical sections. The preponderance of the formula in these homiletical contexts confirms our conclusion that the clause is a rhetorical device.

concluding exhortation of the central paraenesis, 10:12-11:32. The promulgation formula is the final clause of the rhetorical question which opens this section (10:12-13). Then, after three scattered appearances in 10:14-11:25, the climactic section of the exhortation has a three-fold repetition of the formula. The two appearances in 11:26 form a striking combination: first, blessing, שׁמע, promulgation formula with היום; then, cursing, the negative particle, שׁמע, promulgation formula with היום. This sets before Israel with stark simplicity the choice which it faces. The final occurrence of the formula is the last clause of chapter eleven, the conclusion to the central paraenesis.

Despite the quite ordinary language of the promulgation formula, it plays a significant rhetorical role in chapters 5-11. In the first and last sections, the clause occurs once in the introductory pericope and then recurs in the concluding pericope in drumming repetition. This pattern raises these sections to an inexorable climax and leaves the audience no doubt about the nature of the message: this is the commandment of God to be obeyed for blessing or ignored at great peril.

Rounding off 5:1 is a series of verbs: למד and שׁמר in the perfect consecutive and עשׂה in the infinitive construct. Lohfink has shown that these along with שׁמע are the four verbs most commonly used in calling for obedience to the commandments.[16] As here, they are frequently strung together for reinforcement. However, in the other occurrences of the imperative of שׁמע, the verb stands alone. Only here in the opening verse of chapters 5-11 do we encounter reiteration with the force of the imperative. Indeed, this is the only place in Deuteronomy where all four verbs appear together. Consequently, the verbs work together to deliver an extremely forceful call to obedience. Further, the use of all four verbs gives the audience a preview of the author's vocabulary. Each further use of one of these verbs reiterates and recalls God's demand to obey. The use of these verbs in combination as a rhetorical device is further illuminated by the conclusion to the exhortation in 6:3. As we have already seen, the verse begins with the call "Hear, O Israel" (although not in the imperative). It is followed immediately by שׁמר and עשׂה.[17] This

---

[16]Lohfink, *Hauptgebot*, 64-72, 299-302.

[17]Although all the verbs are repeated in 5:2-6:2, there is never a series of three of the verbs connected. Thus, special emphasis falls upon 5:1 and 6:3.

concluding series recapitulates the opening one and further echoes the call to obedience.

Seen in the context of chapters 5-11, Deut 5:1 has tremendous rhetorical impact. Moses announces a call to obedience, identifies it, locates it in time, and drives it home with emphasis and repetition. Each word and phrase links together to heighten the total impact of the verse. Through this tight construction the author encapsulates several rhetorical elements which he repeatedly uses for exhortatory emphasis in these chapters.

The notable rhetorical feature of 5:2, one which continues in 5:3, is the use of the first person plural by Moses to refer to himself and the people of Israel as a unit. While this use of we/us/our is common in Deut 1-4,[18] this verse provides the only similar instance in Deut 5-11. The function and impact of the use of the first person plural are apparent only in contrast to the use of pronouns in the remainder of chapters 5-11. Throughout these chapters the second person singular and plural pronouns predominate, as Moses addresses the people and establishes a certain distance between himself as deliverer of the law and the people as recipients. The only significant variations, apart from 5:2-3, occur in 5:24-31 and 6:20-25.

Deut 5:24-31 is part of the conclusion to the decalogue, 5:22-6:3, which establishes the role of Moses as mediator between God and the people. Two deviations from the general pattern of pronoun use occur in this section. The first is in verses 24-27. This section is a speech of the people to Moses, couched in the first person plural. The use of we/us/our fourteen times in the course of four verses is clearly a rhetorical device. It not only calls attention to these verses but also sets them in sharp contrast to the words of Moses. The limits of the speech are firmly set, and no doubt remains about the identify ot the speaker.[19]

A similar device is used in 5:28-31. Here Yahweh is the speaker and the speech is put in the first person singular. Once again we encounter repetition (six times in four verses) and emphasis at the

---

[18]See Deut 1:19-21; 2:1,8,13,30,32-37; 3:1,3-7,12.

[19]The difference is further sharpened by clusters of the first person plural at the beginning of the speech (the first and third words) and at the end of the speech (three of the last four words).

beginning and end of the speech (אָנֹכִי is the opening word and I/me/my occurs three times in the last verse).

The change in person in these two sections clarifies the narrative, enlivens it, and emphasizes the point being made. It clarifies by giving each speaker a separate pronoun: Moses speaks in the second person (with one lapse into the first person singular in 5:28); the people use the first person plural; Yahweh uses the first person singular. Consequently, each speaker is clearly identified and the extent of the speech sharply defined. It enlivens the narrative by breaking up the address by Moses and introducing other speakers. This change in voice is useful in maintaining interest in the exhortation. The point of the narrative is the establishment of Moses' mediatorial role. Instead of merely explaining the role, the writer demonstrates it by allowing the various participants to make speeches. Each speech is directed to Moses; the people and God never have a direct encounter.

The changes in person in this section are a highly effective rhetorical device that performs several interrelated functions. It is an indication of the sophisticated literary ability of the author of this section. While the device in 5:2-3 is the same as in 5:24-27, the effect is quite different. In the former the use of we/us/our indicates the solidarity of Moses and the people; in the latter it serves to distinguish one from the other and to define their separate roles.

The other encounter with the first person plural occurs in 6:20-25. Here it appears in response to a rhetorical/catechetical question: "What is the meaning of the testimonies?" The people respond in the first person plural, repeated fifteen times in six verses. Its use here indicates the solidarity of later generations with the generation of the exodus. However, the effect is still quite different from that of 5:2-3. In the earlier pericope the emphasis is upon the identification of two specific generations at a specific place, Horeb. In 6:20-25 the effect is a timeless identification: instead of a speech by Moses, one receives a recital of events which includes all generations, past, present, and future. The absence of the time identification, הַיּוֹם, enhances this sense.[20]

---

[20]The one time reference which occurs is כְּהַיּוֹם הַזֶּה in 6:24. It has the sense of "like today" in this context (see DeVries, *Yesterday,* 52). It does not carry the force of הַיּוֹם.

To summarize, we should note that each set of we/us/our in Deuteronomy occurs in a different setting and functions differently. Deut 5:2-3 appears in the exhortatory introduction. Coupled with הַיּוֹם, it creates a sense of solidarity and immediacy for a later generation. This sense ties it to a particular moment in time: the giving of the law at Horeb. After the ringing command to obey in 5:1, which implies a distance between Moses as proclaimer and the people as recipients, the author switches to the inclusive first person. This switch stresses the people's intimate involvement with the commandments which follow. The covenant is not an "other," but a present reality with which they are inextricably entwined.

The second appearance, in 5:24-27, occurs in a narrative section of Moses' address. It is a sophisticated rhetorical device which functions quite differently in this context. Instead of creating solidarity between generations, it dramatizes the distinction between Moses (and ultimately Yahweh) and the people. The final occurrence in 6:20-25 responds to a rhetorical question, where it becomes a timeless "we."

Consequently, the use of the first person plural in Deuteronomy does not indicate the vivid immediacy of chronological actualization. This change in persons may serve various functions. Only once in the central paraenetic section of the book does the author use it to create a sense of immediacy. This is slim evidence indeed for constructing a unique sense of time. Instead, the varied, elegant use of the change in persons in Deuteronomy indicates the rhetorical skill of the author and his ability to intensify and enliven language for exhortatory effect. These conclusions emphasize the need to study such devices in context rather than in isolation.

Verse three continues -- indeed, redoubles -- the emphasis upon we/us/our and reiterates the time identification of verse one. We have postponed the discussion of time identification until now to show that the frequent repetition of הַיּוֹם in Deuteronomy is not as unusual a feature as the proponents of chronological actualization would make it seem. Repetition is a rhetorical characteristic of the book and applies to all the other elements of this pericope -- the call to obedience, the words for the commandment, the verbs used, the promulgation formula, the use of the first person plural -- as much as it does to הַיּוֹם.[21] No

---

[21]Indeed, both שמע and the promulgation formula appear more frequently than הַיּוֹם and its equivalents, which have only 61 occurrences in Deut.

special time sense is necessary to explain the frequent appearance of
הַיּוֹם; the rhetorical nature of Deuteronomy's language is sufficient
cause. This explanation of the phenomenon is enhanced by the
frequency with which הַיּוֹם occurs in conjunction with the other devices
we have considered.[22]

In addition to the time identification in 5:3 a particularly good
example of the repetitive use of הַיּוֹם occurs in 11:26-32, the
concluding pericope of the central paraenesis. We have already noted
the presence of other rhetorical features in these verses: שְׁמַע as a
demand for obedience, and the promulgation formula. In addition הַיּוֹם
appears four times, thrice in a promulgation formula. However, it is
the positioning of הַיּוֹם in the passage that is particularly significant.
It appears in the opening clause of 11:26 in a non-emphatic position.
Then in 11:27-28 it occurs twice in the promulgation formula coupled
with שְׁמַע. The final instance is in 11:32, where it is the concluding
word of the central paraenesis, again in the promulgation formula.
Despite the repetition of הַיּוֹם in this passage it acts merely as an
ancillary rhetorical device. The stress lies upon the choice between
blessing and cursing which Moses places before the people. הַיּוֹם acts
to emphasize the urgency of that choice, reiterating the need to make it
"right now." However, an exhortation to decide at this moment in time
is quite different from creating a unique time sense or dissolving the
time barrier. Although the central paraenesis, which opens with an
emphasis upon "today" in 5:1-3, closes with a reiteration of the same
theme, the element of time identification is almost incidental in the
concluding pericope.

However, a different situation pertains in 5:3. The repeated use of
הַיּוֹם and the first person plural in this verse places the emphasis
squarely upon the identification of two generations separated in time.
The result is an awkward syntax that pounds the point home with great
effect: אִתָּנוּ אֲנַחְנוּ אֵלֶּה פֹה הַיּוֹם כֻּלָּנוּ חַיִּים ("with us, we, these
here today, all of us living").

Von Rad and other commentators make much of the identification
posed here, stating that this emphatic affirmation of the people and time

---

[22]In addition to 5:2-3 and 11:26-32 there are several other good examples: 6:4-6
combines שְׁמַע יִשְׂרָאֵל, the promulgation formula, and הַיּוֹם; 9:1-3 has שְׁמַע יִשְׂרָאֵל,
הַיּוֹם, and a rhetorical question; 10:12 has the vocative, a rhetorical question, the
promulgation formula, and הַיּוֹם.

transports the audience at the period of Josiah back to Horeb. Through a rationalizing identification this verse supposedly carries the primitive power of the cult, which obliterates the time gap.

In fact such a facile identification misses the subtlety of the writer's artifice. Since Moses is delivering this speech after the wilderness wandering, the generation of Horeb is dead. We would expect Moses to utter such words, striving to make this later generation identify with their fathers who stood at Horeb. The device by which the author identifies the people of Josiah's time with the generation of Horeb is in fact a *double entendre:* they identify with the people to whom Moses speaks, the generation of the conquest, who are then related to the earlier generation at Horeb.[23] This is neither a primitive formulation nor a matter of the author "forgetting his part" as Noth suggests.[24] This verse demonstrates a use of language that is subtle, consistent, and engaging.

The identification of two separate generations is undoubtedly present in this verse. However, that identification is a conscious problem for the author. He is not governed by a special sense of time but creates a fictional identification by his manipulation of time words. This is evident from his use of the same rhetorical devices for differing purposes.

In conclusion, we have found that these verses act as an exceedingly effective introduction both to the decalogue and to the larger context of Deut 5-11. The introduction continues in 5:4-5, but with a diminution of the repetitive phrases and exhortatory style which are the central elements to our present study. Therefore, a consideration of Deut 5:1-3 is sufficient for our purposes. The effectiveness of these verses lies in the exhortatory nature of the language: it is intense, attention-getting, involving. However, its controlled use and subtle artifice suggest careful thought and literary construction rather than the primitive cult or the uncontrolled residue of that cult.

A full understanding of the use of language in Deut 5:1-3 emerges only in relation to its context. When the repetition of one word (such

---

[23] Several other examples of this problem of the generations occur in the Deuteronomic paraenesis (see particularly 11:2 and 29:9-14). Each of them promotes the identification of the people with earlier times with great rhetorical skill.

[24] Noth, "Re-presentation," 82.

as הַיּוֹם) in Deuteronomy is stressed apart from that context, the function of the word in the book can be distorted. When we perceive that such a word is part of a cluster of repetitious phrases, we can understand that it is part of a group of ideas that are stressed together in the exhortatory sections of Deuteronomy. Indeed, various configurations of phrases, by altering the stress or combining them with other key words, can emphasize different ideas. The same rhetorical device can perform different functions.

Consequently, there is no need for a unique time sense in Israel to explain the stress on "today" and the first person plural in Deuteronomy, as von Rad and Noth have postulated. To do so exhibits a certain naiveté concerning the function of language. They recognize the homiletical nature of Deuteronomy, but neglect to see how this influences the use of language. The purpose of exhortation is to persuade, not merely to entertain, to tell a story, or to impart wisdom. Neither is homily to be confused with history writing. Language functions differently in each of these settings. In exhortation the primary need is to engage the audience, to vivify the point being made. This is precisely the function of the repetition of הַיּוֹם and the other phrases in Deuteronomy. The time identifications in the book are part of an exhortatory scheme of elevated language and audience engagement, not of a separate time sense.

Does this mean that actualization is not present in Deuteronomy? In the sense of cultic or chronological actualization, it certainly is not. However, one method of persuading an audience through exhortation is to make a particular point immediately relevant. This may be regarded as a type of actualization, one that centers on audience engagement. This is an actualization in which the author is clearly aware of his art. In Deuteronomy the author has set up a studied fiction through the speech of Moses and actualizes this fiction by careful control of numerous rhetorical devices. Thus, we may refer to his use of language as actualization. However, it is a type of actualization related to the literary or aesthetic sphere, and not the unique category of chronological actualization set up by von Rad.

Through our study of the language of Deut 5:1-3 in its context, we have reached a very different sense of the verses than did von Rad or Noth. However, our study is not unrelated. It affirms the homiletical nature of the material and finds a type of actualization present. The contribution and corrective of our study lie in its stress upon the literary function and linguistic level of the words in a pericope and upon an analysis of those words in their larger context.

Amos 9:11-15: The Problem of Atomization

The treatment of Amos 9:11-15 by the historical-critical method highlights the problem of the atomization of the text which we discussed in chapter three. The majority of scholars holds that this unit is a later addition to the words of Amos. This conclusion has in turn focused discussion of the passage upon two issues: first, what evidence can be mustered to support the authenticity or the secondary nature of the passage; second, what is the meaning of the unit in and of itself, apart from the remainder of Amos? Indeed, once they have established the secondary nature of the passage, many commentators have regarded 9:11-15 as essentially meaningless to the rest of the book. The historical separation is translated into literary inferiority and theological unimportance.[25]

The proponents of actualization who have commented upon this passage (von Rad and Wolff in particular) have moved beyond this extreme negativity. They have sought to recover a positive theological message for the passage, although in very different ways. Von Rad uses actualization in a surprising manner in relation to 9:11-15. He defends the authenticity of the unit on the basis of Amos being a Judean:

> Things wear a different look, however, once we see the prophets as men who addressed themselves to definite sacral traditions as these still survived in the nation, and once we regard their whole preaching as a unique discussion of these ancient inherited traditions, a discussion which submitted them to criticism and made them relevant *(aktualisierenden)* for the prophets' own day and generation. Now, Amos was a Judean. Would it not surprise us if there had been absolutely no mention of the traditions in which he was most at home?[26]

He proceeds to comment on the restrained nature of the Messianic promise in the passage. However, he avoids discussing any of the

---

[25]For a particularly good example, see William R. Harper, *A Critical and Exegetical Commentary on Amos and Hosea* (New York: Scribner's, 1915) 195-200.

[26]Von Rad, *Theology*, 2.138.

arguments against attributing this oracle to Amos. More importantly, he fails to relate this oracle to the rest of the book. Even though it is the work of Amos, the oracle is seen in isolation from the remainder of the prophet's message. Since the passage forms a discrete form-critical unit and uses traditions not otherwise present in the book, he treats it as a unique, unrelated section.

Wolff uses actualization in a quite different manner. He views the oracle as secondary to Amos, yet related to his message because of actualization. Wolff separates Amos into several redactional layers, each of which is an actualization of the earlier material for a later time. In this vein Amos 9:11-15 updates Amos for the post-exilic period. The dating of the oracle, its form and meaning in isolation, and its parallels in other prophetic literature are Wolff's primary concerns. However, his concern for actualization has freed him to grant the oracle a positive theological value and to consider its relationship to the rest of Amos. His primary concern in this regard is to see how Amos' reinterpreted message fits the post-exilic period. He mentions a few of the points of contact between Amos 9:11-15 and the rest of the book. However, by failing to pursue these connections any further, he relegates them to a minor role in his analysis.[27] In his history of the post-Old Testament interpretation of the passage, he even uses the final paragraph to interpret the book as a whole.[28] His observations, although limited in scope, do open new windows on Amos as a unity.

Consequently, we can see that actualization has enabled Wolff to move beyond both the negative assessment of Amos 9:11-15 found in most historical-critical studies and the positive interpretation of von Rad which is isolated from its context. He is able to interpret the passage positively and begin to relate it to the bulk of the book. However, Wolff's interpretation still views the pericope as a separate, historically conditioned layer and fails to pursue fully its relationship to the book.

In the analysis which follows, we wish to push beyond Wolff to explore the literary relations between Amos 9:11-15 and the rest of the book. The study will deliberately ignore the usual historical-critical questions concerning the date and the specific historical situation of the various passages considered. Instead, in an effort to break the isolation

---

[27]Hans Walter Wolff, *Joel and Amos* (Philadelphia: Fortress, 1975) 353.

[28]Wolff, *Joel and Amos,* 355.

of Amos 9:11-15, we will focus upon the literary interpretation in its context. This method will consist of seeking out the linguistic and conceptual allusions -- without regard to the author's intention -- which connect the passage to the remainder of Amos and to the entire prophetic corpus.

The literary connections between the concluding oracle and the bulk of Amos are quite substantial. They begin with the connective phrases which introduce the two parts of the oracle: "in that day" (9:11a) and "behold, days are coming, says Yahweh" (9:13a). The former is a frequently used redactional connective in prophetic literature.[29] However, it occurs only one other time in Amos (8:13). The latter phrase is more distinctive: in this full form it occurs only in Jeremiah (fourteen times) and twice in Amos (9:13a and 8:11). The close proximity between the two phrases in each case (8:11,13; 9:11,13) leads one to look for literary relations between the two sets of material which they introduce. Indeed, such a relationship exists -- in the form of a double reversal.

The first reversal is a formal one: the order of occurrence of the phrases is changed. "Behold, days are coming, says Yahweh" is the initial phrase of 8:11-14. In this position it tends to dissociate 8:11-14 from the prior oracle without making a complete break. "In that day," following in 8:13, forms a synchronic connection to the preceding section, 8:11-12. Thus, one reads 8:11-14 as a unit with a loose synchronic connection to the previous material.

In the concluding oracle, "in that day" is the initial introductory phrase in 9:11a. Here also the phrase is a synchronism, which has the effect of tying the concluding oracle to the Amos context. Then "behold, days are coming, says Yahweh," with its more complex and independent structure, acts as a climactic and emphatic phrase which strengthens the conclusion to Amos.

To draw these conclusions from two fairly standard redactional phrases might be pushing the evidence too far if they were not accompanied by a relation in content between the two sets of oracles. However, such a content relationship exists in the form of a second reversal. In comparing 8:11-12 with 9:13-15, the reversal is conceptual

---

[29]See: Peter Munch, "The expression bajjom hahu, is it an eschatological terminus technicus?," *Avhändlinger utgitt av det Norske Videnskaps-Akademi* (1936) 5-69, DeVries, *Yesterday*, 55-136, 279-332.

rather than linguistic. Two images dominate 8:11-12: famine and wandering. Both images are metaphorical, referring to the lack of the word of God in the land rather than to physical actions or needs. In 9:13-15 the images are reversed and concretized: the land will be paradisically abundant and the people will be firmly planted in it.

The reversal between 8:13-14 and 9:11-12 rests upon linguistic as well as conceptual grounds. The concluding line of 8:14 states that those who worship other gods "will fall (נפל) and never rise (קום) again." Verse 9:11b speaks of raising up (קום) the fallen (נפל) booth of David. The Hebrew verb roots are the same in both instances, but the image is reversed. Consequently, a brief look at the two introductory phrases in Amos 9:11-15 reveals a literary relationship to material in the rest of Amos in the form of a double reversal. The first is formal, a mere reversal of phrases; the second is substantial, applying the same set of images to judgment in 8:11-14 and then to salvation in 9:11-15.

Our noting the relationship between 8:14 and 9:11 leads naturally to a more complete discussion of 9:11b: "I will raise up the fallen booth of David." Most commentators focus upon the booth of David in this line, since it is a unique phrase and adds the Davidic tradition to Amos. The chief point of discussion has been the identification of the booth as either Judah or Jerusalem. What has been overlooked is the integration of this phrase into the context of Amos. The phrase itself may be unique, but the accompanying words are not. The two verbs, הַנֹּפֶלֶת ... אָקִים, are forms of the same root used in Amos 5:2 ("fallen no more to rise, virgin Israel") as well as 8:14 (which is probably derived from 5:2). The literary association connects 9:11b with one of the best-known oracles in Amos, again by reversal: Israel will not be resurrected, but Judah/Jerusalem shall be revived from her abject state.[30]

Following this opening line which draws associations with the rest of Amos are three lines which expand upon the same idea poetically. The literary associations here are not so much with Amos as with Isa 58:12: "And some from you will build (וּבָנוּ) the ancient (עוֹלָם) ruins; /You will raise (תְּקוֹמֵם) the ancestral foundations, / And you will be

---

[30]A further association is through the feminine aspect: virgin" of 5:2 with the feminine "booth" and the pervasive feminine imagery associated with Zion. A further literary relation is the double occurrence of the root קום in both 5:2 and 9:11-12.

called "Repairer of Breaches" (גֹּדֵר פֶּרֶץ). The Hebrew words transliterated above appear in inverted order in Amos 9:11cde. The central promise of rebuilding the city is the same in both verses. The difference lies in the active agent: God is the restorer in Amos; the people in Isaiah. The striking relationship between the two verses is the parallel of גֹּדֵר פֶּרֶץ to וְגָדַרְתִּי אֶת-פִּרְצֵיהֶן (9:11c: "and repair its breaches"), the only two places in the Old Testament in which these words are used in conjunction. This phrase also supplies the literary connection between these three lines and the context of Amos: "breaches" also appears in Amos 4:3 in a judgment oracle against Samaria.[31] Consequently, literary allusion connects Amos 9:11cde both to a salvation oracle outside of Amos and a judgment oracle inside the book, leading us both in to the context of Amos and out to the broader horizon of the prophetic literature.

The next verse of this oracle returns our focus to Amos.[32] The association is primarily conceptual, although there are several loose linguistic associations. The linguistic connections occur in 9:12a, "... possess the remnant of Edom." Each of these words appears in the string of indictments which open Amos: "to possess the land of the Amorite" (2:10); "the remnant of the Philistines" (1:8); "Edom" (1:11). As a summary phrase 9:12b, "and all the nations which are called by my name," recalls the entire list of nations in 1:3-2:16. Whether or not this is a conscious allusion by the author, the effect is to call the readers' attention to the opening indictment and to have them view that list of nations as now being the possession of a restored Israelite people. Consequently, Amos 9:12 expands the promise of a rebuilt Jerusalem uttered in 9:11 to include a re-established empire which will include the remnants of most of the peoples originally subject to David.[33]

In summary, while Amos 9:11-12 is distinct from the rest of the book in form, style, and meaning, it does not appear in isolation.

---

[31]פֶּרֶץ occurs 25 times in the Old Testament. Of the 11 occurrences in the prophetic literature, 3 are involved in these literary associations.

[32]Most commentators adjudge this verse as prose, although a poetic scan is possible: accentually they are 4:4 (minus the closing phrase); syllable count runs as 12:14; there is a semblance of parallelism (a b c d // d e f g).

[33]Thematically, this verse is reminiscent of the conclusion of Obadiah (vv 17-21), in which Israel is given possession of numerous other nations: Esau/Edom, Philistia, Ephraim, Gilead, Phonecia, the Negev.

Regardless of its origin, one can read it as part of Amos because of the literary allusions, both conceptual and linguistic. These allusions lead us both in to the book of Amos and out to the larger context of prophetic literature. The outward allusion which occupies the center of the oracle is the most complex, involving the repetition of five words of Isa 58:12 in inverted order. The thrust of both Isa 58:12 and Amos 9:11cde is the restoration of Jerusalem. Even this outward allusion is connected briefly to Amos through the seldom-used word, "breaches," in Amos 4:3. In addition the outward allusion is encased by the inward. Amos 9:11b is linguistically connected to Amos 5:2 and 8:14. Amos 9:12 is conceptually related to the list of nations in Amos 1:3-2:16. These inward allusions all operate through a reversal of imagery: from judgment in the body of Amos to salvation in the conclusion. Consequently, Amos 9:11-12 allows us to read the Davidic promise of the restoration of Jerusalem and the return to empire as a salvation which grows out of and reverses the judgment of Amos.

The second section of the concluding oracle, 9:13-15, opens with a picture which sets before the reader the paradisical fertility of the land to which Israel will be restored. There are no striking literary allusions to either Amos or to other prophetic literature in the first two lines, 9:13bc. Although several words appear both in the body of Amos and in these lines, they call forth no imagistic connections and appear to be mere happenstance.[34] We have already mentioned the conceptual reversal between 8:11 and 9:13, from threat of famine to promise of fecundity. This connection applies to the whole verse and offers no linguistic associations.

However, an indisputable link with Joel 4:18 occurs in the two closing lines of the verse: "and the mountains will drip with wine/ and all the hills will melt with it" (9:13de). The first line is identical with Joel 4:18[35] and the second is a significant variation upon it. This variation, the substitution of תְּהְמוֹגֵגְנָה ("melt with it") for the תֵּלַכְנָה חָלָב ("flow with milk") of Joel, is the element which provides a linguistic link to the rest of Amos. The verb "melt" also appears in Amos 9:5. In this passage it connotes the power of Yahweh over the earth. The use of the two verbs מוֹג and אבל in parallel suggests that

---

[34]See Amos 4:7 (קצר), 4:13 (דרך); 6:12 (חרשׁ).

[35]The only difference is insignificant: the line in Amos begins with the *waw*-conversive.

it is Yahweh's power of judgment that is being exercised in this case.[36] In 9:13de we once again have a reversal of the image. The melting is now part of the natural fecundity of the land, indirectly under the power of God. More importantly, the process is one connected with restoration, abundance, and salvation rather than judgment. In 9:13d הֶהָרִים furnishes a further literary allusion to Amos. Three times the book refers to the "mountain(s) of Samaria" (3:9; 4:1; 6:1), all in contexts of judgment upon the northern kingdom. In 9:13d these mountains which have been a symbol of God's punishment now flow with his salvation. That which was the assembly point for Assyria (3:9) and the home of the covenant-breakers (4:1; 6:1) is now the source of sweet wine. Thus, as in 9:11-12 we find in 9:13 both an outward focus through the linguistic allusion to Joel 4:18 and an inward connection, by the substitution of a synonym and the use of a catchword, to the rest of Amos. This creates resonances with both the judgments of Amos and the promised salvation of the prophetic corpus.

In 9:14 the theme of reversal which we have been pursuing is made explicit. The first line of the verse contains the oft-used idiom שׁוּב שְׁבוּת. Although the precise meaning and derivation of the idiom has been debated, its sense is indisputable: it refers to a reversal of fortunes for the people of Israel, a change from being under God's judgment to experiencing his restoration. On the basis of its frequent use, the phrase itself is independent of Amos. However, its appearance here provides two linguistic allusions to the bulk of the book. The phrase itself connects with Amos 4:6-11. In a series of striking oracles Yahweh states the chastisements which he has sent against his people: famine, drought, plague, pestilence, and destruction. His lament at the end of each of these oracles is that even after such chastisement, Israel did not return to him (וְלֹא־שַׁבְתֶּם עָדַי). These occurrences of שׁוּב set the two oracles in sharp contrast: my people did not return to me, but I will restore them nonetheless. There is a further reversal of images in the two. The judgment in 4:6-11 comes primarily through natural disaster; restoration in 9:13-15 includes the superabundance of nature.

---

[36]מוּג is usually taken in the sense of "flow" in this verse, as retaining the same sense as תֵּלַכְנָה in Joel. If this is correct, it is a unique use of the verb. Only in four instances is מוּג used to describe Yahweh's power to destroy the earth: twice in the *qal* (Amos 9:5; Ps 46:6, once in the *niphal* (Ps 74:4), and once in the *hithpolel* (Nah 1:5). Amos 9:5 is part of a doxology which is generally regarded as late. In terms of literary resonance this is significant only in showing that resonance may occur in any strata of the book.

Yahweh manipulates nature for either the blessing or the cursing of his people.

The second linguistic connection is through the accompanying vocative, עַמִּי יִשְׂרָאֵל ("my people, Israel"). This phrase appears in Amos 7:15 and 8:2 in prophecies of exile and destruction. Once again we encounter the opposition of judgment and salvation.

The explicitness of the reversal continues in the next two lines: "they will build the desolated cities and they will dwell/ they will plant vineyards and drink wine" (9:14bc). These lines are clearly drawn from Amos 5:11. The first line differs only in the object of the building: stone houses in 5:11; desolated cities in 9:14b. The second line is completely parallel to 5:11. The reversal comes from Amos 5:11 being phrased in the negative ("you shall not dwell ... you shall not drink") while 9:14bc is the positive counterpart. Amos 9:14bc depicts the successful restoration of city and farm abandoned in the execution of God's judgment which was foretold in 5:11.

Although these lines are primarily related to Amos, they also lead us to the other prophetic literature. The image of rural and urban restoration is a frequent one in the prophets. Linguistic similarities are apparent between Amos 9:14bcd and some prophetic passages, especially Isa 65:21 and Jer 29:5,28.[37] This relationship is strengthened when one includes Amos 9:14d. The structure of 9:14bcd is such that 14b speaks of restoring the cities, 14c and 14d are in parallel describing the rejuvenated agriculture. Lines 14bc are related to Amos 5:11, but 14d has no linguistic associations with Amos. However, the related passages in Isaiah and Jeremiah each consist of two lines, one referring to the city, the other to the countryside. The parallels in each passage are primarily to 14b and 14d, with only passing reference to 14c. The linguistic parallels in Amos 9:14bcd to the prophetic passages mentioned above are as follows:

14b   וּבָנוּ ... וְיָשָׁבוּ ("rebuild ... and inhabit")

14c   וְנָטְעוּ... ("plant")

14d   ... גַּנּוֹת וְאָכְלוּ אֶת-פְּרִיהֶם ("... gardens and eat their fruit")

Consequently, Amos 9:14cd may be regarded as an expansion of the prophetic parallels -- or the prophetic passages as a contraction of 9:14cd. Both Isaiah and Jeremiah contain the verb from 14c and the

---

[37]Deut 28:30 also bears a strong resemblance to Amos 9:14cde.

remainder of the line from 14d. Thus, in 14bcd we again encounter our double focus. Lines 14b and 14c allude to Amos 5:11 in a striking manner. However, a concluding line is added which has no parallels in Amos. This line leads us outward, since the same wording is used in similar oracles in Isaiah and Jeremiah. Only this double focus accounts for the entire structure of Amos 9:14bcd. It does more than reverse the meaning of Amos 5:11; it does more than refer to similar salvation oracles in Jeremiah and Isaiah. The entirety of Amos 9:14 acts as a centerpiece and summary of the concluding section of the book by encapsulating both the inward and outward movements and the reversal from judgment to salvation.

The final verse of the book offers further allusions of the same type that we have been investigating, although in far less spectacular fashion than the preceding verse. The focus of 9:15 is clearly upon the land, with the repetition of אֲדְמָתָם. The agricultural imagery is continued from the previous verse, but here it is used only metaphorically: the people will be planted and not uprooted. The focus upon the land offers the connecting link between this verse and Amos. Twice in the book אֲדְמָתָם occurs in prominent judgment oracles. The first is Amos 5:2, which also has literary allusions to 9:11b. The mention of the land offers a further connection to 9:15a. Whereas Israel was forsaken (נטש) upon the land in 5:2, it is planted (נטע) upon the land in 9:15a. The word play calls forth yet another imagistic reversal. The land again appears in Amos' prophecy against Israel in 7:11 (repeated in 7:17). Here Israel is thrust out of the land into exile. In both verses the phrase is מֵעַל אַדְמָתוֹ, the same wording as in 9:15c. The latter is phrased in the negative, so we again encounter an explicit reversal: from uprooting for exile to firm and irrevocable planting.

The phraseology used in Amos 9:15 is quite common in the prophetic literature, especially in Jeremiah. The most striking allusive connection is with Jer 24:1-10. This is a vision report about baskets of good and bad figs. In the interpretation of the vision we encounter in the midst of several Jeremianic phrases וּנְטַעְתִּים וְלֹא אֶתּוֹשׁ ("and I will plant them and not uproot") in 24:6, which combines wording from Amos 9:15a and 9:15b. Then at the conclusion to the oracle we encounter a word-for-word parallel to Amos 9:15c, "out of the land that I have given them." All of these words are quite common in the prophets; the connection is certainly one of allusion, not quotation. However, the similarity in wording leads one to compare the visions of salvation in both oracles. The one in Amos is markedly restrained compared to the one in Jeremiah. Amos 9:11-15 concentrates upon the external features of salvation: the political restoration of the Davidic kingdom, the restoration of the cities, renewed agriculture (with superabundant returns), the security of the nation. These are stated as unconditional acts of God. No response is needed from the people; they are merely to accept his bounty as they have his judgment. There is no intimation of the conditionality of the salvation set forth in Jer 24:1-10, where the people are divided into good and bad figs and restored or judged accordingly. Nor is there a hint of the internal change in the individual which Jeremiah details. The people do not receive a new heart (Jer 24:7) which enables them to know Yahweh in a new way. Jer 24:1-10 is consonant with the interiorization of both judgment and salvation, the questioning and the probing of the inner nature of God's people that is characteristic of the book. Amos 9:11-15 contains none of this, remaining on the level of exterior reality. This is consistent with the outlook of the book of Amos, where judgment is based upon external, visible violations of the covenant. The spirit of the salvation conferred in the concluding oracle is true to the tone of Amos the prophet.

In summary, we have demonstrated that a study of the literary allusions in Amos 9:11-15 uncovers a complex interaction among this pericope, the remainder of Amos, and the prophetic corpus. These allusions move in two directions. First, they focus our attention inward upon the book of Amos itself. This aspect includes allusions through form (the ordering of the sections of the oracle signaled by the introductory phrases), through concepts (the nations governed by Yahweh), through images (famine and superabundance), and through linguistic parallels (the similarities of Amos 5:11 and 9:14). All of these allusions reinforce one point: judgment has been reversed. Words, images, concepts, and forms which signaled judgment before now proclaim deliverance. The outward direction of the allusions leads us to the prophetic corpus. We are reminded of salvation oracles in other books, particularly Deutero-Isaiah, Joel, and Jeremiah. Thus, Amos cannot be read in isolation, but must be taken in context. The salvation is of the same type described elsewhere in the prophets, but it is singularly consonant with Amos. Compared to Jeremiah, Amos 9:11-15 is external and unconditional, just as is the judgment of Amos.

As Wolff has pointed out, every legalistic interpretation is excluded.[38] The salvation is the free gift of God.

What may we conclude from this study? We have concentrated upon literary allusions and contextual readings in contrast to an isolated, atomized interpretation of the text. We have carefully avoided discussing subjects such as the intention of the author, its meaning for its own generation, and the historical context. All of these are important topics, but they obscure as much as they uncover. In looking at allusions and context we have shown that Amos 9:11-15 is much more thoroughly integrated with the rest of Amos than other commentators have suggested. Every verse contains allusions which enrich the meaning of both this pericope and the rest of the book. As Wolff states, the "eschatology of salvation" has not "penetrated the preceding book of Amos"[39] in the sense that the oracles of deliverance are not inserted in Amos 1:1-9:10. However, in terms of literary allusions the two are thoroughly intertwined. This interrelation affects and enriches meaning.

The interpretation which we have given Amos 9:11-15 is not essentially new, nor are the parallels which we have drawn unique discoveries. Many of the parallels are mentioned in one commentary or another. However, the atomization resulting from the application of the historical-critical method has prevented commentators from interpreting the pericope in relation to the parallels. They are neither drawn together nor explored to any great extent. By using a different perspective, we have found that the sum total of the parallels forms a significant network of literary allusions. These parallels enrich the meaning of Amos 9:11-15 in both comparison and contrast.

We have carefully avoided stating whether or not this multitude of allusions is intentional on the part of the author. Intentionality is difficult, if not impossible, to prove. The dependence between Amos 5:11 and 9:14 is clear enough that one may speak of intention. "Mountains" and "land" on the other hand are such common words that their appearance in Amos 9:13 and 15 could be coincidental. However, both words resonate strongly with important passages in Amos. Whether or not this resonance is intentional, the effect is very real and present. In the final state of Amos these words help connect salvation

---

[38]Wolff, *Joel and Amos*, 355.

[39]*Ibid.*, 354.

and judgment in the book. Focusing on intention prevents the full investigation of parallels and increases the atomization of the text. To alter our vision and examine the effect of the parallels cuts down this isolation and enables us to see oracles in a new light.

This study does not question the validity of an historical-critical investigation; it does question the sufficiency of the method. The establishing of the secondary nature of Amos 9:11-15, the investigation of its form, and the ascertaining of the historical situation of the passage are all important steps in a full understanding of the passage. However, one must then recognize that the pericope is related to its context and conduct a thorough investigation of that relationship as an integral part of the interpretive process. As we have demonstrated, this involves shedding some of the preconceptions of the historical-critical method and regarding literary allusions with an open mind.

Our discussion of Amos 9:11-15 has focused upon the literary sphere and the effects of an historical-critical atomization of the text upon our understanding of the book. In relating our study to actualization, however, we must move beyond this level to discuss the hermeneutical implications. This is an easy step to make, since this literary atomization leads to a hermeneutical isolation as well. Although von Rad's chronological actualization permits him to view this passage as originating with Amos, his theological interpretation still occurs in isolation from the remainder of the book. He interprets the promise as a contradiction to the remainder of Amos' message. Since he does nothing to resolve the contradiction, the passage stands in complete isolation from Amos, with its only theological connection being a vague association with the prophets' re-use of the Davidic tradition. Wolff's approach, although it regards the pericope as secondary, actually does more to integrate Amos 9:11-15 theologically with the rest of the book. He interprets the aim of the passage as being an unconditional promise of God juxtaposed with the unremitting picture of judgment painted by Amos. However, he retains the perspective of this passage as a late, limited redaction of the book and emphasizes the lack of penetration of the promise into the body of Amos.

We wish to suggest that a more integrated theological interpretation is justified. In moving beyond historical-critical methods to examine literary allusions, we have demonstrated that a remarkable nexus of allusions connects Amos 9:11-15 both to the remainder of the book and to the prophetic corpus. These connections make it possible to interpret this final oracle as integrally related to Amos and not merely as an isolated and non-penetrating redaction. Its placement at the conclusion of the book allows the judgment of Amos to stand forth in its stark, brooding power and historical specificity. Without the literary allusions which we have detailed, the isolation of the final oracle would be the major interpretive factor (as it has been in most critical studies). However, the literary allusions allow Amos 9:11-15 to draw upon the images of Amos for a sense of depth through its series of reversals and to gain strength from the striking contrast of judgment and promise.

Consequently, the final oracle constitutes an expansion of Amos centered upon literary features rather than historical. The historical setting of the pericope (other than being of the general post-exilic period) is rather vague, while the literary relation to Amos is quite detailed and complex. It does not eliminate or disguise the historical specifics in the book, but relates to them through literary images. This interaction produces a unity for the book which is not possible if one works within the framework of chronological actualization with its emphasis upon historical specificity. However, it is possible to speak of this final expansion of Amos as an actualization. It makes the book of Amos relevant to a later period in Israel's life. Indeed, it spreads this relevance beyond the bounds of a single generation, because it transcends the historical specifics of Amos' judgment and casts the book in the light of a less specific promise. We may characterize this type of contemporization as the actualization of a literary whole. It is literary because it utilizes literary interpenetrations, allusions, and parallels to reinterpret the material; it is holistic because it interrelates and reinterprets the entire book, not just isolated oracles, from its own point of view.

Isaiah 36-39:   The Problem of Historical Reconstruction

The two passages which we have already considered are ones which von Rad used to explain and develop the concept of actualization. We demonstrated that chronological actualization, while giving helpful insights into these passages, leads to an incomplete and distorted interpretation. Modifications in the concept of actualization were necessary to do full justice to the interpretation of Deut 5:1-3 and Amos 9:11-15.

We encounter a different situation with Isa 36-39, because von Rad has great difficulty incorporating the interpretation of these chapters into his system. While he cautiously raises the question of the continuing effectiveness *(Weiterwirken)* of the passage and its later reinterpretation *(Interpretation)*, he avoids referring specifically to actualization in regard to this section. His reasons for this circumspect approach emerge in his analysis: these stories are "already a thing of the past," and "lack the specifically historical interest in the political event which is closing in on Zion."[40] The typifying of the foe in the narrative and the waning interest in salvation history preclude Isa 36-39 from being an example of actualization: "Faith is now on the way to becoming something almost divorced from history and belonging to the individual's encounter with God."[41]

This is very peculiar interpretation of the passage. A rescension of the same narrative appears in II Kings 18-20. Many elements in both rescensions indicate the shaping hand of the Deuteronomistic historian upon the material. Yet von Rad holds the Deuteronomist in high regard for his theology of history and use of actualization. Why should he speak of Isa 36-39 in such completely different terms?   His individualizing of the narrative also strikes a peculiar chord. Although his reference is quite vague, he may be referring to the significance of Hezekiah's role in the narrative. However, as Childs has shown, Hezekiah's part is the type of the righteous king, epitomized by David and Solomon in the Deuteronomistic history.[42] The most common elements of the encounter of king and prophet are also still present here: God's word of salvation or judgment is mediated through the prophet; the prophet offers and interprets a sign; the prophet acts as a healer; the king offers a prayer of confession. Von Rad has not placed an individualistic interpretation upon other such encounters containing these same elements.[43]

Clearly, von Rad has great difficulty in interpreting Isa 36-39. This problem stems from the interrelationship which he establishes between actualization and historical reconstruction and specificity.

---

[40]Von Rad, *Theology*, 2.168.

[41]*Ibid.*, 169.

[42]Brevard S. Childs, *Isaiah and the Assyrian Crisis* (London: SCM, 1967) 92, 100.

[43]See his interpretation of the encounter between Ahaz and Isaiah in von Rad, *Theology*, 2.158-61.

Although this passage purports to be an historical narrative, the actual historical lineaments are quite blurred. Von Rad recognizes this aspect of the passage, but he is unable to cope with it. Since he is unable either to reconstruct the original historical events or to pin down its re-use to a specific historical situation, his interpretive method leads him far afield in his attempt to explicate the passage.

The question we need to answer here is how one can fruitfully approach the interpretation of Isa 36-39. Childs and Ackroyd have laid considerable groundwork in their attempts to break the impasse in the interpretation of this passage. Their work is so extensive and the passage is so long that we will not present a detailed analysis of Isa 36-39. Instead, we will refer first to the considerable advances in interpretation made by Childs and Ackroyd. Then, we will consider how these chapters relate to their present context and influence the interpretation of the book of Isaiah as an example of a fruitful redefinition of actualization.

In *Isaiah and the Assyrian Crisis* Childs focuses upon the problem of the historical interpretation of the material concerning Sennacherib's invasion of Judah, including Isa 36-37. He concludes:

> The largely negative results of our historical conclusions are a warning against trying to understand these texts exclusively from an historical point of view. We have seen the extent to which the texts simply do not lend themselves to answering this set of questions. Also this predominant historical interest has obscured the understanding of the manner in which the texts themselves really function.[44]

He finds that the structuring of the Biblical material is dependent upon many factors other than the underlying historical events, such as prior traditions, the influence of other responses, and the shifting contexts of the various pericopes.[45]

In reference to Isa 36-37 in particular, Childs discovers two distinct sets of material outlining the Assyrian threat. Each set follows the same pattern: threat to Israel (Isa 36:4-20//37:9b-13); lament of Hezekiah (Isa 37:1-4//37:14-20); Yahweh's reasurrance (Isa 37:5-

---

[44]Childs, *Isaiah*, 121.

[45]*Ibid.*

7//37:21-35); the final effect (Isa 37:8-9a, 37:38//37:36).[46] These accounts are linked by a catchword connection centering on Isa 37:7-9.[47] Both the pattern and the connection are literary in form, not historical. The patterning and repetition convey a growing tension in the narrative and emphasize the final message: the repentence of king and people result in Yahweh's deliverance. To interpret these chapters based upon a reconstruction of historical events would distort the form in which they now exist. We must look to literary, not historical, criteria for the interpretation of Isa 36-37, since literary forces have determined the final shape of the material.

In "An Interpretation of the Babylonian Exile: A Study of 2 Kings 20, Isaiah 38-39," Ackroyd picks up where Childs left off, both in subject matter and method. He accepts Childs' conclusions on the impossibility of an historical reading of the material and utilizes some of his interpretive suggestions to deliver a "reading as a whole" of the subsequent Hezekiah-Isaiah narratives.

In both of these chapters he finds pointed references to the Babylonian exile. In chapter 38 Hezekiah's illness and deliverance act as a type for the exile and restoration of the nation. The inclusion of Hezekiah's psalm in the Isaianic rescension emphasizes this point with its references to consignment to Sheol, the return from the pit, and the restoration to life. Ackroyd finds parallels to these themes in Lamentations and Jeremiah which also act as metaphors for the Babylonian captivity and restoration.[48] Isaiah 39 offers clear references to the exile. Repetition places the emphasis of this story upon two elements: the place of origin of the ambassadors (Babylon, a far country); and the fact that Hezekiah showed them everything. These themes appear in the opening narrative, in Hezekiah's speech, and in Yahweh's indictment.[49] The indictment itself relates them to the brutal fact of exile. Consequently, Ackroyd has demonstrated that the major thrust of Isa 39 and an attendant metaphor of Isa 38 is the prefigurement of the exile.

---

[46]For Childs' outline in relation to the II Kings rescension, *Ibid.*, 96.

[47]*Ibid.*, 74-75.

[48]Peter Ackroyd, "An Interpretation of the Babylonian Exile: A Study of 2 Kings 20, Isaiah 38-39," *SJT* 27 (1974) 345.

[49]*Ibid.*, 333-35.

He also isolates elements pertaining to the exile in Isa 36-37. He interprets the Rabshakeh's speech as a parody of the divine promise of the land in an ironic reflection upon the exilic loss. He locates Deutero-Isaianic elements in Isaiah's indictment of Assyria (II Kings 19:21-28//Isa 37:22-29). He concludes that the entire section of Isa 36-39 must be viewed in relation to the exile, with the Isaianic rescension functioning specifically as a preface to Deutero-Isaiah.

While Ackroyd acknowledges that Isa 36-39 has been shaped by forces outside the original historical events, he still sees the primary shaping force as an historical one: the experience of the exile. For him a "reading as a whole" means understanding II Kings 18-20//Isa 36-39 in its internal relations and in connection with that specific historical experience. He is not concerned with its context in the book of Isaiah except where it furthers his thesis of an exilic interpretation. For example, he mentions these chapters as a preface to Isa 40-66 to demonstrate their exilic context, not to contribute to the understanding of the literary setting of the material.

In the comments which follow, we accept the basic conclusions of both Childs and Ackroyd: 1) that the shaping forces upon the material have been non-historical; 2) that the material, especially Isa 39, bears an exilic stamp. However, we wish to push beyond these statements and suggest that the shaping force for Isa 36-39 is not so much the historical exilic experience, but the literary setting of the material. In their present context these chapters function as a bridge between first and second Isaiah. To demonstrate the validity of this suggestion, we must show that the present shape of the material fits this role to a remarkable degree.

The most obvious place in which Isa 36-39 betrays the literary shaping is in the order of the pericopes. Even with our questioning of the historical reconstructions of the events surrounding these chapters, we can conclude from the generally accepted dates of Merodach-Baladan's reign (721-710, 703 B.C.) and Sennacherib's invasion (701 B.C.) that the sending of the ambassadors from Babylon preceded the invasion. In both rescensions of the stories the ambassadors' visit follows the Assyrian threat. Both chapters 38 and 39 are only loosely tied to the previous account of the invasion. The synchronic connectives בַּיָּמִים הָהֵם ("in those days") in 38:1 and בָּעֵת הַהִיא ("at that time") in 39:1 are redactional and do not specify a time. As Ackroyd points out, this order possibly occurred through ignorance or sloppiness, in which case it would carry no particular significance.[50] However, a more likely solution is that such a rearrangement is purposeful. One possible reason is strikingly apparent in the Isaianic setting: chapter 39 refers explicitly to the Babylonian exile and acts as a herald for Deutero-Isaiah. With the present arrangement of stories we are forcefully reminded of the exile just prior to the oracles of deliverance.

Of course this reordering occurs not just in the Isaianic rescension, but also in the Deuteronomistic. If one follows Ackroyd's reading of the material, the impending tragedy becomes increasingly obvious through the sequence of stories. However, in II Kings 18-20 this climactic awareness of the exile leads to -- nothing. Therefore, to detect a purposive ordering of the stories, one must look to the Isaianic setting, where the climax of Isa 39 focuses the reader's attention upon the Deutero-Isaianic deliverance. Consequently, the order of stories in Isa 36-39 appears tailored to the Isaianic context and reflects a purpose lacking in the Deuteronomistic context. This in turn suggests that the reason for the order is not the actual event of the exile, but the literary setting of the chapters which calls for an introductory reference to that event.

Clearly, the question of the adaptation of these narratives to their Isaianic setting is a complicated one, since the shaping appears to have influenced the rescension in II Kings as well. We may draw this conclusion from the identical order of the narratives, even though the order has no evident purpose in II Kings. Since the Deuteronomistic version is generally the longer of the two, we can isolate very few elements that are unique to the Isaianic version. Therefore, the most clear-cut method of ascertaining the influence of the Isaianic context yields little material with which to work.

However, two elements unique to Isaiah do point to an adaptation to this context. The first of these is Hezekiah's psalm in Isa 38:10-20. This constitutes the only notable expansion of the Isaianic text compared to the Deuteronomistic. Ackroyd has already analyzed this passage as a metaphorical reference to the exile and a prelude to chapter 39. He points out that the addition of such a psalm to a narrative context is a Deuteronomistic technique to highlight important elements

---

[50]*Ibid.*, p. 332.

in the narrative.[51] The second elements unique to Isaiah is the addition of צְבָאוֹת to the Isaianic version in three instances.[52] This is an appellation of Yahweh that appears frequently in both first and second Isaiah, but rarely in the Deuteronomistic history. Consequently, its addition is an adaptation to the entire Isaianic milieu, albeit a minor one.

Many elements in the Isaiah-Hezekiah narratives are present in both rescensions, yet supply links to either first or second Isaiah. To speak of these elements as adaptations is a bit rash. A more cautious explanation is that they are elements of the stories which made them suitable as a link between the parts of Isaiah. If the evidence for a particular link is strong enough, we shall discuss it as a possible adaptation.

The thematic and linguistic connections to first Isaiah are the most obvious. Shebnah and Eliakim appear in an independent narrative in Isa 22:15-25. The element of trust (בטח) which is central to the Rabshakeh's speech also plays an important role in Isa 30:15.[53] The Rabshakeh's emphasis upon the impotence of Egypt and his description of their weakness recall several of Isaiah's anti-Egyptian oracles. The arrogance of the Assyrians and particularly the boast in the first person in 37:23-25 closely parallel Isaiah's oracles against the Assyrians (especially Isa 10:8-11) and against kingly pride (Isa 14:13-14). While other references could be listed, this brief summary demonstrates that numerous connections are present which relate Isa 36-39 to first Isaiah. Virtually all of these are integral to the text of the narratives. Only the boast in 37:23-25 occurs in what is generally regarded as a secondary expansion of the stories. Therefore, the links between Isa 36-39 and

---

[51]*Ibid.* We find the Deuteronomist at work even in the uniquely Isaianic elements. This may be the reason that there are so few unique elements in the Isaianic version: the same school redacted both versions.

[52]Isa 37:16,32; 39:5. The divine name appears much more frequently without the addition of צְבָאוֹת than with it in Isa 36-39.

[53]See Childs, *Isaiah,* 85. The use of בטח here is a good example of why I speak of suitability to the context rather than adaptation. Trust plays a more important role in the Deuteronomistic corpus than it does in Isaiah, and, therefore, is primarily an example of the Deuteronomistic hand at work in the formation of these stories. However, once these stories are located in the book of Isaiah, בטח also calls to mind the oracle against Egypt in Isa 30:1-17 and acts as a connective between the two.

first Isaiah are almost all cases of "suitability" to its context and function rather than adaptation.

Links to Deutero-Isaiah are also present in these chapters, although they are not as readily apparent. The strongest links, apart from Isa 39, cluster around the conclusion of Israel's deliverance from the Assyrians in Isa 37:19-35.

The majority of these occur in the poem in verses 23-29, which is probably an expansion of Isaiah's originally brief oracle of deliverance.[54] The clearest link between this poem and Deutero-Isaiah lies in 37:26. In this verse the predetermined plan of Yahweh is put forth as a rhetorical question. Several times in Deutero-Isaiah we encounter not just the theme of Yahweh's plan, but the same rhetorical format as well.[55] Many of the same words and phrases occur in both Isa 37:26 and Deutero-Isaiah.[56] The connections of theme, form, and phraseology that the reader encounters in 37:26 immediately calls Deutero-Isaiah to mind.

Several other connective links are also present in this poem. The קְדוֹשׁ יִשְׂרָאֵל ("Holy One of Israel") of 37:23 is an appellation of Yahweh which appears only in first and second Isaiah and Psalms. Hence, it provides a connection to both parts of the book. In verse 25 the Assyrian king boasts that he "dried up (חרב) ... all the streams of Egypt." Since the thrust of 37:23-25 is that the tyrant has raised himself to the status of God, this image may well refer to the exodus. The same verb חרב is applied to the deliverance at the exodus in Deutero-Isaiah (51:10; also see 44:27 and 50:2). The image of grass as transient and easily blighted in 37:27 recalls the opening oracle of Deutero-Isaiah in 40:6-8.

The strength of the connections between this poem (especially 37:26) and Deutero-Isaiah are such that one thinks of this as an adaptation of the narrative to the Isaianic context. This is an especially

---

[54]*Ibid.*, 96-97, 103. One possible explanation of this expansion is that it served to strengthen the connection to Deutero-Isaiah. It also has several links to the context of Isa 36-37, particularly the wording of verses 23-24.

[55]See Isa 40:21; 41:4,26; 44:7-8; 45:21. For the same theme without the rhetorical question, see 46:9-11; 48:3-5; 51:9-10.

[56]Some of the linguistic connections are, for example: הֲלוֹא שְׁמַעְתָּ (Isa 40:21; 44:7); מִימֵי קֶדֶם (Isa 51:9); קֶדֶם (Isa 45:21; 46:10); יצר (Isa 46:11); the *hiphil* of בוא (Isa 46:11; 48:3,5).

plausible reading because the poem is regarded as a secondary addition. While it is not modeled directly on any one Deutero-Isaianic text, the frequent literary allusions constantly call that body of material to mind. We also have links to first Isaiah in the poem in the use of קְדוֹשׁ יִשְׂרָאֵל and the boast of the tyrant. There are further allusions to the poem's immediate context of chapters 36-37. The use of חרף and גדף in 37:23 characterize the Rabshakeh's taunting of the people of Israel (37:4,6,17). Consequently, we conclude that this poem functions as a strong connecting link between the immediate context of Isa 36-39 and Deutero-Isaiah with some allusions to first Isaiah as well.

Two further links to Deutero-Isaiah are present in the verses immediately surrounding this poem. The first is the mention of idols in Hezekiah's prayer. The reference to these figures as human workmanship is reminiscent of the scorn heaped upon idols by Deutero-Isaiah (for example, see Isa 40:19-20; 41:6-7; 44:9-20; 45:16-17). The second connection is the conclusion to Isaiah's promise of deliverance in 37:35. Otto Kaiser points out that this verse "explicitly takes up 31:5, the Deutero-Isaianic 'for my sake' (cf. 43:25; 48:9; 55:5) and the Deuteronomic 'for the sake of my servant David' (cf. I Kings 11:13,34; 15:4 and II Kings 8:9)."[57] While both of these links reflect the suitability of the passage for its context and function rather than being a specific adaptation, they do reinforce the connection to Deutero-Isaiah.

In summary, we have found that Isa 36-39 functions admirably in its context as a connecting link between the oracles of Isaiah of Jerusalem and Deutero-Isaiah. The material contains formal, thematic, and linguistic allusions to both sets of prophetic material. In two instances we may reasonably speak of the adaptation of the narratives for their function in the Isaianic context. The first instance is the placement of the visit of the Babylonian ambassadors at the conclusion of the narrative sequence. In this location it leads the reader from the Assyrian threat to the Babylonian one, associating the two and prefiguring the exile and restoration which form the primary focus of Deutero-Isaiah. The second is the secondary addition of the poem in Isa 37:23-29, which contains numerous allusions to Deutero-Isaiah as well as connections to both first Isaiah and the preceding narrative chapters.

The other links which we have discussed, including virtually all the connections to first Isaiah, show little evidence of being intentional

---

[57]Otto Kaiser, *Isaiah* 13-39 (Philadelphia: Westminster, 1974) 395.

adaptations. Instead, they are elements which are integral to the narrative but which provide allusive connections to their context. These allusions make them suitable for their role as a link between the two Isaiahs. The need to distinguish between such fine points as adaptation and suitability underlines the difficulty in treating this text in historical terms, either to reconstruct the actual historical events underlying the text or to identify the historical setting for its later re-use.

Regardless of the history of the shaping of the text, it has clearly been re-used in its Isaianic setting. Its Deuteronomistic tone and a host of other factors rule out the Isaianic setting as the original home of these traditions. The evidence which we have presented is sufficient to regard its re-use here as purposive and not merely a move to collect all the material concerning Isaiah in the book of that name.

Its re-use in this particular context, moreover, leads us to seek that purpose in literary factors, not historical ones. The close relationship between the two rescensions of the narrative indicate that we are not discussing the simple re-use of traditions. Isa 36-39 is a block of material which has already assumed a definite, although not a fixed, literary form. It is more than a disparate set of traditions which may be freely combined and re-used, as we found in Amos 9:11-15. Rather, the narratives are re-used *en masse* with relatively minor changes in the overall composition. Isa 36-39 is first and foremost a literary unit.

Furthermore, the nature of its re-use is literary. Its purpose is not to interpret the exile to a specific audience, as Ackroyd implies. Instead, it interprets the relationship of two blocks of prophetic material. The nature of first and second Isaiah make it logical, indeed imperative, that they be linked by material concerning the exile. The Assyrian threat which pervades first Isaiah needs to be linked to the later Babylonian menace; the promise of restoration in Deutero-Isaiah must be placed in the context of exile. Through the intermediary nature of Isa 36-39 this is accomplished; and we may read the book of Isaiah as a unit, which, even in its disparate nature, is theologically and literarily related.

What are the hermeneutical implications of this reapplication of a set of historical traditions to the literary sphere? As we have indicated, the historical events to which this material refers have become hopelessly blurred in the process of reinterpreting the traditions for their new literary function. However, this reinterpretation has done more than merely cloud the historical lineaments of the traditions; it has occasioned a shift in the semantic level of the language used. In its Isaianic context the language functions metaphorically, not historically. Ackroyd has suggested this shift in his mention of metaphors of restoration to life in Hezekiah's psalm. Most of the features which we have discussed also highlight this shift from historical function to metaphor. The switch of the story of the ambassadors from its historical position to the end of this set of traditions enables it to function as a metaphor for the exile, especially with the reiteration of the images of Babylon and "everything."[58] The expansion in Isa 37:23-28 contains several metaphorical references to both first and second Isaiah. The whole image of the tyrant in verses 23-25 is idealistic, with no historical referent. Finally, the non-historical double pattern which Childs discovered in Isa 36-37 indicates a sequence of threat and deliverance that is now metaphorical rather than historical.

Consequently, these chapters function as a literary connective on the semantic level of metaphor and image. To interpret the material historically would be to falsify its present shape. The semantic shift results in a re-use of the traditions which is quite different from chronological actualization. While a metaphorical reinterpretation may originate in a specific historical situation, its application is not limited to that situation. A shift to metaphor both de-historicizes and universalizes the underlying themes of the material. As a result, the traditions in Isa 36-39 are actualized for all subsequent generations. The images are no longer restricted to Sennacherib's invasion -- nor even to the experience of the Babylonian exile -- but to all situations of exile and restoration. Since Isa 36-39 acts as a literary connective, it also affects the surrounding material. While these chapters lack the impact to impose an a-historical interpretation upon the whole book of Isaiah, they do move the book in that direction. Isa 36-39, especially when viewed in relation to similar materials,[59] help to de-historicize Isaiah and cast the book in a metaphorical light. Therefore, we may describe the contemporization encountered here as actualization through metaphor: it functions in the literary sphere and acts as a contemporization for all generations.

---

[58]Ackroyd, "Babylonian Exile," 334-35.

[59]Isa 13-14 seem to have undergone a similar de-historicizing process, with the tyrant described there assuming idealistic proportions. The description in Isa 14:13-15 is reminiscent of Isa 37:24-25.

Redefining Actualization

The goal of this chapter has been to refine our analysis of the concept of actualization by approaching it on a different basis, that of textual studies. The object of this analysis is not merely to criticize chronological actualization further, but to reach a redefinition of the concept which is more generally and consistently applicable to the Biblical material.

In these studies we have noted several features of chronological actualization which can distort the interpretation of a Biblical passage rather than illuminating the pericope. First, we discovered that the peculiar constructions in Deuteronomy which von Rad and Noth have cited as evidence for chronological actualization do not necessarily point to either a unique sense of time and identity or to a primitive level of cultic material. The unique style of expression is more easily explained by literary and linguistic criteria, and the positing of a special time sense obscures the nature and function of religious language in the book. Second, the atomization of a text, as a result of the interaction of form and tradition criticism with the hermeneutical procedures of chronological actualization, can obscure the literary and theological connections which that text may have with the material surrounding it. Both Amos 9:11-15 and Isa 36-39 contain evidence that these units did not function in isolation, but in an integral relationship with their literary setting. Third, a reliance upon historical criteria for determining the theological significance of a passage can lead the interpreter away from its real function, as von Rad's inability to deal convincingly with Isa 36-39 demonstrates. With this passage theological and literary concerns dominate its interpretation and must be considered as the primary hermeneutical factors. While these last two features of chronological actualization (considering the text in isolation and interpreting the passage on the basis of historical criteria) can play an important role in Old Testament interpretation, they must be applied with discretion and form only a part of the overall hermeneutical procedure.

However, this chapter has also provided us with some clues on how to transcend these weaknesses and generate a broader concept of actualization more applicable to the whole of the Old Testament. First, actualization may include or result from a shift in the semantic level of language. The method of contemporizing Isa 36-39 is to move from historical language to a metaphorical use of the same material. In

Deuteronomy a similar shift takes place from historical and cultic traditions to a homiletical style. In both instances the shift is occasioned by a re-use of old traditions which renders them relevant to a new setting or situation. Therefore, we may regard this re-use as a type of actualization.

Second, actualization may focus upon the literary interaction of a passage with its context. Amos 9:11-15 provided an excellent example of this feature, with the complex of literary allusions and images dominating the theological meaning of the pericope. The literary features of the passage enable us to overcome the sense of isolation experienced when historical criteria form the primary interpretive categories and reveal the theological significance of the passage for the book of Amos. Similar literary interactions play a significant role in interpreting Deut 5:1-3 and Isa 36-39 as well. Therefore, actualization may also be based upon literary allusion and interaction.

Third, actualization may encompass a literary whole. The complex of allusions created by Amos 9:11-15 penetrates the entire book of Amos and ties images together in a manner that creates a new unit. The theological interpretation of this pericope should not remain in isolation but involve a fresh look at the whole book. The final effect of this actualization is a reinterpretation of all of Amos that transcends the separate historical origins of its different layers. Isa 36-39 is less successful in this regard than the conclusion to Amos, but the setting of these chapters as a literary bridge between first and second Isaiah requires us to interpret them in relation to the entire book, not in historical isolation. Deut 5:1-3 focuses upon a different aspect of holistic actualization. The uniform nature of the language of Deuteronomy is an acknowledged feature of the book. Therefore, we must consider the language about time in relation to this whole rather than as an isolated phenomenon. In this instance interpretation from the whole reveals the true nature of a single element of the book.

Fourth, actualization must have the freedom to employ varied interpretive mechanisms. At times the historical criteria central to chronological actualization will predominate in the reinterpretation of a set of traditions. In other instances different methods such as literary interaction, semantic shifts, or holistic interpretations may more accurately reflect the hermeneutical procedure operative in the re-use of Old Testament materials. Actualization must have the freedom to focus upon the appropriate mechanism and not force the interpretation of a passage into a predetermined mold. In this way actualization can reflect the varied methods of reinterpretation present in inner-Biblical exegesis.

As stated at the beginning of the chapter, these ideas are more suggestive than definitive. However, we have demonstrated inner-Biblical evidence for a broader definition of actualization, one that draws Biblical contemporization much closer to that which we have described as literary actualization. In so doing, we have further undercut the uniqueness of the Biblical phenomenon and strengthened the ties between the Old Testament and other types of literature and literary analysis. This delineation of Biblical actualization conforms more closely to the final shape of the Old Testament as a written, literary document than does the hybrid category of chronological actualization.

Conclusions

This study has approached the broad problem of Old Testament theology: how can a modern interpreter appropriate writings as old, as foreign, as disparate as those of the Old Testament in a manner that is theologically relevant to a contemporary audience? This question has faced exegetes since the beginning of the traditionary process which produced the Old Testament, and the ages have proposed numerous answers. However, the twentieth century has posed its own particular constellation of factors influencing the solution to that problem. Only in this century has the discipline of historical criticism been faced with a sweeping revival of interest in the theological application of scripture. In previous periods either historical criticism as we know it was non-existent or theological interest in the Old Testament was at a low ebb. In the last few decades both have occupied positions of importance, and the situation has demanded a resolution to the conflict between the two disciplines.

We have chosen to investigate one of the most influential and successful attempts to resolve this conflict: the theological enterprise initiated by Gerhard von Rad. We have determined that his hermeneutical method centers in the device called actualization, which refers to the continual updating of religiously important traditions for each generation of Israel. While this method is not easily defined because of von Rad's ambiguity and vagueness at key points, we isolated enough central characteristics to show that he envisioned a concept considerably different from the manner in which actualization is usually employed (either as cultic or literary contemporization). We labeled his formulation chronological actualization. The importance of this formulation lies in the unique sense of identity, time, and history which it provides for the Old Testament, the traditio-historical unity which it imposes on scripture, and the central place which it occupies in inner-Biblical exegesis. On the basis of these factors chronological actualization forms the overarching hermeneutical method for Biblical interpretation.

Other scholars accepted (and participated in the formulation of) von Rad's basic premises. Actualization's influence upon the study of the Old Testament was particularly strong in Germany, where it became the regnant Protestant hermeneutical method in the fifties and sixties. It played an important, although less dominant, role in England and America during the same period. These other scholars developed, adapted, and applied actualization to cover various aspects of Old Testament studies. While many of these studies proved useful, they also revealed some of the underlying weaknesses of the concept.

From an investigation of the internal logic of chronological actualization we concluded that it forms an inadequate hermeneutic for Old Testament theology. Apart from criticisms leveled by advocates of other systems of thought, the method collapses from the weight of its own inconsistencies. We may briefly summarize the major flaws as follows:

1. The special senses of identity, time, and history are unproven assumptions. The peculiarities of expression in the Old Testament which gave rise to these formulations may be better explained by other theories.

2. While actualization claims to provide an overarching unity for the whole Bible, it in fact fails to link the Old and New Testaments convincingly and neglects significant portions of the Old Testament. It is one inner-Biblical hermeneutical device among many.

3. It takes concepts based upon oral transmission which is still in a state of flux and applies them to written, canonized materials without considering the consequences of such a change.

4. Its reliance upon the historical-critical method leads actualization away from the Old Testament text because of the distortion caused by fragmentation, historical reconstruction, and historical specificity. While these techniques may be legitimate for historical inquiries, they form a questionable basis for theological investigation.

5. Despite its claim to use Biblical categories, chronological actualization introduces modern Protestant concepts as the basis for its theological program. This procedure results

in unresolved tensions in the theological-historical equation.

In the final analysis chronological actualization is a hypothetical category which fails to reconcile the opposites which von Rad wished to preserve: identity and an historical sense. One may speak legitimately of actualization in a cultic sense where the participants experience an identity with the event being celebrated. Likewise, one may speak of an aesthetic or literary actualization where the interpreter is conscious of the historical time gap and seeks to understand and communicate in spite of it. Von Rad tried to combine the best of each sense of actualization in order to demonstrate the uniqueness of the Biblical faith. This proved to be an impossible task. The uniqueness which he contrived, the bridge between the historical method and faith, foundered on the inconsistencies listed above.

Nevertheless, actualization exerted a powerful influence upon the theological interpretation of the Old Testament. More than any other theological-historical method emerging in this century, actualization responded to the needs of the times. While von Rad's reliance upon an analogical relationship between the theological rubrics of the Bible and modern theological categories created strains in the method, it also lent his theological program a vitality and relevance absent in most other attempts. Thus, although flawed, his own charismatic, eclectic procedure resulted in an effective contemporary actualization.

Furthermore, his methodology rested upon a firmly based insight: that the adaptation and application of older material is an important feature of the Old Testament traditionary process. This concept of the re-use of traditions proved particularly effective in understanding the development and internal relationships of the various historical materials and the growth of the prophetic corpus. Von Rad did not originate this concept: it was present and active in Gunkel's work. Rather, von Rad's genius lay in his perceiving the theological nature of the re-use of tradition. Consequently, even though the particular connection which he drew between the historical-critical method and the theological dimension of the Old Testament was deeply flawed, it rested upon a valid insight into the theological nature of the Old Testament traditions. This basic insight, coupled with his sensitive, illuminating exegesis of particular passages or books of the Old Testament, enabled him to respond to the currents of his time more appropriately and sensitively than any other Biblical theologian of that day.

Growing out of this traditio-historical insight is the re-evaluation of the so-called secondary materials of the Old Testament. Von Rad opened the door to an appreciation of the interpretive value of the later reworkings of tradition. While in his work this value was limited to the historical and prophetic corpora, other scholars have demonstrated its applicability to virtually all areas of the Old Testament. Although he envisioned this re-use as a further layer of tradition added to the preceding ones, this initial step has opened the door to more thorough reappraisals of the value and the role of later additions, as we have suggested in the textual studies in chapter four.

As with most interpretive schemes, actualization presents some essential insights with contemporary applicability locked into a flawed and inconsistent method. Our study of actualization has enabled us to sort out both the strengths and weaknesses of the concept and given us a basis upon which to posit some corrective insights. These insights, suggestive rather than definitive in nature, can point the way toward a redefinition of actualization which is more in line with the Biblical material and more useful in changing theological contexts than the narrowly defined chronological actualization.

First, actualization may not be tied to any specific theological program. Its strong links to the confessional nature of Protestant neo-orthodoxy severely restricted the theological vision derived from the Old Testament. James Sanders has demonstrated that a different theological understanding can employ many of the insights of actualization, breaking away from the strict talk of confessions and credenda which governs von Rad's work. Two precepts of actualization related to its theological program must also be jettisoned. These are the attempts to have actualization account for the uniqueness and the unity of the Bible. We have found that the concept is inadequate to explain either one. The various types of actualization that one encounters in the Bible highlight its theological diversity instead. Therefore, a proper concept of Biblical actualization will open the Old Testament up to multivalent theological interpretations rather than tie it to one school of thought.

Second, actualization must not be tied exclusively to historical-critical procedures. While historical criticism has been essential in understanding and sorting out the different layers of tradition in the Old Testament, it has also distorted the interpretation of many passages. Von Rad correctly discerned that the procedures governing the reconstruction of Israel's religion were not always applicable in theological interpretation, even though his application of this insight was somewhat limited. Our textual studies have suggested that actualization is frequently governed by such non-historical factors as changes in the semantic level of language, literary allusion and interaction, and the interpretation of literary wholes. Only when these factors are allowed their due will the full interpretive range of actualization in relation to the Old Testament be realized. Once again, this is a move away from the uniqueness of scripture to an acknowledgement of the connection between the Bible and other literature. Consequently, actualization must be viewed as a force binding the Old Testament to other literary traditions and procedures rather than setting it apart from them.

Third, we must acknowledge the religious dimension of actualization. Von Rad was correct in seeing a religious impulse behind every re-use of tradition. However, we must not connect a general religious impulse with a specific manifestation such as proclamation, as he did. The impulse to re-use traditions may assume many different forms: didactic, visionary, historiographic, among others. Acknowledgement of the multivalent forces at work allows us to connect actualization to the theological dimension, but with a much broader range than that present in chronological actualization. In this sense Biblical actualization is different from a general theory of literary actualization. The religious motive for the re-use of old traditions gives Biblical actualization an intensity and complexity lacking in most other applications of the general concept. To understand fully this aspect of the phenomenon, one would need to investigate the nature and function of religious language in the Old Testament, especially in relation to the use of language in other religious traditions and in relation to the phenomenon of canonization. Only in this way can the complex interaction of the literary and religious dimensions be studied in depth.

In summary, we may properly speak of the presence of actualization in the Bible, although in a different sense than the chronological actualization proposed by von Rad and others. Actualization in the Old Testament centered upon the re-use of older material in a way that renders that material theologically relevant for a later time (whether that time be a single generation or all generations to come). While an acknowledgement of the religious nature of this actualization is essential, the religious aspect does not establish such actualization as a unique procedure. It is one method by which people everywhere handle their past -- especially their religious past. Consequently, Biblical actualization is both broader and narrower than von Rad acknowledged: broader because it is kin to the actualization practiced by many cultures and ages; narrower because it fails to encompass the hermeneutical complexities of the Old Testament. Therefore, in any strict evaluation chronological actualization is a failure; it falls short of its own high standards of being an overarching interpretive device for Old Testament theology. The uniqueness of the Bible lies elsewhere than in its hermeneutical methods; the search must continue for any grand design which may enable a comprehensive linkage of the theological and historical enterprises in Old Testament studies. However, actualization redefined remains a valuable tool for Old Testament interpretation, offering insight into the traditionary process of the Bible and into both the faith of its people and the relevance of that faith for us today. As such, actualization functions as one element among many in reaching a theological evaluation of the Old Testament.

List of Works Consulted

Abramowski, Rudolf. "Vom Streit um das Alte Testament." *TRu* 9 (1937) 65-93.

Achtemeier, Elizabeth. "The Relevance of the Old Testament for Christian Preaching." *A Light Unto My Path: Old Testament Studies in Honor of Jacob Meyers.* Ed. H. Bream, R. Heim, and C. Moore; Philadelphia: Temple University, 1974. 3-24.

Ackroyd, Peter. "An Interpretation of the Babylonian Exile: A Study of 2 Kings 20, Isaiah 38-39." *SJT* 27 (1974) 329-51.

_____. "The Vitality of the Word of God in the Old Testament." ASTI 1 (1962) 7-23.

Albrektson, Bertil. *History and the Gods: An Essay on the Idea of Historical Events as Divine Manifestations in the Ancient Near East and in Israel.* Lund: Gleerup, 1967.

Alt, Albrecht. "The Origins of Israelite Law." *Essays on Old Testament History and Religion.* Trans. R.A. Wilson; Garden City, New York: Doubleday, 1968. 101-72.

Anderson, Bernhard. "Martin Noth's Traditio-Historical Approach in the Context of Twentieth-Century Biblical Research." In Martin Noth. *A History of the Pentateuchal Traditions.* Trans. and introd. Bernhard Anderson; Englewood Cliffs: Prentice Hall, 1972. xiii-xxxii.

Barr, James. *Biblical Words for Time.* London: SCM, 1962.

_____. "Gerhard von Rad's *Theologie des Alten Testaments." ExpTim* 73 (1962) 142-46.

_____. *Old and New in Interpretation: A Study of the Two Testaments.* New York: Harper & Row, 1966.

_____. "The Problem of Old Testament Theology and the History of Religion." CJT 3 (1957) 141-49.

_____. "Revelation Through History in the Old Testament and in Modern Theology." *Int* 17 (1963) 193-205.

_____. *The Semantics of Biblical Language.* Glasgow: Oxford University, 1961.

Barth, Karl. "The Authority and Significance of the Bible: 12 Theses." *God Here and Now.* Trans. Paul van Buren; New York: Harper & Row, 1964.

_____. "Biblical Questions, Insights, and Vistas." *The Word of God and the Word of Man.* Trans. Douglas Horton; Boston: Pilgrim, 1928.

_____. *Church Dogmatics.* Trans. G.T. Thomson; Edinburgh: T&T Clark, 1936-1956.

_____. *The Epistle to the Romans.* Trans. Edwyn Hoskyns from the 6th ed; London: Oxford University, 1933.

_____. *Evangelical Theology: An Introduction.* Trans. G. Foley; New York: Holt, Rhinehart, Winston, 1963.

_____. *Die kirchliche Dogmatik.* 1/1. Munich: C. Kaiser, 1932.

_____. *Die kirchliche Dogmatik.* 1/2. Zollikon: evangelischen Buchhandlung, 1938.

_____. *Protestant Theology in the Nineteenth Century: Its Background and History.* Trans. Brian Cozens and John Bowden; Valley Forge: Judson, 1973.

Baumgärtel, Friedrich. "Gerhard von Rad's *Theologie des Alten Testaments.*" *TLZ* 86 (1961) 801-16, 895-908.

_____. "The Hermeneutical Problem of the Old Testament." Trans. Murray Newman; *Essays in Old Testament Hermeneutics.* 134-59.

_____. *Verheissung: Zur Frage des evangelischen Verständnisses des Alten Testaments.* Gütersloh: C. Bertelsmann, 1951.

Baumgartner, Walter. "Die Auslegung des Alten Testament im Streit die Gegenwart." *Schweizeriche Theologische Umschau* 11 (1941) 17-38.

Becker, Joachim. *Israel deutet seine Psalmen: Urform und Neuinterpretation in den Psalmen.* Stuttgart: Katholisches Bibelwerk, 1966.

Birkeland, Harris. *Zum Hebräischen Traditionswesen. Avhändlinger utgitt av Det Norske Videnskaps-Akademi,* 1938. 5-96.

Bloch, Renée. "Midrash." *DBSup* 5 (1957) 1263-81.

Boman, Thorlief. *Hebrew Thought Compared with Greek.* Trans. Jules Moreau; London: SCM, 1960.

Brown, Raymond. "Hermeneutics." *JBC.* 1968 ed.; 605-23.

_____. *Sensus Plenior of Sacred Scripture.* Baltimore: St. Mary's University, 1955.

Brueggemann, Walter. "The Kerygma of the Priestly Writers." *ZAW* 84 (1972) 397-413.

_____. *Tradition for Crisis: A Study in Hosea.* Richmond: John Knox, 1968.

Childs, Brevard S. *Biblical Theology in Crisis.* Philadelphia: Westminster, 1970.

_____. "The Canonical Shape of the Prophetic Literature." *Int* 33 (1978) 46-55.

_____. *Isaiah and the Assyrian Crisis.* London: SCM, 1967.

_____. *Memory and Tradition in Israel.* London: SCM, 1962.

_____. "Prophecy and Fulfillment." *Int* 12 (1958) 259-71.

_____. "The Old Testament as Scripture of the Church." *CTM* 43 (1972) 709-22.

Clements, Ronald. *A Century of Old Testament Study.* London: Lutterworth, 1976.

Conzelmann, Hans. "Fragen an Gerhard von Rad." *EvT* 24 (1964) 113-25.

Cross, Frank. "The Divine Warrior in Israel's Early Cult." *Biblical Motifs: Origins and Transformations.* Ed. Alexander Altmann; Cambridge: Harvard University, 1966. 11-30.

_____. "Yahweh and the God of the Patriarchs." *HTR* 55 (1962) 225-59.

Cross, Frank, and Freedman, David Noel. "The Song of Miriam." *JNES* 14 (1955) 237-50.

Davies, G. Henton. "Gerhard von Rad." *Contemporary Old Testament Theologians.* Ed. Robert Laurin; Valley Forge: Judson, 1970. 63-90.

Déaut, Roger le. "Apropos a Definition of Midrash." *Int* 25 (1971) 259-82.

Dentan, Robert. *Preface to Old Testament Theology.* Rev. ed.; New York: Seabury, 1963.

DeVries, Simon. "The Development of the Deuteronomic Promulgation Formula." *Bib* 55 (1974) 301-16.

_____. *Yesterday, Today, and Tomorrow.* Grand Rapids: William B. Eerdmans, 1975.

Dreyfus, F. "L'Actualisation à l'interieur de la Bible." *RB* 83 (1976) 161-202.

Eichrodt, Walther. "Is Typological Exegesis an Appropriate Method?" Trans. James Barr. *Essays in Old Testament Hermeneutics.* 224-45.

_____. "Offenbarung und Geschichte im Alten Testament." *TZ* 4 (1948) 321ff.

214   Actualization and Interpretation in the Old Testament

_____. "The Problem of Old Testament Theology." *Theology of the Old Testament*. 1.512-20.

_____. *Theology of the Old Testament*. 2 vols. Trans. J.A. Bakers; Philadelphia: Westminster, 1961.

Eissfeldt, Otto. "Geschichtliches und Übergeschichtliches." *TSK* 109 (1937) 37ff.

_____. "Israelitische-jüdische Religiongeschichte und alttestamentliche Theologie." *ZAW* 44 (1926) 1-12.

Ellis, Peter. *The Yahwist: The Bible's First Theologian*. Notre Dame: Fides, 1968.

Frazer, James. *Folk-lore in the Old Testament*. New York: Macmillan, 1923.

_____. *The Golden Bough*. New York: Macmillan, 1922.

Frei, Hans. *The Eclipse of Biblical Narrative*. New Haven: Yale University, 1974.

Gese, Harmut. "The Idea of History in the Ancient Near East and the Old Testament." *JTC* 1 (1965) 49-64.

Gillies, Alexander. *Herder*. Oxford: Basil Blackwood, 1945.

Girgensohn, Karl. *Grundriss der Dogmatik*. Leipzig: A. Deichert, 1924.

Goppelt, Leonhard. *Typos: Die typologische Deutung des Alten Testaments im Neuen*. Gütersloh: C. Bertelsmann, 1939.

Gunkel, Hermann. "The Close of Micah: A Prophetic Liturgy." *What Remains of the Old Testament*. 145-83.

_____. *Einleitung in die Psalmen: Die Gattungen der religiösen Lyrik Israels*. Göttingen: Vandenhoeck & Ruprecht, 1933.

_____. "Fundamental Problems of Hebrew Literary History." *What Remains of the Old Testament*. 58-68. Originally published as "Die Grundprobleme der israelitischen Literaturgeschichte." *Deutsche Literaturzeitung* 27 (1906) 1797-1800, 1861-66.

_____. *Genesis: Übersetzt und erklärt von Hermann Gunkel*. Göttingen: Vandenhoeck & Ruprecht, 1901.

_____. "Jacob." *What Remains of the Old Testament*. 151-83.

_____. "Die Komposition der Joseph-Geschichten." *ZDMG* 76 (1922) 56-71.

_____. *The Legends of Genesis: The Biblical Saga and History*. Trans. W.H. Carruth. 1901; rpt. New York: Schocken, 1965.

_____. *What Remains of the Old Testament and Other Essays*. Trans. A. Dallas; New York: Macmillan, 1928.

Harper, William. *A Critical and Exegetical Commentary on Amos and Hosea*. New York: Scribner's, 1915.

Hasel, Gerhard. *Old Testament Theology: Issues in the Current Debate*. Grand Rapids: Eerdmanns, 1972.

_____. "The Problem of History in Old Testament Theology." *AUSS* 8 (1970) 32-35, 41-46.

_____. "The Problem of the Center in the Old Testament Theology Debate." *ZAW* 86 (1974) 65-82.

Hellbart, Hans. "Die Auslesung des Alten Testaments als theologische Disziplin." *TBl* 16 (1937) 140ff.

Herder, Johann Gottfried von. *Briefe, das Stadium der Theologie betreffend*. Weimar: in der Hoffmannischen Hofbuchhandlung, 1816.

_____. *The Spirit of Hebrew Poetry*. 2 vols. Trans. James Marsh; Burlington: Edward Smith, 1833. Originally published as *Vom Geist der Ebräischen Poesie*. 1782; rpt. Stuttgart: J.G. Eottaschen, 1827.

_____. *Yet Another Philosophy of History*. Trans., ed., and introd. Frederick Barnard. *J.G. Herder on Social and Political Culture*. Cambridge: Cambridge University, 1969.

Hirsch, Eric. *Validity in Interpretation*. New Haven: Yale University, 1967.

Hofmann, Johann Christian Konrad von. *Interpreting the Bible*. Trans. Christian Preus; Minneapolis: Augsburg, 1959.

_____. *Weissagung und Erfüllung im Alten und im Neuen Testaments*. Nordlinger: C. Beck, 1841.

Honecker, Martin. "Zum Verständnis der Geschichte in Gerhard von Rads *Theologie des Alten Testaments*." *EvT* 23 (1963) 143-68.

Jones, Douglas. "The Traditio of the Oracles of Isaiah of Jerusalem." *ZAW* 67 (1955) 226-46.

Kaiser, Otto. *Isaiah 13-39: A Commentary*. Philadelphia: Westminster, 1974.

Kierkegaard, Søren. *Repetition: An Essay in Experimental Psychology*. Trans. Walter Lowrie; Princeton: Princeton University, 1946.

_____. *Training in Christianity*. Trans. Walter Lowrie; Princeton: Princeton University, 1944.

Klatt, Werner. *Hermann Gunkel: Zu seiner Theologie der Religionsgeschichte und zur Entstehung der formgeschichtlichen Methode*. Göttingen: Vandenhoeck & Ruprecht, 1969.

Knight, Douglas. *Rediscovering the Traditions of Israel.* Missoula: SBL, 1973.

Knight, Douglas, ed. *Tradition and Theology in the Old Testament.* Philadelphia: Fortress, 1977.

Kraeling, Emil. *The Old Testament Since the Reformation.* New York: Harper & Bros., 1955.

Kraus, Hans-Joachim. *Die Biblische Theologie: Ihre Geschichte und Problematik.* Neukirchen-Vluyn: Neukirchener, 1970.

_____. *Geschichte der historisch-kritischen Erforschung des Alten Testaments von der Reformation bis zur Gegenwart.* Neukirchen Kreis Moers: Buchhandlung des Erziehungsvereins, 1956.

Lohfink, Norbert. *Das Hauptgebot: Eine Untersuchung literarischer Einleitungsfragen zu Dtn 5-11.* Rome: Pontificio Institutio Biblico, 1963.

Long, Burke, and Coats, George, eds. *Canon and Authority: Essays in Old Testament Religion and Theology.* Philadelphia: Fortress, 1977.

McKenzie, John L. *Myths and Realities: Studies in Biblical Theology.* Milwaukee: Bruce, 1963.

_____. *A Theology of the Old Testament.* Garden City, New York: Doubleday, 1974.

_____. *The Two-Edged Sword: An Interpretation of the Old Testament.* Milwaukee: Bruce, 1955.

Marsh, John. *The Fulness of Time.* London: Nisbet, 1952.

Mays, James. "Exegesis as a Theological Discipline." Inaugural address delivered April 20, 1960. Richmond, Virginia: Union Theological Seminary, 1960.

Mowinckel, Sigmund. *The Old Testament as Word of God.* Trans. R. Bjornard; Nashville: Abingdon, 1959.

_____. *Prophecy and Tradition: The Prophetic Books in the Light of the Study of the Growth and History of the Tradition. Avhändlinger utgitt av det Norske Videnskaps-Akademi.* 1946. 3-117.

_____. *Psalmenstudien.* 1921-24; rpt. Amsterdam: P. Schippers, 1961.

Munch, Peter. "The expression bajjom hahu, is it an eschatological terminus technicus?" *Avhändlinger utgitt av det Norske Videnskaps-Akademi.* 1936. 5-69.

Nicholson, Ernest W. *Deuteronomy and Tradition.* Philadelphia: Fortress, 1967.

_____. *Exodus and Sinai in History and Tradition*. Richmond: John Knox, 1973.

_____. *Preaching to the Exiles: A Study in the Prose Tradition in the Book of Jeremiah*. New York: Schocken, 1971.

Noth, Martin. *Die Gesetz im Pentateuch*. Halle: M. Niemeyer, 1940. Rpt. in *Gesammelte Studien zum alten Testament*. Munich: C. Kaiser, 1966. 9-141.

_____. *The History of Israel*. Rev. trans. Peter Ackroyd; New York: Harper & Row, 1960.

_____. *A History of the Pentateuchal Traditions*. Trans. and intro. Bernhard Anderson; Englewood Cliffs, New Jersey: Prentice Hall, 1972.

_____. *The Laws in the Pentateuch and Other Studies*. Trans. D.R. Ap-Thomas. Intro. Norman Porteous; Philadelphia: Fortress, 1967.

_____. "The Re-presentation of the Old Testament in Proclamation." Trans. James Mays; *Essays in Old Testament Hermeneutics*. 76-88.

_____. *Überlieferungsgeschichtlichen Studien: Die sammelnden und bearbeitenden Geschichtswerke im Alten Testament*. 1941; rpt. Tübingen: M. Niemeyer, 1967.

Pidoux, G. "À propos de la notion biblique du temps." *RTP* 3 (1952) 120-125.

Porteous, Norman. "Actualization and the Prophetic Criticism of the Cult." *Tradition und Situation*. Ed. E. Wurthwein and O. Kaiser; Göttingen: Vandenhoeck & Ruprecht, 1963. Rpt. in *Living the Mystery: Collected Essays*. Oxford: Basil Blackwell, 1967. 127-42.

_____. *Living the Mystery: Collected Essays*. Oxford: Basil Blackwell, 1967.

Procksch, Otto. "Pneumatische Exegese." *Christentum und Wissenschaft*, 1 (1925) 145ff.

_____. *Theologie des Alten Testaments*. Gütersloh: C. Bertelsmann, 1950.

Rad, Gerhard von. "About Exegesis and Preaching." *Biblical Interpretations in Preaching*. Trans. John Steely; Nashville: Abingdon, 1977. 11-18.

_____. "Ancient Word and Living Word: The Preaching of Deuteronomy and Our Preaching." Trans. Lloyd Gaston; *Int*, 15 (1961) 3-13.

_____. "Antwort auf Conzelmanns Fragen." *EvT* 24 (1964) 388-94.

_____. "The Beginnings of Historical Writing in Ancient Israel." *The Form-Critical Problem of the Hexateuch and Other Essays*. 166-204.

_____. "Das Christuszeugnis des Alten Testaments: Eine Auseinandersetzung mit Wilhelm Vischers gleichnämigen Buch." *TBl*, 14 (1935) 249-54.

_____. "The City on the Hill." *The Form-Critical Problem of the Hexateuch and Other Essays*. 232-42. Originally published as "Die Stadt auf dem Berge." *EvT* 8 (1948-49) 439-47.

_____. *Deuteronomy: A Commentary*. Trans. Dorothea Barton; Philadelphia: Westminster, 1966.

_____. "The Deuteronomic Theology of History in I and II Kings." *The Form-Critical Problem of the Hexateuch and Other Essays*. 205-221.

_____. "Eichrodt, Walther: *Theologie des Alten Testaments*." *Christentum und Wissenschaft*, 10 (1934) 427-48.

_____. "Die falsche Propheten." *ZAW* 51 (1933) 109-20.

_____. *The Form-Critical Problem of the Hexateuch*. *The Form-Critical Problem of the Hexateuch and Other Essays*. 1-78. Originally published as *Das formgeschichtliche Problem des Hexateuchs*. Stuttgart: W. Kohlhammer, 1938.

_____. *The Form-Critical Problem of the Hexateuch and Other Essays*. Trans. E. Dicken; New York: McGraw Hill, 1966.

_____. *Genesis: A Commentary*. Trans. J. Marks; Philadelphia: Westminster Press, 1961. Originally published as *Das erste Buch Mose: Genesis*. Göttingen: Vandenhoeck & Ruprecht, 1950-53.

_____. *Genesis: A Commentary*. 2nd rev. ed. Trans. J. Marks; Philadelphia: Westminster, 1963.

_____. *Das Geschichtsbild des chronistischen Werkes*. Stuttgart: W. Kohlhammer, 1930.

_____. "Gesetz und Evangelium im Alten Testament. Gedanken zu dem Buch von E. Hirsch: *Das Alte Testament und die Predigt des Evangeliums*." *TBl* 16 (1937) 41-47.

_____. *Das Gottesvolk im Deuteronomium*. Stuttgart: W. Kohlhammer, 1929.

_____. "Grundprobleme einer biblischen Theologie des Alten Testaments." *TLZ*, 68 (1943) 225-34.

_____. "The Levitical Sermon in I and II Chronicles." *The Form-Critical Problem of the Hexateuch and Other Essays*. 267-80.

_____. "Literarkritische und Überlieferungsgeschichtliche Forschung im Alten Testament." *VF* (1947-48), Part 3 (1950) 172-94.

_____. "Offene Fragen im Umkreis einer Theologie des Alten Testaments." *TLZ* 88 (1963) 401-16. Trans. as "Postscript" to *Old Testament Theology* 2.410-29.

_____. *Old Testament Theology* 1. Trans. David Stalker; Edinburgh: Harper & Row, 1962.

_____. *Old Testament Theology* 2. Trans. David Stalker; Edinburgh: Harper & Row, 1965.

_____. *Die Priesterschrift im Hexateuch literarisch untersucht und theologisch gewertet.* Stuttgart: W. Kohlhammer, 1934.

_____. "The Promised Land and Yahweh's Land in the Hexateuch." *The Form-Critical Problem of the Hexateuch and Other Essays.* 79-83.

_____. "Rückblick und Ausblick." Postscript to *Theologie des Alten Testaments.* 2.437-47. 4th ed.

_____. *Studies in Deuteronomy.* Trans. David Stalker; London: SCM, 1953. Originally published as *Deuteronomium-Studien.* Göttingen: Vandenhoeck & Ruprecht, 1947.

_____. "The Theological Problem of the Old Testament Doctrine of Creation." *The Form-Critical Problem of the Hexateuch and Other Essays.* 131-43.

_____. *Theologie des Alten Testaments* 1. 1st ed. Munich: C. Kaiser, 1957.

_____. *Theologie des Alten Testaments* 1. 4th ed. Munich: C. Kaiser, 1962.

_____. *Theologie des Alten Testaments* 2. 1st ed. Munich: C. Kaiser, 1960.

_____. *Theologie des Alten Testaments* 2. 4th ed. Munich: C. Kaiser, 1965.

_____. "There Remains Still a Rest for the People of God: An Investigation of a Biblical Concept." *The Form-Critical Problem of the Hexateuch and Other Essays.* 94-102. Originally published as "Es ist noch eine Ruhe vorhanden den Volkes Gottes." *Zwischen den Zeiten* 11 (1933) 104-11.

_____. "Typological Interpretation of the Old Testament." Trans. John Bright; *Essays on Old Testament Hermeneutics.* 17-39.

_____. "Weiser: *Glaube und Geschichte im Alten Testament.*" *Christentum und Wissenschaft* 8 (1932) 37.

_____. *Wisdom in Israel*. Trans. J. Martin; Nashville: Abingdon, 1972. Originally published as *Weisheit in Israel*. Neukirchen-Vluyn: Neukirchener, 1970.

Rendtorff, Rolf. "Geschichte und Überlieferung." *Studien zur Theologie des alttestamentlichen Überlieferungen: Festschrift für Gerhard von Rad zum 60. Geburtstag*. Ed. Rolf Rendtorff and Klaus Koch; Neukirchen-Vluyn: Neukirchener, 1961.

Robinson, James M. "The New Hermeneutic at Work." *Int* 18 (1964) 346-59.

_____. *A New Quest for the Historical Jesus*. London: SCM, 1959.

Robinson, James, and Cobb, John, eds. *New Frontiers in Theology: The New Hermeneutic* 2. New York: Harper & Row, 1964.

Rogerson, J.W. *Myth in Old Testament Interpretation*. Berlin: W. de Gruyter, 1974.

Ruppert, Lothar. "Der Jahwist -- Künder der Heilsgeschichte." *Wort und Botschaft: Eine theologische und kritische Einführung im die Probleme des Alten Testaments*. Ed. Josef Schreiner; Würzburg: Echter, 1967. 88-107.

Sanders, James A. "Adaptable for Life: The Nature and Function of Canon." *Magnalia Dei, the Mighty Acts of God: Essays on the Bible and Archaeology in Memory of G. Ernest Wright*. Ed. Frank Cross, Werner Lenke, and Patrick Miller; Garden City: Doubleday, 1976. 531-60.

_____. "Hermeneutics." *IDBSup*. 1976. 402-07.

_____. *Torah and Canon*. Philadelphia: Fortress, 1972.

Schmidt, Joh. Michael. "Vergegenwärtigung und Überlieferung." *EvT* 30 (1970) 169-200.

Seeligmann, Isaac. "Voraussetzungen der Midraschexegese." *VTSup* 1 (1953) 150-181.

Sellin, Ernst. *Das Alte Testament und die evangelische Kirche der Gegenwart*. Leipzig: A. Deichert, 1921.

Soggin, J.A. "Geschichte, Historie, und Heilsgeschichte im Alten Testaments." *TLZ* 89 (1964) 721-36.

Spriggs, D.G. *Two Old Testament Theologies*. London: SCM, 1974.

Steck, Odil Hannes. "Theological Streams of Tradition." *Tradition and Theology in the Old Testament*. Ed. David Knight; Philadelphia: Fortress, 1977. 183-214.

_____. *Überlieferung und Zeitgeschichte in den Elia-Erzählung*. Neukirchen-Vluyn: Neukirchener, 1968.

Steck, Odil Hannes, and Barth, Hermann. *Exegese des Alten Testaments.* Neukirchen-Vluyn: Neukirchener, 1971.

Strauss, David. *Das Leben Jesu.* Tübingen: C. Osiander, 1835.

Tucker, Gene. *Form Criticism of the Old Testament.* Philadelphia: Fortress, 1971.

Vesco, Jean-Luc. "Abraham, actualisation, et relectures." *RSPT* 55 (1971) 33-80.

Vickery, John. *The Literary Impact of the Golden Bough.* Princeton: Princeton University, 1973.

Vischer, Wilhelm. *The Witness of the Old Testament to Christ.* Trans. A. B. Crabtree; London: Lutterworth, 1949.

Vriezen, Theodorus. "Geloof, openbaring en geschiedenis in de nieuwste Oud-Testamentische Theologie." *Kerk en Theologie* 16 (1956) 97-113, 210-18.

Weiser, Artur. *Glaube und Geschichte.* Stuttgart: W. Kohlhammer, 1931.

_____. *The Psalms: A Commentary.* Trans. Herbert Hartwell; Philadelphia: Westminster, 1962.

Wellhausen, Julius. *Prolegomena to the History of Ancient Israel.* Trans. J. Sutherland Black and Allen Menzies; Edinburgh: Adam & Charles Black, 1885.

Westermann, Claus. *Basic Forms of Prophetic Speech.* Trans. Hugh White; Philadelphia: Westminster, 1967.

_____. *Creation.* Trans. J. J. Scullion; London: S.P.C.K., 1974.

_____. "Das hermeneutische Problem in der Theologie." *Forschung aus Alten Testaments; gesammelte Studien.* Munich: C. Kaiser, 1974. 2.68-84.

_____. *Isaiah 40-66: A Commentary.* Trans. David Stalker; Philadelphia: Westminster, 1969.

_____. "The Interpretation of the Old Testament." Trans. Dietrich Ritschl; *Essays on Old Testament Hermeneutics.* 40-49.

_____. *The Old Testament and Jesus Christ.* Trans. O. Kaste; Minneapolis: Augsburg, n.d.

_____. *Our Controversial Bible.* Trans. and ed. D. Beckmann; Minneapolis: Augsburg, 1969.

_____. *The Praise of God in the Psalms.* Trans. Keith Crim; Richmond: John Knox, 1965.

_____. "Remarks on the Theses of Bultmann and Baumgärtel." Trans. Dietrich Ritschl; *Essays on Old Testament Hermeneutics.* 123-33.

222   Actualization and Interpretation in the Old Testament

_____. "Vergegenwärtigung der Geschichte in den Psalmen." *Zwischenstation Festschrift für Karl Kupisch zum 60. Geburtstag.* Munich: C. Kaiser, 1963. 253-80.

_____. "Was ist eine exegetische Aussage?" *ZTK* 59 (1962) 1-15.

_____. "The Way of Promise Through the Old Testament." Trans. Lloyd Gaston and Bernhard Anderson. *The Old Testament and Christian Faith.* Ed. Bernhard Anderson; New York: Herder & Herder, 1969. 200-24.

Westermann, Claus, ed. *Essays on Old Testament Hermeneutics.* Richmond: John Knox, 1966.

Wimsatt, William. "The Intentional Fallacy." *The Verbal Icon.* New York: Noonday, 1966. 3-18.

Wolff, Hans Walter. "Das Alte Testament und das Probleme der existentialen Interpretation." *EvT* 23 (1963) 1-17.

_____. *Anthropology of the Old Testament.* Trans. M. Kohl; London: SCM, 1974.

_____. "The Elohistic Fragments in the Pentateuch." Trans. Keith Crim. *The Vitality of Old Testament Traditions.* 67-82. Originally published as "Zur Thematik der elohistischen Fragmente in Pentateuch." *EvT* 29 (1969) 59-72.

_____. "Hauptprobleme alttestamentliche Prophetie." EvT 15 (1955) 116-68.

_____. "The Hermeneutics of the Old Testament." Trans. Keith Crim; *Essays on Old Testament Hermeneutics.* 160-99.

_____. "Hoseas geistige Heimat." *TLZ* 81 (1956) 83-94.

_____. *Joel and Amos: A Commentary on the Books of the Prophets Joel and Amos.* Trans. Waldemar Jantzen, S. Dean McBride and Charles Muenchow; Philadelphia: Fortress, 1977.

_____. "The Kerygma of the Deuteronomistic Historical Work." Trans. F. Prussner. *The Vitality of Old Testament Traditions.* 83-100. Originally published as "Das Kerygma des deuteronomistischen Geschichtswerks." *ZAW* 73 (1961) 171-86.

_____. "The Kerygma of the Yahwist." Trans. W. Benware. *The Vitality of Old Testament Traditions.* 41-66. Originally published as "Das Kerygma des Jahwisten." *EvT* 24 (1964) 73-97.

_____. *The Old Testament -- A Guide to its Writings.* Trans. Keith Crim; Philadelphia: Fortress, 1973.

_____. "The Old Testament in Controversy." Trans. James Mays; *Int* 12 (1958) 281-91.

_____. "The Understanding of History in the Prophets." Trans. Keith Crim; *Essays on Old Testament Hermeneutics*. 336-56.

Wolff, Hans Walter; Rendtorff, Rolf; and Pannenberg, Wolfhart. *Gerhard von Rad: Seine Bedeutung für die Theologie*. Munich: C. Kaiser, 1973.

Wolff, Hans Walter, and Brueggemann, Walter. *The Vitality of Old Testament Traditions*. Atlanta: John Knox, 1975.

Wright, G. Ernest. *God Who Acts: Biblical Theology as Recital*. London: SCM, 1952.

Zimmerli, Walther. "Die historisch-kritische Bibelwissenschaft und die Verkündigungsaufgabe der Kirche." *EvT* 23 (1963) 17-31.

_____. "Promise and Fulfillment." Trans. James Wharton; *Essays on Old Testament Hermeneutics*. 89-122.

Zirker, Hans. *Die kultische Vergegenwärtigung der Vergangenheit in den Psalmen*. Bonn: P. Hanstein, 1964.